Routledge International Studies in Business History
Series Editor: Geoffrey Jones

Religion, Business and Wealth in Modern Britain

Edited by David J. Jeremy

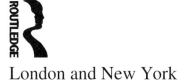

London and New York

First published 1998
by Routledge
11 New Fetter Lane, London EC4P 4EE

Simultaneously published in the USA and Canada
by Routledge
29 West 35th Street, New York, NY 10001

© 1998 Edited by David J. Jeremy

Typeset in Times by
Ponting–Green Publishing Services,
Chesham, Buckinghamshire
Printed and bound in Great Britain by
Biddles Ltd, Guildford and King's Lynn

British Library Cataloguing in Publication Data
A catalogue record for this book is available from the
British Library

Library of Congress Cataloguing in Publication Data
Religion, business and wealth in modern Britain / edited by
    David J. Jeremy.
    p.   cm.
    1. Capitalism–Religious aspects–Protestant churches.
    2. Great Britain–Economic conditions–19th century.
    3. Great Britain–Economic conditions–20th century
    4. Great Britain–Church history–19th century.
    5. Great Britain–Church history–20th century.
    I. Jeremy, David J.
    BR115.C3R45   1998
    306.6'0941–dc21   97–29571
    CIP

ISBN 0–415–16898–8

Contents

Part IV   Ethnicity, religion and wealth

Illustrations

Contributors

Dr Stanley Chapman, Professor of Business History, University of Nottingham.

Mr T. A. B. Corley, Visiting Research Fellow, Economics Department, University of Reading.

Dr Douglas A. Farnie, formerly Reader in Economic History, University of Manchester, currently Visiting Professor, Centre for Business History, The Manchester Metropolitan University.

Dr A. J. Boyd Hilton, University Reader in History and Fellow of Trinity College, Cambridge.

Dr David J. Jeremy, Professor of Business History, Centre for Business History, The Manchester Metropolitan University.

Dr Maurice Kirby, Reader in Economic History, University of Lancaster.

Dr Patrick K. O'Brien, Professor of Economic History and Director of the Institute of Historical Research, University of London.

Dr Ann Prior, Research Associate in Economic History, University of Lancaster.

Dr W. D. Rubinstein, Professor of Modern History, University of Wales, Aberystwyth.

Dr W. R. Ward, Emeritus Professor of Modern History, University of Durham.

Dr Chris Waters, Associate Professor of History, Williams College, Massachusetts.

Dr B. W. Young, Lecturer in Intellectual History, School of English and American Studies, University of Sussex.

Introduction

Debates about interactions between religion, business, and wealth in modern Britain

David J. Jeremy

In the Judaeo-Christian tradition the tensions between riches and religion date from ancient times. The Psalmist warned, 'If riches increase, set not your heart upon them' (Psalm 62: 10 AV). In the New Testament, Jesus observed that 'it is easier for a camel to go through a needle's eye, than for a rich man to enter into the kingdom of God' (Luke 18: 25 AV). The experience of the early and the medieval Church frequently demonstrated the force of these warnings.[1] Both religious collectivities within the Church, like diocesan foundations or religious orders, and religious individuals, like priests and prelates, fell prey to the temptations of worldly wealth. Nor did wealthy individuals among the laity escape the snare. However, the pre-modern world, familiar with merchant wealth, knew little if anything of industrial capitalism. It knew nothing of factories where work was governed by steam-driven machines and the mill-owner's clock. It certainly knew nothing of a world in which giant managerial corporations shift high volumes and values of goods, services, knowledge, and wealth across national boundaries at the stroke of a pen or the depression of a computer key. In short, with the emergence of industrial society in Britain in the eighteenth century, the issues intertwining the Christian religion (the traditional source of the country's social values) and economic theory and behaviour extended in number and complexity, as this collection of essays illustrates.[2]

Since the late eighteenth century a string of controversies has erupted between religion and business. Naturally, the disputants and their concerns were (and are) prisoners of their own times and experience. Nevertheless, many of the questions which occupied academics and others in the past (ranging from clerics to industrialists and bankers) continue to have relevance to issues in the present. To help to place these new essays in context I have related them to some of the questions which still intrigue historians today. Some of the writings and episodes which have fuelled these controversies are set out in the chronological and interim tabulation I have assembled in Table 1.1. This is supplemented by Table 1.2 which lists the main Christian church denominations in Britain over the period covered by the essays. In this introduction references to Table 1.1 are cited in parentheses as '(item 1, etc.)'.

Table 1.1 Some landmarks in the history of interactions between religion and business (excluding benefactions) in modern Britain, 1770s–1990s[1]

Date	Publication, movement, episode, business practice or debate	Content or inspiration	Vehicle	Origin (business (B) or church (C) or academia (A))
1770s–1936	1. Tithes had been paid in kind by farmers to the established Church (or to lay tithe owners) since the Middle Ages. Dissenters especially objected, for religious as well as economic reasons. In 1836 tithes were commuted to annual money payments which were finally abolished in 1936	social injustice	social and political campaign	C and B
1770s–1850s	2. Debate among classical economists on the relationship between economics and ethics	political economy	debate	A and C
1776	3. Adam Smith (former Professor of Moral Philosophy in Glasgow University) published An Inquiry into the Nature and Causes of the Wealth of Nations: the cornerstone of classical economics	political economy	publication	A
1780s–1829	4. Struggle by Dissenters, among whom there were leading manufacturers, for religious toleration	social injustice and religious issue	political campaign	C
1780s–1833	5. The anti-slavery movement, in which Quakers and Churchmen like William Wilberforce and the 'Clapham sect' fought against the slave traders of Liverpool (the centre of the trade), Bristol, and London	social injustice	political campaign	C
1798	6. Revd Thomas R. Malthus (curate of Albury, Surrey, and later Professor of Political Economy at the East India College, Haileybury), An Essay on the Principle of Population published. Only misery (famine, pestilence, war), moral restraint, and vice (sexual), he argued, prevented population growth from outstripping food supplies. Such a pessimistic view was used to support social inequality and to counter notions of personal indulgence and pleasure	political economy	publication	C
1816–present	7. Debate about Nonconformity's contribution to the first generation of industrialists and hence the process of industrialisation. Claims for Nonconformists seem first to have been publicly registered by the Unitarian cleric Israel Worsley (d. 1836) in his Observations on the State and Changes in the Presbyterian Societies of England during the Last Half Century:	history	debate	C

also on the Manufactures of Great Britain; Which Have Been for the Most Part Established and Supported by the Protestant Dissenters: Tending to Illustrate the Importance of Religious Liberty and Free Inquiry to the Welfare and Prosperity of a People (1816)

1826	8. Revd Thomas Chalmers (Church of Scotland minister and professor at St Andrews University) published *The Christian and Civic Economy*, vol 3: important for its application to the business cycle of Malthus's concept of checks to population growth, i.e. Chalmers proposed that capital as well as labour were subject to a divinely ordained natural law. This was a foundational view in evangelical attitudes to business	political economy	publication	C
1826	9. Chalmers' *The Christian and Civic Economy* is also important for providing a theological underpinning for the social duties of the ruling classes. Romantic poets, Tories and Anglicans also publicised the duties of the ruling classes, giving wide credence to a theory of paternalism	political economy	publication	C
1828	10. Revd John Bird Sumner (evangelical, assistant master at Eton, vicar of Mapledurham, Oxfordshire,and future Bishop of Chester) published *A Treatise on the Records of Creation, and on the Moral Attributes of the Creator*. Sumner harmonised Malthusian theory with Scripture	political economy–theology	publication	C
1830–1850	11. The campaign against child labour in industry in which Tory and Anglican priests, doctors, and some merchants, led by Richard Oastler and Lord Shaftesbury, joined with Radical millowners like John Fielden, to campaign against Nonconformist (and other) masters	social injustice	political campaign	B and C
1837	12. Samuel Jones Loyd (later Lord Overstone), a banker and well-known advocate of the use of coin and paper money rather than credit, published *Reflections . . . on the Causes and Consequences of the Pressure on the Money Market*, which, following Chalmers, related the business cycle to morality and Providence	political economy	publication	B
1838	13. Revd J. F. D. Maurice (chaplain to Guy's Hospital and later Professor of Moral Philosophy at Cambridge) published *The Kingdom of Christ*, one of the first expressions of 'incarnational' Christianity	theology	publication	C

Date	Publication, movement, episode, business practice or debate	Content or inspiration	Vehicle	Origin (business (B) or church (C) or academia (A))
1838–1846	14. The Manchester Anti-Corn Law Association, formed by manufacturers, many of them Nonconformists, fought for free trade against Anglican landowners. This gave rise to the 'Manchester school' of free trade economics	political economy	political campaign	B and C
1830s–1870	15. Statutory requirements for educational provision under the Factory Acts led to conflicts over control of schools between Nonconformist and Anglican manufacturers, and to Nonconformist resistance to the introduction of state-controlled education, until 1870	political economy	political campaign	C and B
1830s–1868	16. The Nonconformists' battle against Church rates, involved manufacturers like John Bright and Samuel Courtauld III	social injustice	political campaign	C and B
1830s–1920s+	17. The temperance movement which aimed at the prohibition of the manufacture and sale of alcohol. The movement saw Nonconformists oppose an alliance of brewers and bishops	social injustice	political campaign	C
1840s onwards	18. Other Nonconformists joined with the Quakers in the Peace Society which, among other tactics, opposed arms manufacturers	social injustice	political campaign	C
1850	19. The *Christian Socialist*, edited by J. M. Ludlow and inspired by the incarnational theology of Frederick Denison Maurice, first appeared. It stressed co-operation between masters and men	social injustice	publication	C
1854	20. Repeal of the usury laws. The laws, deriving from Old Testament precept and upheld by canon law since the Middle Ages, from 1713 imposed a ceiling of 5 per cent on interest charged on loans. This was widely evaded by the early nineteenth century	business practice	political pressure	C
1856–1865	21. Publications by James William Gilbart (1794–1863), manager of the London & Westminster Bank and author of a number of practical texts on joint-stock banking, published opinions on the moral duties of public companies: in *The Moral and Religious Duties of Public Companies* (1856) and in sections of *A Practical Treatise on Banking* (2 vols, 1865)	business ethics	publication	B

Date		ethics of wealth-holding	publications	C and B
1850s–1870s	22. Movement for systematic beneficence and the use of wealth by rich people for Christian purposes			C and B
1864	23. Sir Francis Crossley, a Congregationalist and carpet manufacturer of Halifax, and his two brothers converted their partnership into a public company, partly in order to allow some of their 4,100 employees to buy some of the shares	business ethics	business practice	B
1865	24. Profit-sharing (allowing employees a pre-determined share of company profits) viewed by some Christian employers as the most proper expression of stewardship in business because labour gained at the same rate as capital, pioneered by Henry Currer Briggs, Yorkshire coalmine owner and Unitarian, who converted his business into a public company and instituted profit-sharing at the same time	business ethics	business practice	B
1866	25. Collapse of Overend, Gurney & Co., Quaker bank and leading discount house in London	business scandal	business practice	B
1867–1868	26. The bankruptcy of Sir Samuel Morton Peto, railway contractor, and the subsequent investigation of his business behaviour by the deacons of Bloomsbury Baptist Chapel of which he was a member: an investigation which faulted him for lack of moderation and prudence	business scandal	church court	B and C
1871–1992	27. Nonconformists and evangelicals in the Church of England agitated to defend the observance of Sunday as a day of minimal trading	religious issue	political and social campaign	C
1878	28. City of Glasgow Bank failure. In this collapse, which incurred losses of £4,250,000 for over 1,800 stockholders, one or two of the prime culprits in the Bank were Free Church of Scotland local church office-holders	business scandal	criminal court	B
1883	29. Anonymous pamphlet (published under the auspices of the Congregational Union and written either by Andrew William Mearns or William Preston), *The Bitter Cry of Outcast London* published. Catching wide public attention it signalled the beginning of a move from private and individual to public and eventually state solutions to social problems – and in the churches a definitive shift to 'social Christianity'	campaign for social reform	publication	C

Date	Publication, movement, episode, business practice or debate	Content or inspiration	Vehicle	Origin (business (B) or church (C) or academia (A))
1889	30. Christian Social Union formed aiming to bring the economic realm under Christian ethics, founded by Henry Scott Holland, canon of St Paul's	political economy	society and campaign	C
late 1880s onwards	31. Nonconformists began to oppose the introduction of mass gambling and the business interests behind it	social injustice	campaign	C
1891	32. Pope Leo XIII's encyclical *Rerum Novarum*, on the rights and duties of capital and labour	political economy	publication	C
1892	33. Liberator Building Society failure in which 11,825 shareholders lost £1,661,000. The founder of the Liberator and the man most responsible for its collapse was Jabez Spencer Balfour, former MP for Croydon and a prominent Nonconformist (a Congregationalist) who had tapped the Nonconformist market for customers wishing to build houses or chapels	business scandal	criminal court	B
1896	34. Revd Samuel E. Keeble, Wesleyan Methodist minister, published *Industrial Day Dreams: Studies in Industrial Ethics and Economics*, asserting dominance of ethics over economics	political economy	publication	C
1899	35. Chemical works of J. & J. White & Co., Rutherglen, owned by John Campbell White, Lord Overtoun, a publicly pious member of the Free Church of Scotland, were exposed as filthy and dangerous to workers. Despite the revelations by Keir Hardie, Overtoun did little to improve health and safety on his plant	business scandal	newspaper publicity	B
1902	36. The collapse of J. & J. W. Pease, a Quaker business, which led to the resignation of Sir Joseph Whitwell Pease from the partnership, his effective bankruptcy, and his death the following year	business scandal	civil court	B
1904–present	37. Religion and the rise of capitalism: a debate started by Max Weber, one of the fathers of modern sociology. His two articles '*Die protestantische Ethik und der Geist des Kapitalismus*' ('The Protestant Ethic and the Spirit of Capitalism'), published in 1904–5, and his third article '*Die protestantische Sekten und*	history	debate	A

	der Geist des Kapitalismus' ('The Protestant Sects and the Spirit of Capitalism'), published in 1906, ignited the controversy which has run ever since. The English translation of Weber's essays of 1904–5, by the American sociologist Talcott Parsons, appeared in 1930, giving a fresh wind to the debate. In Britain the most influential contribution to the debate was R. H. Tawney's book *Religion and the Rise of Capitalism* (1926)			
1906	38. Church Socialist League, an Anglo-Catholic group, formed to critique capitalism; by 1912 it included R. H. Tawney, the Oxford historian, and Maurice Reckitt	political economy	society and campaign	C
1907	39. William Whiteley, owner of the country's largest department store and an evangelical Anglican, murdered by a man claiming to be his illegitimate son	business scandal	inquest court	B
1908–1909	40. Cadburys, the Quaker and Liberal chocolate manufacturers, faced charges, published in the Conservative *Evening Standard*, of profiting from slave-grown cocoa supplied by the Portuguese West African islands of São Tome and Principe. The charges were dismissed in a libel case brought by George Cadbury in Birmingham Crown Court in 1909. By 1912 Cadburys and the other UK chocolate manufacturers had switched to suppliers in the Gold Coast (Ghana)	business scandal disproved	newspaper	B
1916	41. The horrors of the First World War led the Anglican bishops to announce a Mission of Repentance and Hope, out of which in 1918 came the Report of the Archbishops' Fifth Committee of Inquiry, *Christianity and Industrial Problems* (1918). This committed the Church to the view that economic activity should be evaluated by Christian moral teaching	religious and social concern	campaign and publication	C and B
1918–1948	42. First of the decennial conferences for Quaker employers was held in 1918, the last in 1948, at Woodbrooke (once George Cadbury's home), near Selly Oak, Birmingham. Their purpose: to allow Quaker industrialists to discuss the economic and business problems of their day in the light of Quaker principles	political economy	national conferences	B
1920	43. The Lambeth Conference, the decennial conference of all bishops in communion with the Church of England, condemned the 'internecine conflict between capital and labour' and urged 'co-operation in service for the common good'	political economy	conference and publication	C

Date	Publication, movement, episode, business practice or debate	Content or inspiration	Vehicle	Origin (business (B) or church (C) or academia (A))
1920	44. Anglo-Catholic Christendom group attacked capitalism, and especially the banks, as unchristian and adopted C. H. Douglas's theory of Social Credit, an underconsumption theory condemned by the Labour Party in 1922 as unsound economics	political economy	publications	C
1924	45. Conference on Christian Politics, Economics and Citizenship (COPEC) assembled 1,500 delegates of all denominations under the chairmanship of William Temple, Bishop of Manchester, to discuss twelve reports including one on 'Industry and Property'	political economy	national conference	C
1926	46. R. H. Tawney's book Religion and the Rise of Capitalism published. It was important in supplying historical evidence for the view that a traditional harmonious form of economic behaviour turned into competitive individualism in the sixteenth and seventeenth centuries	history	publication	A
1926	47. Sir Josiah C. Stamp (LSE and Civil Service-trained, director of Nobel Industries Ltd and shortly to become president of the executive of the London Midland & Scottish Railway, one of the UK's largest employers; and a leading Wesleyan layman) published The Christian Ethic as an Economic Factor, the first of three titles dealing with Christianity and economics. The others were Motive and Method in a Christian Order (1936) and Christianity and Economics (1939). Stamp's views stood opposite Tawney's: for Stamp economic systems were neutral; only individuals in those systems were susceptible to Christian influence and conversion	political economy	publications	B
1934	48. Following the union of most of the Methodist denominations to form the Methodist Church in 1932, the annual Methodist Conference in 1934 adopted a Declaration of the Methodist Church on a Christian View of Industry in Relation to the Social Order (1934). This viewed industry as 'an instrument for establishing the Kingdom of God on earth'	political economy	conference and publications	C

1939–1960s	49. The *Christian News-Letter* edited by Dr Joseph H. Oldham, church statesman and friend of Temple, and its outgrowth, the Christian Frontier Council, formed in 1942, drew together on an interdenominational basis all manner of policy-makers and influential people. They included a number of leading men in business like Samuel Courtauld IV and the 3rd Viscount Hambleden (William Henry Smith of W. H. Smith & Son)	political economy	publications and organisation	C
early 1940s	50. During the Second World War the architects of post-war Britain were heavily influenced by Archbishop William Temple's call to build a more caring society, summarised in his small book *Christianity and Social Order* which sold over 140,000 copies when published in 1942. Temple's ideas and influence helped to shape the welfare state constructed by the Labour Government of 1945–50	political economy	publication and informal influence	C and B
1942	51. Industrial chaplains were appointed by an interdenominational committee to serve employees in the hostels attached to the munitions factories built in 1941. Out of this came the industrial chaplaincy movement	employee welfare	national church committee and individual clergy	C and B
1948 onwards	52. The Church Commissioners (replacing the Ecclesiastical Commissioners and Queen Anne's Bounty) were set up to manage the funds for paying the clergy of the Church of England. They immediately adopted a policy of ethical investment but found it difficult both to follow this principle and to convince the public that they were doing so	business ethics	business practice	C
1951	53. George Goyder, managing director of the Newsprint Supply Co. and a member of the Church Assembly, published *The Future of Private Enterprise* in which he advocated legal reforms that would make a board of directors responsible to employees and consumers as well as shareholders (thereby adumbrating the more recent notion of stakeholders)	political economy	publication	B
1951	54. Ernest Bader, plastic resin manufacturer and Quaker, set up the Scott Bader Commonwealth Ltd, a company limited by guarantee, by which he began to hand all his business assets over to a trust as a radical experiment in fusing the interests of capital and labour	political economy	business practice	B
1963	55. The Marxist historian E. P. Thompson published *The Making of the English Working Class*, triggering the debate about religion as a means of controlling the working classes, wielded by capitalists, in the Industrial Revolution	history	debate	A

Date	Publication, movement, episode, business practice or debate	Content or inspiration	Vehicle	Origin (business (B) or church (C) or academia (A))
1977	56. Ronald J. Sider's *Rich Christians in an Age of Hunger: A Biblical Study* first published in the USA (in the UK in 1978). Coming from the evangelical wing of the Protestant churches, it has had a wide impact in balancing those churches' adventism and other-worldliness with concern for the material needs of the starving and underprivileged in the twentieth-century global village	political economy	publication	C
1979	57. Conservative Government of Mrs Thatcher appealed to Victorian entrepreneurial values to help reverse Britain's relative economic decline	political economy	government policy	politics
1980	58. *North-South: A Programme for Survival.* The Report of the Independent Commission on International Development Issues, chaired by Willy Brandt, published. *North-South* was a clarion call to the developed world to end the misery of the world's starving millions. The British member of the Commission was Edward Heath MP, former UK Prime Minister, who in a 1976 reprint of William Temple's *Christianity and Social Order* acknowledged the enormous debt of his generation to Temple	international political economy	publication	politics
1981 onwards	59. The gentrification debate, attributing Britain's relative economic decline in part to the teaching of Christianity and the classics in Victorian public schools, was revived by Martin J. Wiener in his book *English Culture and the Decline of the Industrial Spirit, 1850–1980.* Another study in a similar vein, Correlli Barnett's *The Audit of War: The Illusion and Reality of Britain as a Great Nation* (1986), derided Temple's influence as 'New Jerusalemism'	history	debate	A and public debate
1985	60. *Faith in the City: A Call for Action by Church and Nation. The Report of the Archbishop of Canterbury's Commission on Urban Priority Areas* published. A careful assessment of inner-city decay in modern Britain and the challenge this presented to the Church of England, *Faith in the City* said little about the role of business, apart from urging the	religious and national crisis	publication	C

	church scandal / political economy	business practice / government policy	C / politics
	government to promote small firms in Urban Priority Areas as a means of beginning their economic revival		
1980s	61. The Church Commissioners made misjudged property investments which were revealed when property values crashed in 1990. As a result, the Church of England's clergy stipends and pensions funds incurred losses of £800 million. Losses were recovered by 1997		
1997	62. (New) Labour government of Tony Blair, in which Christian Socialists are prominent, started to implement its pre-election promise of cleaning up ethical behaviour in the City and business		

Note: [1]The sources for this table are numerous. Most useful for a general reader will be the following:

David W. Bebbington, *The Nonconformist Conscience: Chapel and Politics, 1870–1914* (London, 1982).

David W. Bebbington, *Evangelicalism in Modern Britain: A History from the 1730s to the 1980s* (London, 1989).

Owen Chadwick, *The Victorian Church* (2 vols, London, 1971–72).

Alan D. Gilbert, *Religion and Society in Industrial England: Church, Chapel and Social Change, 1740–1914* (London, 1976).

David Hempton, *Methodism and Politics in British Society, 1750–1850* (London, 1984).

Ursula Henriques, *Religious Toleration in England, 1787–1833* (London, 1961).

A. J. Boyd Hilton, *The Age of Atonement: The Influence of Evangelicalism on Social and Economic Thought, 1785–1865* (Oxford, 1988).

David J. Jeremy (ed.), *Business and Religion in Britain* (Aldershot, 1988).

David J. Jeremy, *Capitalists and Christians: Business Leaders and the Churches in Britain, 1900–1960* (Oxford, 1990).

Hugh McLeod, *Religion and Society in England, 1850–1914* (London, 1996).

Bernard Lord Manning, *The Protestant Dissenting Deputies* (Cambridge, 1952).

Edward R. Norman, *Church and Society in England, 1770–1970: A Historical Study* (Oxford, 1976).

Paul T. Phillips, *A Kingdom on Earth: Anglo-American Social Christianity, 1880–1940* (University Park PA: Pennsylvania State University Press, 1996).

Ronald H. Preston, *Church and State in the Late Twentieth Century: The Economic and Political Task* (London, 1983).

Michael R. Watts, *The Dissenters* (2 vols, Oxford, 1978–95).

Table 1.2 Major denominations and churches in the United Kingdom in the twentieth century

	Date established	Denomination	Theology	Liturgy	Local leaders	Organisation/polity
England	early AD	Roman Catholic church*	Trinitarian	Ritualistic	Priest	Hierarchy under bishops and pope
		Protestant churches				
	16th century	Church of England (Anglican Church)	Trinitarian	Ritualistic and non-ritualistic	Priest	Hierarchy under two archbishops. State church
	16th century	Congregationalists	Trinitarian	Formal worship	Minister	Local church autonomous
	16th century	Presbyterians	Trinitarian	Formal worship	Minister	Hierarchy of courts
	17th century	Baptists	Trinitarian	Formal worship and believer's baptism	Minister	Local church autonomous
	17th century	Unitarians	Unitarian	Formal worship	Minister	Local church autonomous
	17th century	Society of Friends (Quakers)	Trinitarian	Informal worship	Lay elders and ministers	Local meeting under Yearly Meeting
	1784	Wesleyan Methodists	Trinitarian	Formal worship	Minister	Conference of ministers and laity
	1797	Methodist New Connexion	Trinitarian	Formal worship	Minister	Conference of ministers and laity
	1810	Primitive Methodists	Trinitarian	Formal worship	Minister	Conference of ministers and laity
	1830	Christian Brethren	Trinitarian	Formal worship and believer's baptism	Lay elder	Local church autonomous
	1865	Salvation Army	Trinitarian	Informal worship	Officer	Centralised army model
	1907	United Methodist Churches	Trinitarian	Formal worship	Minister	Conference of ministers and laity
	1932	Methodist Church	Trinitarian	Formal worship	Minister	Conference of ministers and laity
	1972	United Reformed Church	Trinitarian	Formal worship	Minister	National union of churches
Scotland	1560	Church of Scotland	Trinitarian	Formal worship	Minister	Presbyterian (see above); state church
	1690	Episcopal Church in Scotland	Trinitarian	Similar to C of E	Priest	Hierarchy under bishops
	1843	Free Church of Scotland	Trinitarian	Formal worship	Minister	Presbyterian (see above)
	1929	union of C of S and F C of S	Trinitarian	Formal worship	Minister	Presbyterian (see above)
Wales	1536	The Church in Wales	Trinitarian	Similar to C of E	Priest	Hierarchy under bishops; state church until 1920
	1639	Welsh Independents	Trinitarian	Formal worship	Minister	Local church autonomous
	1730	Presbyterian Church of Wales	Trinitarian	Formal worship	Minister	Presbyterian (see above)
Ireland	1537	Church of Ireland	Trinitarian	Similar to C of E	Priest	Hierarchy under bishops; state church until 1871
	1642	Presbyterian Church of Ireland	Trinitarian	Formal worship	Minister	Presbyterian (see above)

Note*: the Roman Catholic Church also existed in Scotland, Wales, and Ireland (where it was the dominant religion in the 26 counties which formed the Republic of Ireland in 1922).

Source: D. Jeremy Capitalists and Christians (Oxford, 1990) pp. 18–21.

RELIGION AND THE RISE OF CAPITALISM

This, the most famous historical debate of all, though not the oldest, originated in Germany (item 37). It has instigated a huge literature,[3] partly because Weber, the debate's originator, made major and enduring contributions to what became the discipline of sociology. His ideas resonated beyond Germany not least because in Britain capitalism was experiencing a crisis in the late nineteenth century. Foreign competitors were now catching up and overtaking the first industrial nation. In terms of national economic growth rates and in shares of international markets the United Kingdom was slipping behind.[4] Trying to understand the non-economic springs of capitalist development had relevance to Weber's contemporaries, though his work was not translated into English until 1930, by which time the collapse of the UK's older industries had made Weber's theory even more pertinent. Weber was interested in affinities between the 'spirit' of modern economic life and the rational ethics of ascetic Protestantism. His perceptions came from his own upbringing (his mother was a devout Protestant, his father, who came from a west German family of linen merchants and textile manufacturers, was indifferent to religion); from his observation of American religion (the essay on Protestant sects arose from a visit to the United States in 1904); and from his studies of ancient, rational legal and administrative systems (his doctoral thesis being on the history of commercial, German, and Roman law in agrarian societies).[5]

In a nutshell, Weber's thesis was that Reformation doctrines and lifestyles were conducive to the accumulation of capital. Weber emphasised the contributions of Martin Luther and John Calvin, the sixteenth-century Protestant reformers. From Luther came the doctrine of 'the calling', of a life-task to which the individual Christian felt divinely called. Calvin's doctrine of predestination, Weber argued, introduced a social logic with enormous consequences. For the individual, uncertainty about his eternal fate induced 'a feeling of unprecedented inner loneliness'.[6] Attaining the grace and favour of God required social achievement, i.e. engaging in intense worldly activity, in work, to the glory of God and proof of personal faith. However, worldly activity had to be characterised by denial of the self and the conquest of carnal appetitites. The old monastic code was diverted into secular pursuits. Only through a rational asceticism could assurance of election to eternal life and self-confidence be gained.

Weber also drew upon the teachings of the seventeenth-century English Puritans. Like the Continental Reformers they emphasised work, the curse on man when (in the Genesis story) he fell from grace. As part of the divine order of things in a fallen world, humankind was destined to labour in life. Other Puritan teachings stressed that all individuals had talents and were ultimately and daily accountable to God for the use of their gifts and resources. There was also the Old Testament-inspired view that material success echoed a moral and spiritual obedience which met with God's approval.

Such teachings moulded mindsets and motivated effort. The striving to overcome inner doubts over election, the struggle to deny self, the dedication to prove one's election was sure: these were powerful drives for the believer in the midst of the uncertainties of life. They fed personal attitudes and habits. So the Protestant ethic, most apparent in work and industriousness, time-discipline, idleness-avoidance, moderation, frugality, and thrift, converged with the spirit of capitalism.

R. H. Tawney (item 46) widened Weber's views to include the whole Protestant movement. He also traced the seeds of an individualism which would emerge in the competitive and (as Tawney the Christian Socialist saw it) uncaring capitalism of the nineteenth and early twentieth centuries.

Attempts by historians to apply Weber to modern capitalism have rested on the premise that Protestantism could produce the 'ideal type' of individual whose philosophy and lifestyle coincided with the demands of economic development. However, as Michael Flinn has observed,[7] industrialisation required two new and very different classes, operatives as well as entrepreneurs. From the former, conformity and discipline were required, from the latter, sufficient deviance to engage in risk-taking. At this point Weber's theory offers little help. Other alternatives arrived, however.

For historians the strongest theoretical case against the wholesale application of Weber came from Samuelsson.[8] He found contradictory attitudes towards the making of profit in the writings of Calvin and in those of the English Puritans, the Quakers, and the Methodists. He noted that Benjamin Franklin (whom Weber cited as an archetype of the Protestant spirit) was a deist rather than a Christian. Moreover, Franklin was as much an economic man as any Puritan in the American colonies of his day. Further, Catholic countries, like late medieval Portugal or northern Italy in the Renaissance or Belgium in the nineteenth century, could be as vigorous in seeking economic development as Protestant countries. In England, Samuelsson argued, economic expansion had preceded the Protestant revolution. Professor O'Brien (Chapter 6) sides with Samuelsson.

In linking business and ethnic groups in Britain since the Industrial Revolution in the context of Weber, Professor Chapman (Chapter 9) and Professor Waters (Chapter 11) emphasise the importance of networks and status, rather than individual striving. Need for achievement, acceptance, and security came from the minority religious or ethnic group. Their work underscores what sociologists have earlier found in immigrant studies.

Professor Rubinstein (Chapter 10) finds new possibilities and old problems. I would only add that in using the evidence of the *Dictionary of Business Biography* (*DBB*)[9] both he and I may have been misled by the nature of the sample on which it was drawn. A much more objective sampling is found in my analysis of the chairmen and managing directors of the UK's largest hundred employers in 1907, 1935, and 1955. This found that the Anglicans and the Quakers had a massive over-representation in these business elites. The evidence is shown in Table 1.3.

Table 1.3 summarises findings from an objectively drawn sample of the British business elite in the first half of the twentieth century. Admittedly, it is biased towards labour rather than capital. The upper half of the table sums the numbers in each of the three elites who attended schools with known Anglican and Quaker

Table 1.3 Denominational school and adult affiliations of the chairmen and managing directors of the hundred largest employers in the United Kingdom in 1907, 1935 and 1955

		1907	*1935*	*1955*
religious schooling	**Church of England**			
	numbers of C. of E.	49	50	72
	total in elite	201	203	212
	total known	142	115	153
	percentage in the elite of each year (cases known) divided by religious density in UK population	3.84	5.74	7.06
	Quakers			
	number of Quakers	3	3	2
	total in elite	201	203	212
	total known	142	115	153
	percentage in the elite of each year (cases known) divided by religious density in UK population	44.01	62.11	30.4
adult religious preference	**Church of England**			
	numbers of C. of E.	54	50	33
	total in elite	201	203	212
	total known	145	171	160
	percentage in the elite of each year (cases known) divided by religious density in UK population	4.14	3.86	3.09
	Quakers			
	number of Quakers	3	3	2
	total in elite	201	203	212
	total known	145	171	160
	percentage in the elite of each year (cases known) divided by religious density in UK population	43.13	41.67	29.07

Source: D. Jeremy, *Capitalists and Christians* (Oxford, 1990) pp. 83, 113, 115.

affiliations. The lower half summarises adult religious preferences of members of the elites, which may have been as tenuous as the nature of the rites by which the individual was married or buried. In each case, schooling and adult religious preference, the proportions in the elite are then compared to denominational proportions in the whole of the UK population. As can be seen, the Anglicans were over-represented in the business elites by a factor ranging from four to seven. The Quakers, tiny in absolute numbers in the elites, vastly outperformed all other denominations when compared to their presence in the population as a whole. The other point suggested by Table 1.3 is that the Anglicans were losing their grip on the elite, especially between the 1930s and the 1950s. Over these decades they invested more in schooling the potential business elite than they gained in terms of membership of the current business elite. None of this does more than overturn the calculations I made earlier from the *DBB* data.[10]

THE NONCONFORMIST CONTRIBUTION TO THE INDUSTRIAL REVOLUTION IN BRITAIN

The contribution of the Nonconformists to Britain's first wave of industrial development was unquestionably significant but just how significant has been the bone of contention. One of the earliest publications identifying the Dissenters as a source of economic success appeared in 1816 (item 7). It is almost unknown because it was published as an appendix to a funeral sermon.[11] Israel Worsley, the author, was a Unitarian minister and teacher (Unitarians were those Presbyterians and Independents, members of 'Old Dissent', whose espousal of Enlightenment rationalism led them to deny the divinity of Christ). He was then in Plymouth. Twenty or more years earlier he had been a Dissenting minister in Amsterdam and later Dunkirk, and had been imprisoned in France after the collapse of the Peace of Amiens in 1803. His marginal social status in England and his distant views of England's multiplying factories and fortunes gave him a special perspective on the economic activities of his Dissenting brethren.

In publishing his *Observations* Worsley had a more pointed purpose than social commentary. The Toleration Act of 1688 allowed all religious congregations a legal existence outside the Church of England, apart from Unitarians, Catholics, and Jews. All kinds of Dissenters were officially excluded from offices of power in government and the armed forces until 1828–29 (1858 in the case of the Jews).[12] In 1813 William Smith's Act allowed Unitarians for the first time to claim the benefits of religious assembly granted under the Toleration Act. Emerging from the shadows into which they were driven by charges of sedition in the intolerant aftermath of the French Revolution, these Dissenters were especially anxious to prove their loyalty to the British constitution and their value to British society. Such was the context of Worsley's polemic.

The fifty-five pages of Worsley's tract on British manufactures scanned the technically advanced industries of his day, purposefully claiming manufacturers and inventors (a few of whom he names) as members of Dissenting congregations. His survey passed from Huguenots and the woollen and silk manufacturers of the seventeenth century to Arkwright. The latter, he alleged, gleaned some of his technical ideas from French refugees. William and Joseph Strutt, cotton manufacturers of Derby (and Arkwright's associates), were hailed as 'the enlightened and energetic professors of the Unitarian doctrine'.[13] French and English Presbyterians, Worsley claimed, set up the cotton manufacture in seventeenth-century Lancashire. The following century the Dissenters Jedediah Strutt and William Woollatt introduced the ribbed stocking manufacture. So Worsley's catalogue continued. Anonymous linen manufacturers in Ireland, Josiah Wedgwood, the Stoke-on-Trent potter, an un-named Worcester china manufacturer, iron and steel manufacturers at Birmingham and Sheffield, lace makers in Buckingham and Bedfordshire: all demonstrated Worsley's conclusion,

> that, although the avowal of dissenting principles cannot of itself manufacture either woollen or silken or linen cloth, yet, the freedom of the mind which they enjoy who are bound by no 'tyrant's law' is calculated to promote the general

interests of society; and that a love of religious liberty promotes also a love of civil liberty, and of the arts and sciences, in the improvement of which the dissenters of England are well known to have borne no inconsiderable share.[14]

Curiously, Worsley made no use of the estimate of the size of the Dissenting proportion of the population recently published by Bogue and Bennett.[15] Nor did he seem to know much about the gentlemen clothiers and Unitarians in the West of England.[16]

The role of the Nonconformists was overlooked at the height of mid-Victorian prosperity when the myth of the self-made man carried the day as a popular explanatory model for British industrial success. Carlyle's tomes on heroes and Samuel Smiles's readable sketches projected an ideology of heroic individualism which had little place for networks and communities and none for denominational religion. In *Self-Help* (1859), the key text which sold 20,000 copies in the first year and over 250,000 by the time he died in 1904, Smiles held aloft for emulation several Nonconformist manufacturers, the anti-slavery campaigners, and the missionary David Livingstone, but declined to say anything substantive about their religious impulses. 'Heaven helps those who help themselves', the individualistic maxim with which Smiles opened *Self-Help*, was as far as he ventured in relating religion and business.

Buried under Smiles's bootstrap heroes, the contribution of Nonconformity awaited later generations armed with different historical motives and methods. T. S. Ashton, the Lancashire-born economic historian and pillar of the 'Manchester school', was one of the first modern historians to rediscover the significance of the Dissenters, to whom he gave credit both in his history of the eighteenth-century steel industry in 1924 and in his small and much more widely read history of the industrial revolution twenty-four years later.[17] Ashton observed the relatively strong presence of the Quakers in the iron industry, particularly in the West Midlands where families like the Darbys of Coalbrookdale exemplified the phenomenon. In Chapter 7 in this volume, Drs Prior and Kirby reveal in rich detail the ways in which religious and economic lives intersected.

While Ashton drew attention to Nonconformists, some headway was made by Hagen in estimating their numerical strength and by Flinn in theorising about how they moved ahead. Hagen estimated that of ninety-two leading entrepreneurs in Britain in the early industrial period, 49 per cent were Nonconformist. Flinn applied the results of D. C. McClelland's psychometric studies of high achievers to eighteenth-century evidence on child rearing, arguing that it was this which produced both entrepreneurs and docile factory workers because the educational ideas and practices of the Dissenters clearly distinguished between middle-class and working-class education. Unfortunately the much larger sample of early industrialists later constructed by Crouzet has cast doubt on the representativeness of Hagen's sample. However, Crouzet made no systematic attempt to establish religious affiliations.[18]

Most recently, attention has turned to the intangible factor of trust. In Casson's opinion 'perhaps the single most important set of beliefs, however, relates to the question of who can be trusted'. He argues that lack of trust pushes up the transaction costs experienced within and between firms. If he is right, then the religious and ethnic minorities have non-economic network advantages which could translate into lower costs and swifter transactions. The whole idea of trust has been explored at some length by Fukuyama. He believes that high-trust societies, like Germany and Japan, 'in contrast to familistic societies . . . have had a much easier time spawning large-scale firms not based on kinship'.[19]

RELIGIOUS MINORITIES AND THE CREATION OF WEALTH

While learned divines deployed lengthy treatises in defence of Christian principles of business conduct, the Society of Friends drew on a simpler, more practical code instituted by their seventeenth-century founder which they too enforced through church disciplinary bodies. Ann Prior and Maurice Kirby in Chapter 7 detail the standards expected of Quakers in business and the mechanisms by which they were enforced, most consistently before the 1840s.[20]

Not all scholars studying religious minorities have seen religion as the key to those minorities' material success. In Chapter 9 Professor Chapman argues that the Weber thesis is dead and that much more is to be learned by focusing on ethnicity and international mobility. Personal wealth creation, he says, was for some immigrant merchants a way of achieving social acceptance in their host community.

The possibility that religious teaching was related to the worldly success of religious minorities is one which Professor Rubinstein in Chapter 10 regards as central to the Weber thesis and one which he questions. Educational systems and kin networks might be more important. He suggests that 'place', i.e. the geographical location or the industry where high achievers chose to operate, was more important than ascetic personal habits. His observation that nineteenth-century technological networks (railways, steamships, telegraphs etc.) may have diminished the value of ethnic or religious networks is an interesting one. I would note that the expansion of secrecy and secretive techniques in modern industry and commerce would diminish the force of this argument.[21] Equally interesting is Professor Rubinstein's suggestion that (a) the Methodist sects were better at producing self-made men than the Quakers and Old Dissent; and (b) these new individualistic entrepreneurs were better than older cousinhoods at seizing the market opportunities offered by the competitive factory capitalism of nineteenth-century Britain. Perhaps this helps to explain the success of the Wesleyan lay leaders who figure in Chapter 4 by David Jeremy. Should we then be looking at Smiles rather than Weber for explanations? Professor Waters prefers Weber. At any rate the possibility needs empirical investigation – a point which Professor Waters' comments in Chapter 11 on the Chapman and Rubinstein chapters underlines.

METHODISM AS A CAPITALIST INSTRUMENT OF SOCIAL CONTROL

This issue began as a debate about the social importance of Methodism.[22] William Lecky, the late nineteenth-century Irish historian, alleged that in evangelising and civilising the poor, Methodism saved England from revolution. Elie Halevy, the French historian, in his *England in 1815* (published in France in 1913, translated into English in 1924, and reprinted in 1949 and 1960) hazarded that Methodism explained 'the extraordinary stability which English Society was destined to enjoy throughout a period of revolutions and crises'.[23] On the other hand, the Hammonds in 1917 blamed the Methodists for teaching the working classes resignation.[24]

Seeing Methodism in the light of his religion-and-the-rise-of-capitalism theme, Weber regarded Methodism's main contribution as no more than the addition of emotion (in 'the emotional act of conversion'[25]) to asceticism. The place of emotion was explored further by Wellman Warner who in 1930 investigated links between social psychology, Methodism and mill owners.[26] There the debate rested until 1963 when E. P. Thompson (item 55) developed Warner's ideas and examples to provide a highly provocative account of the roles of Methodism in the early development of England's industrial capitalism. According to this, 'box-like blackening chapels stood in the industrial districts like great traps for the human psyche'. Religion, by Weberian mechanisms, created a work-discipline. But more, Methodism's emotional experiences ('a ritualised form of psychic masturbation') sublimated the workers' anger against their masters. Equally effectively, Methodist child-rearing practices 'terrorised' into submission the rebel spirits of fresh generations of the working class.[27]

Thompson, in selecting and interpreting his evidence, had axes to grind. He was the son of a disaffected Methodist minister and he was a Marxist. And he was a militant whose weapon was historical writing. His evidence was qualitative, impressionistic and carefully selected. He offered no quantitative analysis of early Methodist hymnbooks, for example, to support his Freudian interpretations of what went on in Methodist chapels. And he conveniently overlooked the quantitative evidence, offered by E. R. Wickham, that the industrial working classes were not going to church or chapel in the early nineteenth century anyway.[28] Despite Thompson's impassioned and ingenious interpretations, it was hard for those with Methodist sympathies (and many without them) to see how Methodism could have been systematically and effectively used as an instrument of social control.

Nevertheless, Thompson valuably raised the important question of religion as social control. In the context of the workplace and the church or chapel, did this exist to any great extent? How did it function? What changes emerged over time? Some answers came from Patrick Joyce who explored the cultures of northern mill communities in the late nineteenth-century.[29] However, Joyce's style is dense and his analytical technique lacks a rigorous quantitative framework. We are left with lots of examples but no convincing evidence that they were representative. A more limited but focused study by Jane Garnett and Anthony Howe illustrates the complexities that arose in the relations between mill masters and clerics in Victorian Lancashire.[30]

Religion certainly was used as an instrument of social control by entrepreneurs and proprietors. By the beginning of the twentieth century there was at least one case of this among the hundred largest employers. William Lever, the soap manufacturer of Port Sunlight on the Mersey, utilised religion in the service of his business objectives. With remarkable generosity and ingenuity he hired a clergyman to double as a company welfare officer and company church minister. He built a church whose membership was confined to his employees. And he supported all manner of church organisations. All to little avail: less than a fifth of the adults in his company village bothered to become members of the company church.[31]

Ironically, Thompson's obsession with emotion blinded him to the more obvious and materialist possibility that what Methodists did with their money was as important as what they did with their feelings. Professor Reg Ward, a leading church historian whose work has ranged widely and intensively across Non-conformity and early Methodism in particular, in Chapter 3 roams broadly across the theme of Methodists and wealth. Like Mr Corley in Chapter 8, he is interested in Wesley's teachings. Chapter 4 by David Jeremy reveals some remarkable outcomes of Methodist charitable giving which could be regarded as having diverted considerable sums away from business investment.

RELIGION AND ECONOMICS: UNRELATED?

Possibly the new interest in the classical economists, evident since the 1960s and 1970s, arose from contemporary doubts about Keynesian demand management of the economy. More recently it has gathered momentum from a reaction against the econometric and highly technical side of the economics discipline. And classical political economy has attracted those most interested in the social implications of economic policy.

In the present context (and vastly simplifying the debate), the starting point is Adam Smith's *Wealth of Nations* (1776). Fundamental to Smith's view of economics was the supremacy of the market. The market, asserted Smith, is like an invisible hand which promotes public good out of private self-interest. This paradox, Dr Young reminds us in Chapter 1, had earlier been resolved in an anti-Christian tract by Bernard de Mandeville *The Fable of the Bees* (1714). Private vices and conspicuous consumption (Veblen's much later phrase), rather than Christian virtues and the propensity to save, might serve a secular economy. Such a view affronted clerics both in Mandeville's time and after *The Wealth of Nations* appeared. By implication (though he disavowed this elsewhere) Smith might be seen as supping with Mandeville.

Whereas Dr Young stresses continuities of thought, Dr Boyd Hilton's message in Chapter 2 is that the drift towards a morally neutral and technical understanding of economics and the market, evident in Smith, was halted by the watershed of revolution. From the 1790s, Hilton argues, the views of technical economists (Ricardo, Senior, and Mill) were counterbalanced by those of clerics (usually evangelical) who used sin-and-atonement-centred theology to understand the disturbing events and deep pessimism of their post-Revolution times.

The intellectual battle to subject political economy (economics) to a Christian ethic began with Malthus (item 6). Chalmers (item 8) as Boyd Hilton has shown elsewhere, took Malthusian population theory (in which the positive checks on population growth, of famine, war, and pestilence, and the preventive checks of sexual vices, were viewed as divinely ordered mechanisms) and applied it to the business or trade cycle. For Chalmers, the vices of extravagance and speculation would be punished by the retributive collapse of the trade boom.[32] Evangelical men in business, like the banker Samuel Jones Loyd (item 12) in the early Victorian era accepted this moral interpretation of economic behaviour. Indeed, it is this sort of underpinning which makes explicable the intervention of Nonconformist church courts when any of their prominent businessmen went bankrupt (item 26).[33]

The evangelicals lost their battle after the 1860s. Social problems in industrial society were growing beyond the solvent power of personal discipline and private philanthropy. Doubt, inspired by Darwin, German biblical scholarship, and moral sensibilities, assailed the foundations of the evangelical fortress.[34] Desperate evangelicals turned away from worldly problems and increasingly towards pre-millennial hopes.[35] Meanwhile the rise of organised labour and of socialism heralded fresh assaults on the vast urban problems unveiled by the 'Condition of England' debate in the 1880s. By the 1890s there was a self-evident gap between religion and ethics, on one side, economics and business, on the other. Christian Socialists influenced by the incarnational theology of Maurice and his followers, often on the Anglo-Catholic wing of the Church of England, found a voice (items 13, 19, 30). Among Nonconformists Samuel Keeble, a Wesleyan minister, sounded the alarm (item 34). New answers to the religion–business dichotomy had to be sought. Some were found after the next cataclysm, the First World War. Meanwhile there were still plenty who agreed with Sir Josiah Stamp, president of the London, Midland & Scottish Railway Co. and a leading Methodist layman, when in 1936 he asked 'in what precise sense can . . . the National Union of Railwaymen love the Railway Stockholders' Union?'[36] (item 47). Individuals, not systems, were to be redeemed. Political economy still slid away from the claims of religion and ethics.

CHRISTIAN DUTY AND POWER RELATIONS WITHIN THE FIRM

The influence-of-Methodism debate would come under this heading but has been so important historiographically that it has been noted separately here. On three other issues there has been recent historical debate which has implications for this theme. One is paternalism. Another is profit-sharing and its alternatives. The third is the managerial revolution.

Paternalism

In the early nineteenth century a very small minority of industrialists could be regarded as model employers, perhaps in the early 1840s no more than 40 or 50 among 4,800 factory owners, to say nothing of thousands more mine and workshop owners.[37] These 'best practice' employers were paternalists. Their ideas about their responsibilities to their employees and to the community drew upon two traditions, the aristocratic ethos and the Puritan code.[38] The Scottish divine Thomas Chalmers provided theological support for these 'best practice' paternalist employers (item 9). The essence of the paternalist, and an aspect that has offended twentieth-century historians, was that he stood above his workers not only in working time but at all times. With the best of intentions he provided benefits in addition to wages – housing, schooling, medical treatment, provision for religious education, etc.. – enveloping his employees' lives with welfare and the obligations which that brought. Joyce detected a shift in paternalist relations over the course of the nineteenth century, from dependence to deference. However, Robert Fitzgerald has traced the persistence of employer welfare up to the Second World War.[39] While the effects of paternalism undermined the individual employee's dignity and independence, as William Lever, one of the great paternalists, found and regretted, the Christian motives that have lain behind it have been both lofty and mixed. Corporate paternalism, it is well known, flourishes in Japan and has contributed to Japan's economic miracle since 1945.

Profit-sharing and its alternatives

Profit-sharing was another nineteenth-century solution which Christian (and other) employers applied to the conflict between capital and labour. Profit-sharing was an agreement whereby the employer awarded a fixed percentage of his profits to his employees in addition to wages and salaries. A later variation, labour co-partnership, awarded employees non-marketable shares. Profit-sharing originated apparently with Henry Currer Briggs, colliery owner and Unitarian of Wakefield, Yorkshire (item 24). Following the 1862 Companies Act and inspired by Henry Fawcett, the Cambridge Professor of Political Economy (and possibly by his Unitarian minister, a Christian Socialist), Briggs converted his business into a public company in 1865.[40] By 1912 199 profit-sharing schemes had been started, of which 163 were abandoned. In the late 1980s there were over 700 such schemes.[41]

Historians have debated whether profit-sharing was anything more than a capitalist device to seduce workers away from trade unions and seal their loyalty to corporate proprietors and managements. That was the view of Church, Pollard and Turner, and Matthews.[42] Others, like Perks, Goodall, and Garnett have emphasised that Christian convictions were the main motive.[43] Exploration of the subtleties of mid-nineteenth-century opinions is promised by Jane Garnett.[44]

The Crossley family of Halifax, carpet manufacturers and Congregationalists who employed 4,100 people when they converted the business to a public company in 1864, sought a different answer to the capital–labour conflict (item 23). Their hope was that employees would buy the shares. Much more radical solutions to the capital–labour tension came after the First World War. While some entrepreneurs continued to insist with William Lever that business was not a charity, others took note of new directions. One was the Whitley Councils, set up at the instigation of the Deputy Speaker of the Commons, James Henry

Whitley, Liberal MP, and a member of a family of Halifax cotton spinners and Congregationalists.[45] The Whitley Councils comprised representatives of employers and unions and were given authority to discuss all matters relating to trade and employment in their respective industries.

Another radical solution was that of John Spedan Lewis, a West End department store owner. Having discovered the merits and limitations of profit-sharing which he started in 1920, after the death of his father in 1928, he established the John Lewis Partnership Ltd. Under this arrangement, he took the first step towards surrendering ownership of his business to a trust, which he did in 1950. Under these schemes employees became Partners and shared in the profits. Lewis disavowed both high and low motives for his determination to seek a more just distribution of resources and rewards between capital and labour, other than the satisfaction of 'the invention of a new system of business for its own sake'. He cannot have been unaffected by his educational background, having been exposed to the values of a liberal Christian culture at Westminster School, a public school.[46] However, not until Ernest Bader, a Swiss-born resin manufacturer and Quaker, launched a similar experiment in 1951 could a Christian motivation be definitely ascribed to this the most drastic of all solutions to the capital–labour power relations problem (item 54).[47] Other Quaker responses are outlined by Mr Corley in Chapter 8 which links Christian Socialism to Quaker debate and action.

Another twentieth-century answer to that problem must be mentioned because it has resurfaced in the late 1980s and 1990s. This was the idea that directors should be responsible to all parties to a business. Further developed, it became the concept of stakeholders. The concept was published in 1951 by George Goyder, managing director of a paper company and a devout and knowledgeable member of the Church Assembly, and active in the Christian Frontier Council whose work was deeply influenced by William Temple, Archbishop of Canterbury, and in Christian social engagement (see items 49, 50, and 53).[48]

The managerial revolution

A momentous development for modern business was the arrival of the joint-stock limited liability company. Besides greatly enlarging the possibilities of capital accumulation, it has wholly transformed power relations within the large corporation by shifting corporate power away from absolute owners and into the hands of professional managers.

Limited companies spread after the Companies Acts of 1856 and 1862 which gave Britain the most liberal company law regime in Europe. From the 1880s onwards limited companies mushroomed. By enabling a plurality of owners to pool their capital without incurring unlimited liability for their corporate debts, the Companies Acts opened the way for proprietors to sell out of a business and people with small savings to buy into it. When company ownership was increasingly diffused among a multitude of shareholders, day-to-day control was left in the hands of full-time managers, as it had been in the new railway companies since the 1830s.[49] Churchgoing people in business now faced new questions. How far was the small shareholder, the owner of a tiny fraction of a public company, responsible for the decisions made by the managers of the company? Was a company a moral agent? What were the duties of managers, especially when their moral principles appeared to conflict with instructions coming from the directors (the shareholders delegated to manage the company at its highest level)? Were managers as free as paternalist owners to spread their religious opinions within the company?

Two examples reveal responses to some of these questions. They both come from the banking industry, necessarily in a propertied economy one of the dominant custodians of high morals in business. The first comes from James William Gilbart, former manager of the London & Westminster Bank (see item 21). In a posthumously published text he asked and answered at great length and with ingenious use of scriptural examples the basic question,

> Ought public companies, like individuals, to be regarded as moral agents, and therefore bound to perform moral and religious duties?
>
> We assume, at the commencement of our inquiries, that mankind, as individuals, are moral agents, having had laws laid down for their government by a Superior Being, to whom they are responsible for their actions. . . . And here we would suggest the following considerations:
>
> 1 Public companies are recognised as moral agents by the laws of the country in which they are established.
>   Public companies have, by law, the same rights as individuals; their property is protected by the same laws as that of individuals. . . . Having the same rights, they have necessarily the same duties as individuals. . . .
> 2 Public companies are capable of sustaining many social relations which are the foundation of moral duties.
>   The social relations of public companies are various. They may be buyers or sellers – debtors or creditors – they may employ others, or be employed themselves – they may be receivers or bestowers of favour – they may be friends or enemies, neighbours or strangers – they may be wealthy or indigent – in prosperity or adversity – they may be influential or otherwise – they may be plaintiffs or defendants in a court of law, or be the accusing or the accused party in a criminal court. . . .
> 3 Public companies sustain those relations to the Deity which imply an obligation to the performance of moral and religious duties. . . .
>   Their relation to the Deity is a relation of dependence. . . . Their relation to the Deity is also a relation of obligation. . . .
> 4 Public companies are analogous to other collective bodies who are acknowledged to be moral agents.[50]

A second reply came from another banking text, by George Rae, chairman and managing director of the North & South Wales Bank, and first published in 1885. Rae advised:

With your private convictions in religion or politics you will have no
interference, provided you keep them in reasonable measure to yourself. . . .
When a Bank Manager therefore becomes either a prominent political partisan,
or a pronounced religious zealot, his Directors have the right to admonish him,
that such outbreaks of zeal are incompatible with his duties to the Bank, and
are not included in the services for which they pay him a salary.[51]

RELIGION AND BRITISH INDUSTRIAL DECLINE

The debate about Britain's relative industrial decline reached a new intensity in
the 1970s when a number of economic measures clearly showed that Britain was
falling behind other capitalist economies. Economic historians pointed out that
this relative decline had begun a century earlier. Soon the search for causation
was sending them down networks of research trails. One of these focused on the
quality of Britain's entrepreneurs in the last quarter of the nineteenth century.
Were they responsible for losing British shares of world markets? If they were
responsible, what was the reason? The debate about the failure of entrepreneurship
thus took two courses. On the one hand, there were the econometricians and others
trying to establish whether the performance of British industry could have been
better if other organisational structures and other technologies had been adopted.
On the other hand, social historians assumed that late Victorian entrepreneurs were
guilty and that explanations in the backgrounds of the entrepreneurs had to be
found.

Economic historians had in fact been debating reasons for divergencies between
the British economic experience and that of follower economies for a long time,
since the early 1950s at least when the Anglo-American differentials exposed by
the Second World War were reviewed.[52] It was therefore a prepared field which
the American college professor Martin Wiener harvested when in 1981 he
published *English Culture and the Decline of the Industrial Spirit, 1850–1980*
(item 59).[53] The gist of the volume was that Britain was basically an aristocratic
agrarian society where landed pursuits and gentlemen amateurs ruled for centuries,
absorbing every new wave of enriched upstarts that came along. Thus the first
wave of self-made industrialists were also subverted and their successors diverted
from achievement in business by the lures of gentlemanly careers and culture. The
instruments of that diversion, Wiener argued, were the public schools and the
Church of England into whose hands self-made fathers entrusted their sons.
However, from the middle of the nineteenth century the Church increasingly
moved towards Christian Socialism, the high tide coming when Temple occupied
the episcopal throne at Canterbury and his *Christianity and Social Order* flooded
the country in 1942 (item 50).[54] Thereafter, with the Labour Government's bold
experiment of the welfare state and the state ownership of industry, 'antiindustrial
sentiments within the church began to wane'.[55]

In fact Wiener's account of the role of the Church in influencing the
government's wartime policies is woefully deficient.[56] But that did not matter in
1982. The Conservative Government of Mrs Thatcher, subjected to growing

criticism from Church dignitaries, warmly welcomed the Wiener thesis. The national press hailed it as a convincing explanation of British industrial decline. The Director of the London School of Economics made a television series, *On Britain*, in which he gave much credence to the Wiener thesis.[57] More support for Wiener came from the military historian Correlli Barnett who in 1986 published his *Audit of War* (item 59). Like Wiener, he blamed the Christian Socialists epitomised by Archbishop William Temple, and labelled their views as 'New Jerusalemism'. Like Wiener, he neither properly reported the influence of Temple's wider circle nor gave them full credit for their impact on business and industry.[58]

Meanwhile the review columns reported scholarly scepticism among economic and social historians. A conference was held at Glasgow University in May 1986 at which Professor Wiener was present but the modest recantation he then made was not printed in the volume of essays which followed.[59] The Wiener thesis looked as elusive as the Weber one to sustain. And yet resonances remain, as Professor Farnie confirms in his magisterial study of the legacy of John Rylands (Chapter 5). Rylands was a hero of towering Weberian and Smilesean proportions if ever there was one. A century after his death the Metropolitan Borough of Trafford demolished his home, despite its listed status. The anti-industrial spirit survived after all.

THE ROLE AND INFLUENCE OF RICH INDIVIDUALS IN CHURCH LIFE

Last, there is debate about the role of rich individuals in the life of the churches. Weber quoted Wesley's opinion, 'I fear, wherever riches have increased, the essence of religion has decreased in the same proportion.'[60] That hazard has been a constant in the life of the Church.

Looking back in 1934, the former Methodist medical missionary, ecumenical statesman, and tourist firm founder, Sir Henry Lunn, recalled,

> Our pulpits in the seventies [1870s] . . . had largely lost touch with the Catholic idea of poverty as one of the great virtues. Some years earlier a much-revered President of the Wesleyan Conference had written two widely different books. One was a powerful assertion of the need for the Baptism of the Holy Spirit in Christian work; the other was a glorification of a rich Methodist merchant. Both books had a large circulation.[61]

Clearly Lunn was unimpressed by the special attention paid to rich benefactors in the churches. And there were rich men among the Dissenters. Rubinstein identified twenty-five millionaires and sixty-eight half-millionaires among the Nonconformists (not including the Church of Scotland), compared to eighty-five millionaires and 234 half-millionaires in the Church of England, between 1780 and 1899.[62]

Adulation of the rich men (and women, like Mrs Rylands) in the midst of the congregation was certainly one side of the problem. It remained a hazard because all the churches to a greater or lesser degree were dependent on wealthy supporters.

Unlike the Anglicans, the Nonconformists could not fall back on tithes and long-held legacies. Yet after the First World War the Church of England too was urgently seeking new sources of finance.[63] Much bigger problems arose in the other Protestant denominations and sects. As Professor Brown has shown in his excellent study of the Nonconformist ministry, their ministers were pitifully paid in most of their churches and throughout most of the nineteenth century. Thus, while the richest Wesleyan businessmen were cheerfully giving away thousands to the Twentieth Century Fund (see Jeremy, Chapter 4), most ministers in the Methodist sects were earning less than £150 a year, no more than an urban workman and only 50 per cent more than an agricultural labourer.[64] This was a source of friction, not least because the more talented would leave the ministry in search of higher remuneration.

Rich laymen for their part worried about how they should use their gold in the service of the gospel. As Dr Garnett has demonstrated, evangelical laymen in the mid-nineteenth century were greatly exercised about how much of their wealth they should regularly give to charity, including the churches. A tenth (or tithe) was the acceptable norm for them.[65] Associated with this problem was the distinction to be made between capital and wealth – the distinction between money for the business and money for the business owner's private use. Confusion over this distinction led to excessive philanthropy, underinvestment, and sometimes even business collapse.[66]

Given that rich laymen were pillars of local congregations there was the possibility in the Nonconformist denominations that their own moral behaviour, within the business or outside it, might be adjudicated not only by ministers but by other businessmen or even employees. One instance of this among the Baptists came after Sir Samuel Morton Peto's bankruptcy (item 26). Professor Ward (Chapter 3) found instances earlier among the Methodists, and Jane Garnett has cited others among mid-nineteenth-century Congregationalists, Quakers, and Methodists, all in relation to bankruptcy.[67]

So the roles of rich men in the church need much more investigation. In local situations the temptation for a businessman to exploit for business interests his position in the chapel may sometimes have been too great to resist. On the other hand, numerous devout men of business have been impeccable and self-sacrificing supporters of religious and philanthropic causes. Some who have been closely studied emerge well from the examination. One of the most extraordinary examples of a Christian in business who combined high levels of personal integrity and faith with outstanding commercial success and a large philanthropy was John Rylands, as Chapter 5 by Professor Farnie shows. On a smaller scale, there was John Mackintosh, the late Victorian toffee manufacturer who prudently distributed his wealth in his Methodist New Connexion chapel in Halifax.[68] Sir Alfred Owen, an energetic Anglican evangelical, gave much time and personal wealth in support of the early Billy Graham Crusades.[69] So too did Sir John Laing, a leader among the Brethren, who also co-founded the London Bible College and, on winning the contract to rebuild Coventry Cathedral, chose to give all the profit back to the Cathedral authorities.[70] On the other hand, there were scoundrels who in various ways brought their faith into disrepute. Most notable perhaps were Jabez Spencer Balfour (item 33), whose decisions caused the collapse of the largest building society of the day on the heads of investors who included many widows, chapel members, and chapel trustees; Lord Overtoun (item 35) who saw no dilemma in simultaneously practising deep public piety and a neglect of health and safety at his chemical works which horribly injured employees; and William Whiteley (item 39), an evangelical whose murder by a man claiming to be his illegitimate son evoked a huge petition for clemency for his killer, to such an extent were Whiteley's ruthless paternalism and sexual hypocrisy resented in Bayswater and West London.[71] But these judgements skate over complexities of perception and motivation.

Historians have debated about how capitalists saw and discharged their duties as men of wealth and power. Commitment to some form of the Christian faith imposed high standards and raised high expectations which were not always met.[72] Changing markets and technologies presented new problems which church teaching did not always prepare its adherents to face. Many of these religious and ethical problems are still with us. Historical debates often have relevance and instruction for the present. The chapters in this volume give an inkling of some of the ideas and developments in theory and in life where firm ground has beckoned but too often quicksands have lurked.

NOTES

1 See numerous essays in W. J. Shiels and Diana Wood (eds), *The Church and Wealth* (Oxford, 1987).
2 This volume began as a number of conference papers. For an excuse to rekindle my interest in the subject I am indebted to Professor Patrick K. O'Brien, Director of the Institute of Historical Research at the University of London. Responsible for organising the 65th annual Conference of Anglo-American Historians, which in 1996 was considering the theme of 'Religion and Society', he kindly invited me to assemble a number of seminars on the topic of Religion and Wealth. Fortunately an appreciable number of other historians have been working on interactions between religion and economic activity in modern Britain and a dozen or so were persuaded to participate. The result was four seminars and eleven papers at the Anglo-American Conference on 3–5 July 1996. Most of those papers, some in revised form, are published here.
3 See Gordon Marshall, *In Search of the Spirit of Capitalism: An Essay on Max Weber's Protestant Ethic Thesis* (London, 1982).
4 Angus Maddison, *Dynamic Forces in Capitalist Development: A Long-Run Comparative View* (Oxford, 1991), p. 49; B. W. E. Alford, *Britain in the World Economy since 1880* (London, 1996), p. 53.
5 H. H. Gerth and C. Wright Mills (eds), *From Max Weber: Essays in Sociology* (repr. London, 1991).
6 Max Weber, *The Protestant Ethic and the Spirit of Capitalism* (trans. Talcott Parsons, 1930; repr. London, 1968), p. 104.
7 M. W. Flinn, 'Social Theory and the Industrial Revolution', in Tom Burns and S. B. Saul (eds), *Social Theory and Economic Change* (London, 1967), p. 12.
8 Kurt Samuelsson, *Religion and Economic Action* (London, 1961).
9 David Jeremy and Christine Shaw (eds), *Dictionary of Business Biography* (6 vols, London, 1984–86). Hereafter cited as *DBB*.

10 David J. Jeremy, 'Important Questions about Business and Religion in Modern Britain' in David Jeremy (ed.), *Business and Religion in Britain* (Aldershot, 1988), pp. 15–18.

11 Israel Worsley, *Observations on the State and Changes in the Presbyterian Societies of England during the Last Half Century: also, on the Manufactures of Great Britain; Which Have Been for the Most Part Established and Supported by the Protestant Dissenters: Tending to Illustrate the Importance of Religious Liberty and Free Inquiry to the Welfare and Prosperity of a People: Preceded by a Sermon on the Death of the Rev. Dr Joshua Toulmin, in which His Character as a Member of Civil Society is Attempted to Be Improved* (London, 1816; 125 pages). Copy in Manchester Central Reference Library.

12 Ursula Henriques, *Religious Toleration In England, 1787–1833* (London, 1961); Bernard Lord Manning, *The Protestant Dissenting Deputies* (Cambridge, 1952).

13 Worsley, *Observations*, p. 92.

14 Ibid., p. 124.

15 D. Bogue and J. Bennett, *History of Dissenters*, vols 2 (1809), 3 (1810), and 4 (1812), quoted in Flinn, 'Social Theory', p. 23.

16 For which see David J. Jeremy (ed.), *Henry Wansey and His American Journal, 1794* (Philadelphia, 1970). See also on Unitarianism, John Seed, 'Theologies of Power: Unitarianism and the Social Relations of Religious Discourse, 1800–50', in R. J. Morris (ed.), *Class, Power and Social Structure in British Nineteenth-Century Towns* (Leicester, 1986).

17 Thomas S. Ashton, *Iron and Steel in the Industrial Revolution* (Manchester, 1924), pp. 211–25; T. S. Ashton, *The Industrial Revolution, 1760–1830* (London, 1948), pp. 17–22.

18 Everett E. Hagen, *On the Theory of Social Change* (London, 1962); Flinn, 'Social Theory'; Francois Crouzet, *The First Industrialists: The Problem of Origins* (Cambridge, 1985), pp. 52–4.

19 Mark Casson, 'Entrepreneurship and Business Culture', in Jonathan Brown and Mary B. Rose (eds), *Entrepreneurship, Networks and Modern Business* (Manchester, 1993), p. 41; Francis Fukuyama, *Trust: The Social Virtues and the Creation of Prosperity* (London, 1995), p. 12.

20 Maurice W. Kirby, *Men of Business and Politics: The Rise and Fall of the Quaker Pease Dynasty of North-East England, 1700–1943* (London, 1984), pp. 47–72.

21 Douglas Farnie and I have an article on secrecy in the textile industry forthcoming.

22 For the debate see David Hempton, *Methodism and Politics in British Society, 1750–1850* (London, 1984), Chapter 2 especially; and earlier, Stuart Andrews, *Methodism and Society* (London, 1970).

23 Elie Halévy, *England in 1815* (London, 1960), p. 387.

24 John L. Hammond and Barbara Hammond, *The Town Labourer, 1760–1832* (London, 1917).

25 Weber, *Protestant Ethic*, p. 143.

26 Wellman J. Warner, *The Wesleyan Movement in the Industrial Revolution* (London, 1930). See Hempton, *Methodism and Politics*, pp. 231–4 for cautionary comments on Warner.

27 Edward P. Thompson, *The Making of the English Working Class* (London, 1963), pp. 350–400. For Thompson's career see *The Times* 30 August 1993.

28 Edward R. Wickham, *Church and People in an Industrial City* (London, 1957), pp. 89–94. Even in the most religious of industrial societies, like that of South Wales, the ecstasies of revival came unpredictably and at long intervals of years, rather than every weekend as Thompson implies. See E. T. Davies, *Religion in the Industrial Revolution in South Wales* (Cardiff, 1965), pp. 55–61.

29 Patrick Joyce, *Work, Society and Politics: The Culture of the Factory in Later Victorian England* (Brighton, 1980).

30   Jane Garnett and A. C. Howe, 'Churchmen and Cotton Masters in Victorian England', in Jeremy (ed.), *Business and Religion in Britain*.

31   David J. Jeremy, 'The Enlightened Paternalist in Action: William Hesketh Lever at Port Sunlight before 1914', *Business History* 33 (1) (1991).

32   Boyd Hilton, *The Age of Atonement: The Influence of Evangelicalism on Social and Economic Thought, 1785–1865*, (Oxford, 1988) pp. 116–20.

33   See Faith and Brian Bowers, 'Bloomsbury Chapel and Mercantile Morality: The Case of Sir Morton Peto', *Baptist Quarterly* 30 (1984).

34   Doubt is well summarised in Hugh McLeod, *Religion and Society in England, 1850–1914*, (London, 1996) pp. 179–96. See Edmund Gosse, *Father and Son* (London, 1907) for inter-generational dimensions to doubt.

35   David W. Bebbington, *Evangelicalism in Modern Britain: A History from the 1730s to the 1980s* (London, 1989) pp. 81–6; cf. Timothy P. Weber, *Living in the Shadow of the Second Coming: American Premillennialism, 1875–1925* (Oxford, 1979).

36   Josiah C. Stamp, *Motive and Method in a Christian Order* (London, 1936), p. 40.

37   David Roberts, *Paternalism in Early Victorian England* (New Brunswick, NJ, 1979), p. 183.

38   S. G. Checkland, 'Cultural Factors and British Business Men, 1815–1914', in K. Nakagawa (ed.), *Social Order and Entrepreneurship* (Tokyo, 1977).

39   Joyce, *Work, Society and Politics*; Robert Fitzgerald, *British Labour Management and Industrial Welfare, 1846–1939* (Beckenham, 1988).

40   John Goodchild, 'Henry Currer Briggs' *DBB*

41   Derek Matthews, 'The British Experience of Profit-Sharing', *Economic History Review* 2nd ser. 42(4) (1989).

42   R. A. Church, 'Profit-Sharing and Labour Relations in England in the Nineteenth Century', *International Review of Social History* 16: 2–16 (1972); Sidney Pollard and Robert Turner, 'Profit-Sharing and Autocracy: The Case of J. T. & J. Taylor of Batley, Woollen Manufacturers, 1892–1966', *Business History* 18 (1) (1976); Derek Matthews, 'Profit-Sharing in the Gas Industry, 1889–1949', *Business History* 30 (3) (1988); Matthews, 'British Experience of Profit-Sharing'.

43   R. B. Perks, 'Real Profit-Sharing: William Thomson & Sons of Huddersfield, 1886–1925', *Business History* 24 (2) (1982); Francis Goodall, 'Sir George Thomas Livesey' in *DBB*; Jane Garnett, '"Gold and the Gospel": Systematic Beneficence in Mid-Nineteenth-Century England', in Sheils and Wood (eds), *Church and Wealth*, p. 356.

44   Jane Garnett, 'Evangelicalism and Business in Mid-Victorian Britain', in John Wolffe (ed.), *Evangelical Faith and Public Zeal: Evangelicals and Society in Britain, 1780–1980* (London, 1995), p. 77.

45   *DNB*.

46   Geoffrey Tweedale, 'John Spedan Lewis', *DBB*; John Lewis Partnership, *John Spedan Lewis 1885–1963* (London, 1985), p. 11.

47   David J. Jeremy, 'Ernest Bader', *DBB*.

48   See David Jeremy, *Capitalists and Christians: Business Leaders and the Churches in Britain, 1900–1960*, pp. 188–92, 196–209.

49   See Philip L. Cottrell, *Industrial Finance, 1830–1914: The Finance and Organization of English Manufacturing Industry* (London, 1980).

50   James William Gilbart, *A Practical Treatise on Banking* (2 vols, London, 1865), vol. II, pp. 608–18. I am grateful to John Booker, Archivist of Lloyds Bank, for this reference.

51   George Rae, *The Country Banker: His Clients, Cares, and Work. From an Experience of Forty Years* (8th edn, London, 1890). Again I am grateful to John Booker for this reference. For the author see Edwin Green, 'George Rae', *DBB*.

52   John E. Sawyer, 'The Social Basis of the American System of Manufacturing', *Journal of Economic History* 14 (1954) was a pivotal article.

53 Martin J. Wiener, *English Culture and the Decline of the Industrial Spirit, 1850–1980* (Cambridge, 1981).

54 William Temple, *Christianity and Social Order* (London, 1942).

55 Wiener, *English Culture*, p. 118.

56 Wiener overplays the impact of the Christendom Group and misses entirely the much more influential Christian Frontier Council, for which see Jeremy, *Capitalists and Christians*, pp. 188–209.

57 Ralf Dahrendorf, *On Britain* (London, 1982).

58 Correlli Barnett, *The Audit of War* (London, 1986), pp. 11–37.

59 Bruce Collins and Keith Robbins (eds), *British Culture and Economic Decline* (London, 1990).

60 Weber, *Protestant Ethic*, p. 175.

61 Henry Lunn, *Nearing Harbour: The Log of Sir Henry S. Lunn* (London, 1934), p. 10.

62 W. D. Rubinstein, *Men of Property: The Very Wealthy in Britain since the Industrial Revolution* (London, 1981), pp. 150–1.

63 See Jeremy, *Capitalists and Christians*, pp. 247–94.

64 Kenneth D. Brown, *A Social History of the Nonconformist Ministry in England and Wales, 1800–1930* (Oxford, 1988), pp. 147–54; John Burnett, *A History of the Cost of Living* (Harmondsworth, 1969), p. 266.

65 Garnett, 'Gold and the Gospel'.

66 One instance of this was Henry Wilson of the Sheffield Smelting Co. who refused to reinvest his profits: Jane Garnett, 'Evangelicalism and Business', p. 73.

67 Ibid., p. 69. See also note 33 above.

68 David J. Jeremy, 'Chapel in a Business Career: The Case of John Mackintosh (1868–1920)', in Jeremy (ed.), *Business and Religion*.

69 Jeremy, *Capitalists and Christians*, pp. 397–410.

70 Roy Coad, *Laing: The Biography of Sir John W. Laing, CBE (1879–1978)* (London, 1979).

71 Esmond Cleary, 'Jabez Spencer Balfour', *DBB*; Sydney Checkland, 'John Campbell White (Lord Overtoun)', in Anthony Slaven and Sydney Checkland (eds), *Dictionary of Scottish Business Biography*, vol. 1 (Aberdeen, 1986); W. Philpott, William Whiteley', *DBB*.

72 See David J. Jeremy, 'Corporate Responses to the Emergent Recognition of a Health Hazard in the UK Asbestos Industry: The Case of Turner & Newall, 1920–1960', *Business and Economic History* 24 (1) (Fall, 1995).

Part I
The relationship between religion and political economy

1 Christianity, secularisation and political economy

B. W. Young

In one of a series of lectures delivered at Oxford in 1831, Richard Whately made a semi-prophetic observation that just failed to be fulfilled:

> That Political-Economy should have been complained of as hostile to Religion, will probably be regarded a century hence (should the fact be then on record) with the same wonder, almost approaching to incredulity, with which we of the present day hear of men sincerely opposing, on religious grounds, the Copernican system.[1]

As the century wore on, and aided, especially from the 1860s onwards, by the polemics surrounding Darwinism, the disjunction between science and religion which Whately hinted at became a cliché in a way that he would have deplored. That political economy should thus have begun to be perceived to have detached itself from religion was part of this simplified depiction of the movement of science away from theology which some nineteenth-century practitioners of both the natural and the evolving social sciences frequently and deliberately promoted.[2]

Alongside the more consciously secular representatives of science were the pious promoters of religion as the supreme antidote to worldliness, whom it suited to denounce such compromising notions as the confessionally efficacious union between Christianity and political economy of the sort advocated by Whately. The very particular dimensions of this debate, so far as it concerned political economy, were at their most emphatic in the 1830s and 1840s. Relations between the two had been somewhat easier in the middle decades of the eighteenth century, although they were to begin to grow more complicated after the publication of Adam Smith's *Wealth of Nations* in 1776. The question that this chapter will address is thus twofold: how far was political economy a secularising science, and how far was it itself secularised both by its practitioners and by the disavowals of its opponents? For Whately such a question would have seemed all but unintelligible; by 1843, however, the barrister Samuel Richard Bosanquet, a follower of John Henry Newman and John Keble (Whately's younger colleagues at Oriel College, Oxford), would denounce the very science which Whately had so vigorously and so recently championed:

> This empire of commerce has its code of laws. The legislators of this table are the doctors of the school of political economists. 'These sages in the satanic

school in politics,' as they have been justly called, have framed a code of maxims, which are characterised as much by their direct opposition to the precepts of the Gospel, as they are by any other peculiarity.[3]

Despite the reservations of the likes of Bosanquet, Whately continued his mission in promoting a profoundly Christian account of political economy when he became Archbishop of Dublin, and in so doing he continued a tradition which had characterised much of the initial progress of political economy in eighteenth-century Britain. A clerical economist of the calibre of Thomas Robert Malthus, for example, had worked in the wake of such predecessors as Josiah Tucker, a former dean of Gloucester, who had devoted much of his energy to clarifying issues in economic policy, especially as these involved trade, foreign relations, and the need for charitable provision for the poor.[4] Similarly, William Paley, the favoured apologist for natural theology in the late eighteenth and early nineteenth centuries, occasionally concerned himself with aspects of economic thought.[5] Of these thinkers only Malthus would ultimately secure himself a place in the canon of classical political economy as this emerged over the nineteenth century, but this ought not to blind us to the contributions of the likes of Tucker and Paley to this emerging science. It is the prevalence of this otherwise predominantly secular canon of classical economists in the work of historians of economic thought which has tended to preclude a proper appreciation of a specifically Christian contribution to its development, whether it be provided by a Tucker or a Whately.

The analogous problem of 'the canon' of literary texts has become central for the academic study of English literature, the field which extended the idea from its original place in theology. Interestingly, canon formation in literature was very much a creation of the early and mid-nineteenth century, the very time when the canon of classical political economy was also being taxonomised by Marx and others.[6] The emergence of the literary 'canon' has itself been related by some literary theorists to the economic, social and aesthetic theories of Adam Smith;[7] the founding figure of the canon of political economy has thus been seen as playing a considerable role in the formation of a literary canon by scholars influenced by Marx, one of the principal architects of the analogous canon of political economy.

This chapter will follow this periodisation of the development of the canon of political economy, and in so doing it will pose the intimately related questions of how far the first period witnessed a secularisation of political economy, and how far, during the second period, efforts were successfully made to Christianise the discourse of political economy.

FROM MANDEVILLE TO SMITH: THE SECULARISATION OF POLITICAL ECONOMY?

It is literary scholars as much as historians of economic thought who have rediscovered a major text in what has been assumed to be the largely secularising discourse of political economy: Bernard de Mandeville's *The Fable of the Bees*. Nor yet is it difficult to see why Mandeville's implicitly anti-Christian account of the relationship between private vices and public benefit has attracted the attention of scholars who have long tended to interpret the role of the burgeoning social and economic sciences as inherently secularising discourses. Mandeville's notoriously amoral tract led contemporaries to denounce his flagrantly anti-Christian stance regarding the way men ought to conduct their affairs.[8] Mandeville's work initiated what was to become, for many of its later combatants, a contest between a firmly Christian moral economy and a consciously secular political economy. This division became a genuinely binary affair: at one extreme stood the Nonjuror William Law, whose reply to the *Fable* concentrated on its supposed immorality and tendency to the promotion of atheism; on the other, stood Mandeville himself.[9]

Mandeville was particularly deplored by clerical commentators for his defence of luxury, and he quickly became identified as the major theorist of self-interested consumption.[10] Clerical theorists were plainly more exposed by this question: Joseph Priestley, the prominent Dissenter, stressed the beneficial effects of luxury, while others, such as Tucker and Paley, were more typically ambivalent.[11] Tucker's work concentrated on the inter-relationship of public and private morals, and the emphasis in his political economy was frequently on the *political*.[12] For some sense of the explicitly Christian nature of Tucker's preoccupations, it is worth comparing him with a contemporary economist, Sir James Steuart, whose work covered much of the same ground in the evolving study of political economy.

Steuart's work is more usually compared with that of his fellow Scot Adam Smith, but it is worth comparing him with Tucker not least as the work of both men has tended to be obscured by the attention paid to Smith. It is difficult to ascertain Steuart's religious position with any degree of accuracy. A Jacobite who had to clear his name in order to win back favour in a Britain from which he had been exiled as a traitor, Steuart was unusually close to European discussion concerning political economy, especially as this subject was understood in France. In this way, the example of Steuart interestingly affirms John Robertson's recent contention that the Scottish Enlightenment's close links with French thought included, as a major component, a doughty concern with the science of political economy.[13] Robertson has also claimed that this cosmopolitan Enlightenment was decidedly secular in its concerns, becoming, at times, deliberately irreligious. Steuart's position in this picture is somewhat more ambiguous. Andrew Skinner, the most recent editor of Steuart's *An Inquiry Into the Principle of Political Oeconomy* (1767), simply described him as a deist, while another commentator, S. R. Sen, had no hesitation in calling him a 'devout Christian'.[14] The truth of the matter is considerably more difficult to disentangle.

Steuart left little published material from which it might be possible to reconstruct his religious position. Writing in 1771 against the 'Common Sense' philosophy of James Beattie, the would-be scourge of Hume (whose publisher, Andrew Millar, lost money in promoting the two volumes of Steuart's political economy), Steuart emphasised the problems surrounding proof of God's existence, whilst stressing his own belief in God. Steuart objected to the metaphysics which clouded the discussion of God promoted by theologians and devout philosophers such as Beattie, concluding simply that:

> I believe in the existence of a Supreme being as much as Dr. Beattie; but I confess, I can no more conceive in what manner a spirit can create matter, than in what manner matter can create a spirit; and therefore I think it prudent, rational and philosophical, to doubt rather than to decide, concerning the existence of the substrata and essences; which is the only thing which perplexes the understanding in this question. What is, most certainly is; and this is known to God alone; not to me.[15]

Steuart challenged Beattie's monolithic interpretation of truth in an epistemologically sophisticated 'middle course' between Humean scepticism (which he defended against Beattie), and the misjudged certainties of Beattian 'believers':

> When I endeavour to clear up my own ideas concerning truth, the best contrivance I can fall upon, is, to call it by different names, according as it relates to different objects. In mathematics, I call it demonstration; in the metaphysics, I call it certainty; in morals, I call it moral certainty; in physics (that is, in our perceptions of our external senses, exclusive of all conclusions drawn from such perceptions), I call it intuition; in religion, I call it faith.[16]

In a piece written in 1779 but which remained unpublished until 1805, Steuart argued for the existence of a God on explicitly deistic grounds. Indeed, he was one of the most explicit exponents of the notoriously deistic clockwork image of divine creation, claiming that 'The universe is a great clock, made by a great clockmaker.' He concluded the piece in tones redolent of Hume's irony on the status of revealed religion, calmly stating that 'nothing but the grace of God, or a direct revelation will make the true Christian'.[17] The advertisement to this short essay, a reply to an atheistic tract by a French thinker, Mirabaud, is even more evidentially perplexing in its claims and counter-claims:

> The Author of these Observations on the System of Nature, in order to exhibit the vast difference between the principles adopted by the most determined modern deists, and those adopted by the Atheist in the System of Nature, has stated the arguments of the deists against the atheist in their fullest extent.
>
> He declares here, notwithstanding, that these arguments ought to determine nothing with regard to his sentiments concerning religion; since he is neither a deist, nor an infidel, with respect to providence, to the grace of God, or a divine revelation; but he believed himself entitled to urge the arguments of the deists in all their force against an atheist, who is rather, if possible, the antipode of the deists than of the true Christians.[18]

The author of the 'Anecdotes of the Life of Sir James Steuart, Baronet' appended to the collected works of 1805, took the author very much at his apparent word when he assumed that 'The plan of his criticism of Mirabaud's odious system consisted, in stating the arguments of the Deists against the Atheists, in their fullest extent, without doubting himself the fundamental principles of the Christian dispensation.'[19] If this is so, one is tempted to ask, why did Steuart not attempt a defence of belief on Christian grounds, rather than resting with the apologetically ambiguous claims of merely deistic thinking?

However this may be, a short tract on the grounds of obedience to God portrayed a belief in a firmly eighteenth-century conception of religion as being grounded in virtue and its consequent rewards, rather than in the divine *diktat* of blind obedience emphasised by Steuart's orthodoxly Presbyterian ancestors and contemporaries. Steuart claimed that his was the religion of 'liberty', that of his opponents 'the religion of despotism', and he stated his belief in the moral efficacy of a religion of virtue undermining vice with considerable clarity:

> It is not here advanced, that this happiness or unhappiness be ranged in the class of immediate consequence. It is sufficient they be certain; and as certain it is, that did we see into the more sublime operations of the divine oeconomy, with the same perspicacity that we behold and feel the similar consequences of moral actions in this world, we should clearly perceive the natural connexion between the whole suit of human actions, from the creation of the species to the extinction of it; and the rewards and punishments which God has prepared for them.[20]

Such a conception of the desirability of religiously-motivated virtue necessarily informed Steuart's interpretation of the relationship between 'the divine oeconomy' and the political economy with which he was more directly concerned. Whether an orthodox Christian or merely an advocate of a religion of virtue, there can be no doubt of the religious resonances of Steuart's work in political economy, however secular it might otherwise appear to be.

It is in this profound respect that it is worth comparing elements of Steuart's political economy with some of those which inform the explicitly Christian conception behind the analogous concerns of Tucker. Both men viewed themselves as contributing to an international debate, and not to a narrowly parochial one. Steuart insisted that the surest way to acquiring a knowledge of the true principles of political economy involved the would-be adherent in doing 'his utmost to become a citizen of the world'; likewise, in his published correspondence with Necker, Tucker claimed to write in the best Enlightenment manner, 'not as an Englishman, but as a Citizen of the World; not as having an inbred antipathy to France, but as the Friend of the whole human Species'.[21] Such would-be internationalism did not preclude Tucker and Steuart from disagreeing on the desirability of the naturalisation of foreign workers by their host country. Tucker, the cleric, proposed a naturalisation act for Protestants to encourage the settlement in Britain of wealth-creating foreign merchants and tradesmen, whilst Steuart, a layman, denounced such a venture as a leap in the dark, piously invoking providence in his dismissal:

> For, however, easy it may be to naturalize men, I believe nothing is so difficult as to naturalize customs and foreign habits; and the greatest blessing any nation can enjoy, is an uniformity of opinion upon every point which concerns public affairs and the administration of them. When God blesses a people, he makes them unanimous, and bestows upon them a governor who loves them, and who is beloved, honoured, and respected by them; this, and this only, can create unanimity.[22]

It is more than a little paradoxical that a former Jacobite, who had been obliged to spend the greater part of his adult years in exile, should have delivered himself of such an exclusive opinion, especially as he did so within twenty years of a Whig cleric declaring himself so differently on the matter.[23]

The question of naturalisation was raised, in part, as an aspect of a larger problem, namely the perceived shortage of inhabitants in a war-torn Europe. Steuart's concern with this matter has led at least one commentator, S. R. Sen, to read in his contribution to a debate which also involved Hume's famous essay 'Of the Populousness of Ancient Nations', a prelude to the work of Malthus.[24] Whereas Malthus berated an excess in population, Steuart, writing after the carnage of the Seven Years' War (which Tucker opposed), was concerned with a need to build up the population. In discussing the relationship between agriculture and population (interestingly detailed by him through the Old Testament story of Joseph and his brothers), Steuart necessarily raised other questions which intersected with concerns already voiced in print by Tucker.[25]

Tucker also believed that the principal strength and riches of a nation were its '*publick* Stock of Inhabitants'.[26] Unlike Steuart, however, he was much more prepared to legislate in its favour. Accordingly, taxes were to be imposed on bachelors and younger widowers without children, both of whom were held to be sources of 'Lewdness and Debauchery', whose failure to reproduce was effectively to undermine the prospects of any population growth.[27] In this respect, Tucker was voicing long and popularly held sentiments: *The Gentleman's Magazine*, as early as its first issue in 1731, had reported a semi-serious proposal to keep out of office all unmarried men, and to forfeit £10 per annum from wealthy bachelors since the multiplicity of a people was necessary for a nation's happiness. In 1740, the magazine reported on a campaign against celibacy, which noted that 'As the Riches of a Country consist more in the Number of its Inhabitants, than in the Extent of its Dominions; *Marriage* has always been encouraged by Politick Societies.'[28] Steuart, by contrast, left the question of celibacy largely unexplored, noting only that Lycurgus and Augustus opposed it as depriving the state of the population that provided its wealth. In Steuart's eyes, 'a sufficient abundance of children are born already', and there was therefore no need to limit marriages, not least since he declared himself 'a friend to liberty, and because such limitations would shock the spirit of the times'.[29] Tucker was much more explicitly concerned with the public consequences of private morality than Steuart would prove to be, querying Mandeville's cynical assertion that public benefits accrued from private vices. Against Mandeville, Tucker noted of the spirit of the times that 'Such *Abounding* of *Lewdness*, and *Superfluity* of *Prostitution*, doth in fact tend to *increase* the more *unnatural Vices*, instead of preventing them, as it is vulgarly, though erroneously, supposed.'[30]

Sexual immorality of this sort was inextricably linked with luxury in Tucker's mind. Steuart undermined this fear, noting the necessary connection between luxury and the peopling of a nation:

> We have supposed a country capable of improvement, a laborious people, a
> taste for refinement and luxury in the rich, an ambition to become so, and an

application to labour and ingenuity in the lower classes of men. According to
the greater or less degree of force, or concurrence of these and like circumstances, will the country in question become more or less cultivated, and
consequently peopled.[31]

Indeed, Steuart would go on to separate the idea of luxury from the more dubious
concept of sensuality in a manner that would radically undercut the moralising
critique of men such as Tucker in favour of the notable ambivalence towards
luxury of such figures as Edward Gibbon. Gibbon's ambivalence was evinced
especially in the argument of *The Decline and Fall of the Roman Empire*, a
work which had much to say, in its own necessarily restricted manner, about
political economy. Like so many eighteenth-century commentators an admirer of
Lycurgus's Sparta, Steuart laid out his separation in terms rooted in the
commonplaces of ancient history:

> *Luxury consists in providing the objects of sensuality, so far as they are*
> *superfluous. Sensuality consists in the actual enjoyment of them, and excess*
> *implies an abuse of enjoyment.* A person, therefore, according to these
> definitions, may be very *luxurious* from vanity, pride, ostentation, or with a
> political view of encouraging corruption, without having a turn for sensuality,
> or a tendency to fall into excess. *Sensuality*, on the other hand, might have been
> indulged in a Lacedominian republic, as well as at the court of Artaxerses.
> *Excess*, indeed, seems more closely connected with *sensuality*, than with
> *luxury*; but the difference is so great, that I apprehend *sensuality* must in a great
> measure be extinguished before *excess* can begin.[32]

The question of charity was not a matter of major interest to Steuart, but it was
one which preoccupied Tucker. Alms-giving was central to early Christian notions
of public morality, and it continued to be a matter of crucial importance to
Christian proponents of political economy in the eighteenth and nineteenth
centuries.[33] Tucker believed that a properly functioning economy could further
the sense of mutuality inherent in conceptions of Christian charity; commerce thus
had a uniquely moral import for him:

> What *general* Rule can we pursue for the *mutual* Benefit of Mankind? And how
> are the Ends both of Religion and Government to be answered, but by the
> System of universal Commerce? – Commerce, I mean, in the large and
> extensive Signification of that Word; Commerce, as it implies a general System
> for the useful Employment of our Time; as it exercises the particular Genius
> and Abilities of Mankind in some Way or other, either of Body or of Mind, in
> mental or corporeal Labour, and so as to make Self-interest and Social
> coincide.[34]

Tucker was certain of the necessary connection between virtue and happiness,
duty and retribution as this was reflected in charitable impulses: 'You will not
only consult the Welfare and Happiness of *your* own immortal Souls, but promote
also the Salvation of *others*, and the *Good* of Mankind.'[35]

Tucker's influence was strongly felt by his stepson, Richard Woodward, a future bishop of Cloyne in Ireland.[36] Woodward continued to share his stepfather's pronounced concern with the welfare and training of the poor in the even more trying conditions of eighteenth-century Ireland. More radical than Tucker, Woodward was a staunch advocate of what he termed the 'rights' of the poor, emphasising that this was a question which united policy with compassion since it was in the interest of the commonwealth that its members should be active and industrious. Woodward accordingly insisted that

> Every Man therefore is bound in *Justice* to contribute in such a Proportion to his Superfluity (that is the Excess of his Income above the Maintenance of a Labourer) as, if universally followed, would leave no one unsupplied with the Necessaries of Life.

This was the amount to be overseen by the legislator; anything beyond this, Woodward argued, 'can be called Charity'.[37] Woodward also proposed erecting county poor-houses, the expenses for which were to be drawn from voluntary subscriptions and 'Taxes on such Things as a good Police would aim to discourage'.[38] In a charity sermon preached in Dublin in 1764, Woodward rehearsed the arguments of optimistic Anglican political economy, noting that 'there is a Natural Tendency in the Scheme of Christian Morals to render Men Industrious and Useful, and of Course, Rich and Happy'.[39] Reciprocity is the main dynamic in Woodward's progressively conservative picture:

> Thus hath Divine Goodness connected our Spiritual and Temporal Good, by a reciprocal Aid, and rendered our Passage to Eternal Happiness a Path of Pleasantness and Peace. For let us represent to ourselves (and it will be a Speculation of much Edification and Comfort) a Society of real Christians, where no shallow Politician or visionary Enthusiast had broken the Links of this admirable Chain: Where each Individual diligent in his Calling (the Poor, that he may have something to contribute, the Rich, because from his larger Sphere of Influence, much will be required from him) is constantly adding to the Wealth and Prosperity of the Whole: Where not Content with abstaining from Wrong, each Man strives to do Good unto all, and labour chearfully that he may be able to give liberally to the Needy, to provide comfortably for his Family, and to form his Children by proper Education, to continue the same Services to the Publick.[40]

In his influential *Principles of Moral and Political Philosophy* (1785), William Paley had likewise argued that the poor had a 'claim founded in the law of nature' not only to the support of the Poor Law but also to private charity dispensed by the comfortably off. His was a broadly utilitarian argument, but it was one which was decidedly congruent with traditional notions of Christian concern for the poor.[41]

These broadly charitable concerns which preoccupied Tucker, Woodward and Paley were also shared by the non-Christian Smith and their fellow-cleric Malthus, as well as by a large number of contemporaries who argued over the nature of voluntary as opposed to state-enforced charity throughout the eighteenth century.[42] The mutual interdependence of citizens in a commercial society, and the plight of the poor are problems which recur in the thought of Smith, while the problem of population pressures received a new and radically divergent analysis in the work of Malthus.[43] Smith was no Christian, and his secularising legacy in this area was as significant in its way as was his actual political economy, as he insisted that: 'Science is the great antidote to the poison of enthusiasm and superstition; and where all the superior ranks of people were secured from it, the inferior ranks could not be much exposed to it.'[44]

FROM MALTHUS TO CHRISTIAN SOCIALISM: A RE-CHRISTIANISATION OF POLITICAL ECONOMY?

The Christian pedigree of Malthus is relatively unproblematic, an Anglican clergyman educated in a Cambridge strongly influenced by former dons such as Paley.[45] Furthermore, scholars have begun to see in Malthus's contribution to the 'dismal science' the foundations of a fledgling Christian tradition in British political economy.[46] This is not to minimise the debate which raged around his critique of the Elizabethan Poor Laws or the problems for a theodicy created by his apparent scepticism regarding a ready solution to the problems induced by population pressure. Nevertheless, by emphasising, for example, how Oriel Noetics such as Edward Copleston and Richard Whately became interested in such questions, historians have delineated a more subtle picture of political economy than that conveyed by an older secularisation thesis.[47] As Donald Winch has reminded us, too much necessary detail is lost in the adoption of 'premature secularisation' by historians of economic thought.[48] Central to this transformation is Thomas Chalmers, whose contribution to a specifically Christian ideal of political economy was definitively registered in his Bridgewater Treatise of 1833.[49]

Fitting his argument neatly to the apologetic of natural religion which underpinned the Bridgewater Treatises, Chalmers both echoed and Christianised Smith's benevolent portrayal of untrammelled political economy through the familiar image of the 'hidden hand':

> The whole science of Political Economy is full of those exquisite adaptations to the wants and comforts of human life, which bespeak the skill of a master-hand, in the adjustment of its laws, and the working of its profoundly constructed mechanisms.[50]

Chalmers' advocacy of economics is now well known, and one historian of economic thought has gone so far as to claim that he should be considered among the founders of classical political economy, thereby extending the canon away from the secular bias which concentration on Smith and Ricardo tends to supply.[51] This Malthusian strand, developed and popularised by Chalmers, had obvious consequences for Christian attitudes towards the charitable provision for the poor, and the practical consequences of their arguments have been made plain in recent work on the origins, predominantly among Whig intellectuals, of the New Poor Law of 1834.[52]

Plainly, then, a good deal of Christian approval was to be found for certain principles of political economy, including those which were controversially to transform attitudes to the poor from the need for private charity to that of publicly funded benevolence. A fissure began to widen at this point between those Christians who were willing positively to learn from political economy and those who decried it as an unwelcome and purely worldly science. Writing in the *British Critic* in 1833, the High Church reviewer of Chalmers' Bridgewater Treatise offered a deeply ambivalent portrayal of Malthus's reputation which is symptomatic of this division:

> And, above all things, let them beware of giving ear to the termagant invectives, wherewith a certain school of philanthropists are perpetually assailing men, who are not less benevolent, and who are much more wise than themselves. As for Mr. Malthus, indeed, we suppose it is a vain thing to attempt to suspend the outpourings of the phials of their wrath upon his head. He is, God help him, as every friend of the poor well knows, in the very gall of bitterness and the bond of iniquity; a dark, incorrigible conspirator against the *rights* of humanity.[53]

Nineteenth-century opposition to classical political economy is well known, especially as this was manifested in the work of Cobbett and Carlyle. Something of their spirit is also apparent in the rambling arguments of Southey's *Colloquies* of 1829, perhaps best known now for their vigorous denunciation by a youthful Macaulay in the *Edinburgh Review*.[54] Southey, a consciously Romantic Tory, mused in the surroundings of 'Druidical stones' that the condition of the poor had never improved over centuries past, and he had the ghost of Sir Thomas More claim that while monasteries accumulated no treasures, they used their incomes better than any other institutions before or since, leaving him to regret that at their dissolution, 'The tenantry were deprived of their best landlords, artificers of their best employers, the poor and miserable of their best and surest friends.'[55] More suspected his interlocutor, Montesinos, of being one who thought England a better country for promoting steam-engines and cotton mills over the older spirit that had endowed monasteries; the greater part of the two volumes is taken up by a meditation on what has supposedly been lost in the process.[56] A pointed reference to Smith and the Scottish school of 'Conjectural History' displays the central defect of eighteenth-century England (the intricacies of North Britain and its Enlightenment are given an Anglocentric turn by Southey): 'But such had your System imperceptibly become, and such were your statesmen, that the wealth of nations was considered as the sole measure of their prosperity.' Pitt's much-trumpeted interest in political economy meant that he became a particular dislike of Southey, for whom the pronounced secularism of such attitudes was their central failing.[57] According to Southey's strongly Anglican views, given public voice at this time because of the 'betrayal' of the Catholic Emancipation Act, 'National happiness must be produced through the influence of religious laws.' Economists were emphatically not of this privileged party: 'You must not suppose that our political economists seek in the Bible for instruction! Moral considerations are allowed no place in their philosophy, . . . how much less should religion be found there!'[58] Similarly, whilst admitting himself an admirer of Robert Owen's schemes (and it is to be remembered that the younger Southey had shared with Coleridge the ideal of a 'Pantisocracy'), Montesinos declares that it was Owen's well-known secular standpoint that undermined all of his attempts at raising money:

> Had he connected his scheme with any system of belief, though it had been as visionary as Swedenborgianism, as fabulous as Popery, as monstrous as Calvinism, as absurd as the dreams of Joanna Southcote, . . . or perhaps even as cold as Unitarianism, the money would have been forthcoming.[59]

A *soi-disant* admirer of Wesley, Southey approvingly adverted to the ideal of a system which Wesley had also once sought to revive: the community of goods mentioned in Acts (and, of course, in More's *Utopia*). Southey, however, regretted the apparent impracticability of the ideal, despite its revival by the Moravians in Saxony.[60] Profit and loss were not the means of assessing such things, or of much else besides; Montesinos recommended a sermon of Wesley on early rising, whilst denouncing Franklin on the same subject for seeing the practice in purely economic terms.[61] Similarly, in appraising the claims of Dissenters to political and social respectability, Southey rather improbably supposed that the techniques of travelling salesmanship were derived from the style of life led by itinerant Quaker preachers.[62] It was not, however, commerce or mercantilism which Southey opposed, but rather the industrialism which had developed in their wake.[63]

Smith and his apologists are the frequently unacknowledged object of much of Southey's ire, and they are clearly the proper objects of More's censure: 'Bad as the feudal times were, they were less injurious than the commercial ones to the kindly and generous feelings of human nature, and far, far more favourable to the principles of honour and integrity.'[64] The Mandevillian strain in Smith is reworked as Southey assumes the mantle of Mandeville's earlier Christian critics in denouncing Smith's occasional pleas for 'benevolence':

> And this, I believe, is true; men are benevolent when they are not selfish but: while gain is the great object of pursuit, selfishness must ever be the uppermost feeling. I cannot dissemble from myself that it is the principle of our social system, and that it is awfully opposed to the spirit of Christianity.[65]

Malthus is even more obliquely present as a troubling figure, as More makes clear in his claim that 'There is abundant room in this country, and its colonies, for any possible increase of population, *incolumi Jove*, till the end of time.' Elsewhere the problem of too many unattached middle-class ladies is linked with the yearnings for monasticism in a solution which suggests the deployment of 'a secular nunnery' for single women.[66] Charitable benevolence is at the core of Southey's critique, if so it can be styled, of political economy, as in his lament that it 'cannot be a durable state of things, in which the increase in riches in a few, occasions an increase of poverty in the many. National wealth is wholesome only when it is equitably diffused'.[67] Such claims, allied with his nostalgia, were the principal sources of Macaulay's criticisms of Southey's unworldly understanding of economics: 'He confesses that he is not well versed in political economy, and that he has neither liking nor appetite for it; and he then proceeds to read the public a lecture concerning it which fully bears out his confession.'[68] Indeed, it could well be argued that Montesinos alluded to more people than he thought when he declared of political economy that it was a science 'concerning which there is a great deal written and talked, and very little understood'.[69]

Macaulay had also been critical of the critique of Malthus developed by Michael Thomas Sadler, a notably pious former MP, in his two-volume study, *The Law of Population* (1830).[70] Sadler had denounced Malthus's theory as being both injurious to the poor and 'degratory' to God, whose goodness and wisdom it impugned. Describing it as the revival of 'the darkest notion of the heathen ages', Sadler saw in the theory the means of a willing abdication of the duties of wealth and power from their proper responsibilities. An opportunity was quickly taken to decry the whole of modern political economy for having adopted a foundation 'unsupported by common sense, experience, or humanity'.[71] Malthus fundamentally misunderstood the nature of population, since, according to Sadler, 'human beings constitute the wealth of the world. It is they only who create that wealth; it is they only who give it its value, when created.' It followed then, in Sadler's terms, that 'No two systems can be more opposite, both in their letter and their spirit, than that of Population, as now expounded, and Christianity.'[72]

Recent work has revealed a somewhat unexpected intensity in the involvement of Tractarians in such socio-economic criticism.[73] The work of the barrister Samuel Richard Bosanquet, much of whose critique of the New Poor Law first appeared in the Tractarian *British Critic* in 1840 and 1842, is particularly interesting in this respect, profitably intersecting as it does with many of the debates about such issues among evangelicals which have recently been made familiar by Boyd Hilton in his stimulating study, *The Age of Atonement*.[74] Reviewing the reports of the Poor Law Commissioners, Bosanquet, a strong believer in providence, lamented that the reports, and allied works, were 'libellous and abusive descriptions of the lower orders of society' which he felt to be so anti-Christian as 'must draw down the heaviest judgments upon the nation, unless happily they may be arrested, and turned again into an opposite channel'. The Poor Law itself he denounced as 'this anti-christian system of philanthropy', regretting its replacement of private charity and alms-giving with state provision. He praised the poor for their own acts of charity, greater, he believed, than those made by the rich to the poor, and much to be preferred to the new 'philosophy of Antichrist'. Worse than merely secular values were, he thought, triumphing over Christianity with a predictably extreme result:

> This country is the most uncharitable country in the world. The sums that we give in charity are a perfect pittance, and are shameful to the name of Christian; though pretty well for a nation governed, as this is, entirely upon heathen

principles. The state of the poor is the greatest disgrace to humanity – let alone the name of Christian which we profess – that ever has existed since the world began. The separation and estrangement of the richer orders from the poorer, is indescribably greater in this country, which professes the religion which makes all men brethren, than it ever was in any country professedly or practically heathen; except perhaps in Rome in her most palmy period, that is, when she was overripe and growing rotten, and tottering, as we now are, to her fall.[75]

He went on to appeal to the example of Jewish injunctions to charity as a reproach to supposed Christians, before extolling the superiority of private alms-giving over telescopic philanthropy, finally regretting, in tones reminiscent of Tucker, the dangerous triumph of mere moneyed 'speculators' over merchants.[76] One simple principle underscored Bosanquet's response to the New Poor Law: 'We assert that *private charity ought to supersede the public provision*, and that the vitality of alms, and the healthiness of our system of poor relief, are in proportion as it does.' The prime agency of such an attitude was, naturally for a Tractarian, the Church, 'the proper dispenser and director of charity, both public and private, general and personal'.[77] Social conservatism, a strong feature of Tractarian thought, played its part in Bosanquet's critique of state provision, especially as this affected the poor, since:

> It places the poor man in a state of war with the rich; from whom he receives all that he can exact as a right, and as given, not from favour and kindness, – as indeed it is not, – but by necessity and compulsion. He naturally thinks it too little; and therefore he feels that all tricks and exaggeration are justifiable . . . The principle and feeling of gratitude is extinct.[78]

In this important respect, Bosanquet and his allies had moved some distance from the attitude to the poor of Paley and Woodward, which is clearly rights-based, albeit in utilitarian terms. Paley and Woodward would have stood denounced by Tractarians as mere latitudinarians (at best), so perhaps this ought not to come as too much of a surprise. Dr Johnson, whose Churchmanship Bosanquet would have found more congenial, had delivered the quintessential eighteenth-century Anglican judgement regarding charity, and its tones dictated much of the discussion which ensued in the early and mid-nineteenth century:

> Charity, or tenderness to the poor, which is now justly considered, by a great part of mankind, as inseparable from piety, and in which almost all the goodness of the present age consists, is, I think, known only to those who enjoy, either immediately or by transmission, the light of revelation.[79]

Charity was very much a Christian duty for Johnson, and it was one which secular thinkers such as Smith tended to replace with the notion of 'benevolence'. This was itself the subject of such pious encomia as that delivered by divines of the ilk of Thomas Balguy, and his work was much approved by Paley.[80] Divisions over the question of the nature of charity were, then, sharp, just as were divisions over the nature and desirability of certain types of intellectual activity, and Bosanquet was happy to repudiate much of the world of ideas opened up to us by Hilton's researches, as so much dangerously senescent foolishness:

> The last fashion and theory in politics and geology, in mesmerism, in phrenology, and often in theology, is just as wise and stable, and well founded in reason, as your wigs and whimples, and your low heads and high heads, and short waists and long waists, and large bonnets and little bonnets, and your hoops and *florines*, and trains, and tails, and hair petticoats.[81]

The question of providentialism was where the pre-millenarian Bosanquet did share in a large part of the world of the evangelicals, as was made apparent in an open letter to Lord Russell published in 1848 in which he warned that 'it is written that even mercantile depravity and corruption shall be reformed at last. The Tyre of trade shall repent of her fornications.' Bosanquet's remedy, were such destruction to be avoided, was to instigate the 'paternal government' so hated by political economists, whom he castigated for being prodigal. The nature of modern capitalist wealth was, he concluded, a very real national calamity:

> this country is already too rich; for its riches bring on all the effects of poverty; and there are added to these the existing disunion and demoralization. Poverty is demoralizing in a rich country, and only in a rich country. Money works disunion everywhere – it has no country, and no patriotism. This strength is our weakness.[82]

The legacies of Tractarian engagement in the style of Bosanquet, and of Tory Romanticism of the sort advocated by Southey, were taken up as much by Christian Socialists as they were by figures more immediately sympathetic to their original proponents. Coleridgean Anglicanism moved into such waters under the advocacy of F. D. Maurice, while the inner-city parishes which attracted Tractarian clergy often had a radicalising affect on their worldly politics. The Christian socialist revival of the last quarter of the nineteenth century up to the outbreak of the First World War inherited a great deal from Tractarian engagements and also from the frequently radical conservatism of Tory Romanticism.[83] Something of a Christian repudiation of classical political economy in the closing decades of the nineteenth century was so strongly made as gradually but effectively to obscure the earlier *rapprochement* between Christian conviction and the principles of political economy. The speculative interest of clerical dons, on the one hand, and the practical activity of evangelical businessmen, on the other, chiefly belong to the early and mid-nineteenth century, and it is to that period and the second half of the eighteenth century that one must turn for an appreciation of the religious repercussions of classical political economy.[84]

To conclude, then, with Southey's Sir Thomas More in best polemical mode: 'The servants of Mammon are, however, wiser in their generation than the children of light. They serve a master who rewards them.'[85] Their generation has indeed enjoyed considerable longevity; historians are finally beginning to challenge them, and to do so, moreover, on their own ground. Their contemporary challengers are beginning to be examined in their turn, as the familiar romantic critique of political economy is critically placed in its historical context.

NOTES

1 Richard Whately, *Introductory Lectures on Political Economy, Being Part of a Course Delivered in Easter Term, MDCCCXXXI* (London, 1831), pp. 29–30. I am grateful to Mishtooni Bose, Jane Garnett and Donald Winch for their comments on an earlier draft of this essay.
2 For discussion of these issues, see Frank M. Turner, *Contesting Cultural Authority: Essays in Victorian Intellectual Life* (Cambridge, 1993).
3 Samuel Richard Bosanquet, 'The Commercial Empire', in *Principia: A Series of Essays on the Principles of Evil Manifesting Themselves in These Last Times in Religion, Philosophy, and Politics* (London, 1843), pp. 279–322, at p. 312. Bosanquet's allusion is to *Memoirs of the Life and Writings of Michael Thomas Sadler, Esq., M.P.* (London, 1842), p. 151.
4 On Tucker, see Robert Livingston Schyler (ed.) *Josiah Tucker: A Selection from His Economic and Political Writings* (New York, 1931), pp. 3–49, and George Shelton, *Dean Tucker and Eighteenth-Century Economic and Political Thought* (London, 1981). For a discussion of Tucker's place in the history of economic thought which develops some of the themes laid out in the first half of this chapter, see B. W. Young, 'Christianity, Commerce and the Canon: Josiah Tucker and Richard Woodward on Political Economy', *History of European Ideas* 22: 385–400 (1996).
5 On Paley, see M. L. Clarke, *Paley: Evidences for the Man* (London, 1974); D. L. Le Mahieu, *The Mind of William Paley: A Philosopher and His Age* (London, 1976); Robert Hole, *Pulpits, Politics and Public Order 1760–1832* (Cambridge, 1989), Chapter 5; A. M. C. Waterman, *Revolution, Economics and Religion: Christian Political Economy, 1798–1833* (Cambridge, 1991), Chapter 4; Mark Francis, 'Naturalism and William Paley', *History of European Ideas* 10: 203–20 (1989).
6 Jan Gorak, *The Making of the Modern Canon: Genesis and Crisis of a Literary Idea* (London, 1991), pp. 46–8, 57–9; Trevor Ross, 'The Emergence of "Literature": Making and Reading the English Canon in the Eighteenth Century', *The Journal of English Literary History* 63: 397–422 (1996). On the canon of classical political economy, see Samuel Hollander, *Classical Economics* (Oxford, 1987), which includes the Physiocrats, and Paul A. Samuelson, 'The Canonical Classical Model of Political Economy', *Journal of Economic Literature* 16: 1415–34 (1978), which does not.
7 John Guillory, *Cultural Capital: The Problem of Literary Canon Formation* (Chicago, 1993), pp. 303–17.
8 Commentary on Mandeville is immense. For some useful exploration of his thought, see E. J. Hundert, *The Enlightenment's Fable: Bernard Mandeville and the Discovery of Society* (Cambridge, 1994); M. M. Goldsmith, *Private Vices, Public Benefits: Bernard Mandeville's Social and Political Thought* (Cambridge, 1985); Goldsmith, 'Liberty, Luxury, and the Pursuit of Happiness', in Anthony Pagden (ed.) *The Languages of Political Theory in Early-Modern Europe* (Cambridge, 1987), pp. 225–51; Dario Castiglione, 'Considering Things Minutely: Reflections on Mandeville and the Eighteenth-Century Science of Man', *History of Political Thought* 7: 463–88 (1986); D. Castiglione, 'Mandeville Moralized', *Annali Della Fondazione Luigi Einaudi* 17: 239–90 (1983).
9 William Law, *Remarks upon a Late Book, Entituled the Fable of the Bees, or, Private Vices, Public Benefits* (London, 1724). For discussion, see B. W. Young, 'William Law and the Christian Economy of Salvation', *English Historical Review* 109: 308–22 (1994).

10   Cf. Hundert, *The Enlightenment's Fable*, Chapter 5.
11   On Priestley's approbation of Smith on this matter, see Alan Tapper, 'Priestley on Politics, Progress and Moral Theology', in Knud Haakonssen (ed.) *Enlightenment and Religion: Rational Dissent in Eighteenth-Century Britain* (Cambridge, 1996), pp. 272–86, at p. 281.
12   For a valuable discussion, see J. G. A. Pocock, 'Josiah Tucker on Burke, Locke and Price: A Study in the Varieties of Eighteenth-Century Conservatism', in *Virtue, Commerce and History* (Cambridge, 1985), pp. 157–91.
13   John Robertson, 'The Scottish Enlightenment', *Rivista Storica Italiana* 108: 792–829 (1996).
14   Andrew Skinner, 'Biographical Sketch of Sir James Steuart-Denham' prefacing his edition of Steuart's *An Inquiry into the Principle of Political Oeconomy* (2 vols, Edinburgh, 1966), I, pp. xxi–lvii, at p. lv; S. R. Sen, *The Economics of Sir James Steuart* (London, 1957), p. 19.
15   Steuart, 'Observations On Dr. Beattie's Essay on the Nature and Immutability of Truth' [1771], in *The Works, Political, Metaphysical and Chronological, Of the Late Sir James Steuart of Coltness, Bart.* (6 vols, London, 1805), VI, pp. 3–39, at pp. 15–16.
16   Ibid., I, p. 33.
17   Steuart, 'Critical Remarks and General Observations Upon a Book, Entitled, System of Nature; Or, Laws of the Physical and Moral World; By M. De Mirabaud', in *Works*, VI, pp. 43–82, at pp. 71 and 82.
18   Ibid., VI, p. 44.
19   Ibid., VI, pp. 361–91, at p. 385.
20   Steuart, 'Dissertation Concerning The Motive of Obedience to the Laws of God', in *Works*, VI, pp. 83–90, at pp. 85, 90.
21   Steuart, *An Inquiry*, I, p. 17; Josiah Tucker, *Cui Bono? Or, An Inquiry What Benefits Can Arise Either To The English or To the Americans, The French, Spaniards, or Dutch, From the Greatest Victories, or Successes in the Present War? Being a Series of Letters Addressed to Monsieur Necker, Late Controller General of the Finances of France* (Gloucester, 1781), pp. 4, 5.
22   Tucker, *A Brief Essay on The Advantages and Disadvantages which respectively Attend France and Great Britain with Regard to Trade*, (2nd edn, London, 1750), p. 85; Steuart, *An Inquiry*, II, p. 86.
23   For an interesting perspective made by a more obviously secular Scot, see Alan Ramsay, *An Essay on the Naturalization of Foreigners* [1762], reprinted in *The Investigator* (London, 1762).
24   Sen, *Economics of Steuart*, pp. 41–5.
25   Steuart, *An Inquiry*, I, pp. 15–139. For the example of Joseph, see I, pp. 35–6. For Tucker's opposition to the Seven Years' War, see *The Cause of Going to War, For the Sake of Procuring, Enlarging, or Securing of Trade, Considered in a New Light* (London, 1763).
26   Tucker, *A Brief Essay*, p. 124.
27   Ibid., pp. 123–4.
28   *The Gentleman's Magazine*, 1: 60–1 (1731); 10: 237–39 (1740).
29   Steuart, *An Inquiry*, I, p. 80.
30   Tucker, *A Brief Essay*, pp. 127–8.
31   Steuart, *An Inquiry*, I, p. 45. For earlier, equally sceptical remarks on the deep-rootedness of disputes concerning luxury, see I, pp. 8–9.
32   Ibid., I, pp. 268–9. Without wishing to trace a direct relationship between Steuart's text and the argument of the *Decline and Fall*, Steuart's reformulation of the 'problem' of luxury has much in common with Gibbon's claim that, 'in the present imperfect condition of society, luxury, though it may proceed from vice or folly, seems to be the only means that may correct the unequal distribution of property'. *The History of The*

Decline and Fall of the Roman Empire, ed. David Womersley (3 vols, Harmondsworth, 1994), I, p. 80.

33 For a thoughtful discussion of alms-giving and the early Church, see Paul Veyne, *Bread and Circuses: Historical Sociology and Political Pluralism*, translated by Brian Pearce (Harmondsworth, 1990), pp. 19–34.

34 Tucker, 'Sermon VII', in *Seventeen Sermons On Some Of The Most Important Points of Natural and Revealed Religion, Respecting the Happiness both of the Present, and of a Future Life* (Gloucester, 1776), pp. 131–49, at pp. 138–9.

35 Ibid., 'Sermon III', pp. 51–62, at pp. 61–2.

36 There is a brief but useful discussion of Woodward in Thomas A. Horne, *Property Rights and Poverty: Political Argument in Britain, 1605–1834* (Chapel Hill, 1990), pp. 131–4.

37 Richard Woodward, *An Argument In Support of the Right of the Poor in the Kingdom of Ireland, to a National Provision* (Dublin, 1766), p. 51.

38 Woodward, *A Scheme for Establishing County Poor-Houses in the Kingdom of Ireland* (Dublin, 1766), p. 14.

39 Woodward, *A Sermon Preached at Christ Church, Dublin, On the 13th of May, 1764, Before The Incorporated Society, for Promoting English, Protestant Schools in Ireland* (Dublin, 1764), pp. 2–3.

40 Ibid., pp. 5–6.

41 William Paley, *Principles of Moral and Political Philosophy* (London, 1785), I, pp. 252–3. For discussion, see Horne, *Property Rights and Poverty*, pp. 131–41; Horne, '"The Poor Have A Claim Founded in the Law of Nature": William Paley and the Rights of the Poor', *Journal of the History of Philosophy* 23: 51–70 (1985).

42 For discussion, see Joanna Innes, 'The "Mixed Economy of Welfare" in Early Modern England: Assessments of the Options from Hale to Malthus (*c*.1683–1803)', in Martin Daunton (ed.) *Charity, Self-Interest and Welfare in the English Past* (London, 1996), pp. 139–80.

43 The work of Donald Winch is especially important on these matters: *Adam Smith's Politics: An Essay in Historiographic Revision* (Cambridge, 1978); *Malthus* (Oxford, 1987); *Riches and Poverty: An Intellectual History of Political Economy in England, 1750–1834* (Cambridge, 1996).

44 Adam Smith, *An Enquiry Into The Wealth of Nations*, ed. R. A. Campbell and A. S. Skinner (2 vols, Indianapolis, 1981), II, p. 796. On Smith's personal religion, see the discussion in Winch, *Riches and Poverty*.

45 John Gascoigne, *Cambridge in the Age of the Enlightenment: Science, Religion and Politics from the Restoration to the French Revolution* (Cambridge, 1989); A. M. C. Waterman, 'A Cambridge "*Via Media*" in Late Georgian Anglicanism', *Journal of Ecclesiastical History* 42: 419–36 (1991). For interesting dissension from this general picture, see Eric K. Heavner, 'Malthus and the Secularization of Political Ideology', *History of Political Thought* 17: 408–30 (1996).

46 A. M. C. Waterman, 'The Ideological Alliance of Political Economy and Christian Theology, 1798–1833', *Journal of Ecclesiastical History* 34: 231–44 (1983); Waterman, *Revolution, Economics and Religion*.

47 Edward Copleston, *A Letter to The Right Hon. Robert Peel, M.P. for the University of Oxford, On the Pernicious Effects of a Variable Standard of Value, Especially as it Regards the Condition of the Lower Orders and the Poor Laws* (Oxford, 1819); Copleston, *A Second Letter to The Right Hon. Robert Peel, M.P. for the University of Oxford, On the Causes of the Increase of Pauperism, and on The Poor Laws* (Oxford, 1819); Whately, *Introductory Lectures*; Waterman, *Revolution, Economics and Religion*, pp. 179–216; Salim Rashid, 'Richard Whately and Christian Political Economy at Oxford and Dublin', *Journal of the History of Ideas* 38: 147–55 (1977); Richard Brent, 'God's Providence: Liberal Political Economy as Natural Theology at Oxford 1825–1862', in Michael Bentley (ed.) *Public and Private Doctrine in Modern*

England: Essays in British History presented to Maurice Cowling (Cambridge, 1993), pp. 85–107.

48   Winch, *Riches and Poverty*, p. 23.

49   The work of Boyd Hilton is especially important in the rehabilitation of Chalmers as a Christian political economist: *The Age of Atonement: The Influence of Evangelicalism on Social and Economic Thought 1785–1865* (Oxford, 1988). For a decidedly critical assessment of Chalmers, see Waterman, *Revolution, Economics and Religion*, Chapter 6.

50   Thomas Chalmers, *On the Adaptation of External Nature to the Moral and Intellectual Constitution of Man* (2 vols, London, 1833), II, p. 36.

51   A. M. C. Waterman, '"The Canonical Classical Model of Political Economy" in 1808, as viewed from 1825: Thomas Chalmers on the "National Resources"', *History of Political Economy* 23: 221–41 (1991).

52   Peter Dunkley, 'Whigs and Paupers: The Reform of the English Poor Laws, 1830–1834', *Journal of British Studies* 20: 124–49 (1981); Peter Mandler, 'The Making of the New Poor Law *Redivivus*', *Past and Present* 117: 131–57 (1987); Mandler, 'Tories and Paupers: Christian Political Economy and the Making of the New Poor Law', *Historical Journal* 33: 81–103 (1990); Mandler, *Aristocratic Government in the Age of Reform: Whigs and Liberals, 1830–1852* (Oxford, 1990), pp. 131–41; David Eastwood, 'The Making of the New Poor Law *Redivivus*: A Comment', *Past and Present* 127: 186–97 (1990); Boyd Hilton, 'Whiggery, Religion and Social Reform: The Case of Lord Morpeth', *Historical Journal* 37: 829–59 (1994).

53   *The British Critic* 14: 239–82 (1833), at p. 271.

54   T. B. Macaulay, 'Southey's Colloquies', *Edinburgh Review* 50: 528–63 (1830). On Southey, see David Eastwood, 'Robert Southey and the Intellectual Origins of Romantic Conservatism', *English Historical Review* 104: 308–31 (1989); Winch, *Riches and Poverty*, Chapters 11–12.

55   Robert Southey, *Sir Thomas More: Or, Colloquies On the Progress and Prospects of Society* (London, 1829), I, pp. 59–60, 84, 88–9. Interestingly, in the light of Tucker's denunciations of slavery, ones largely echoed by the Poet Laureate, Southey none the less had More defend Fletcher of Saltoun's notorious recommendation of a return to slavery in romantically relative terms: 'And in further excuse of Andrew Fletcher, it should be remembered, that he belonged to a country where many of the feudal virtues (as well as most of the feudal vices) were at that time in full vigour', ibid., I, pp. 71–2.

56   Ibid., I, p. 158; II, pp. 35–6, 143. Cf. Woodward, *A Sermon*, p. 4:

> It would be endless to enumerate every Instance, in which the Reformation has in this respect (as well as in numerous others) revived the genuine Spirit of Christianity. Let it suffice to mention the Suppression of Monks and other useless Ecclesiasticks: The Restoration of so many Days lost to Labour, under the Name of Holydays: The Abolition of gaudy sauntering Processions, and of Pilgrimages: And what is too frequently regretted by Persons unacquainted with the Manners of Popish Countries, the indiscriminate Hospitality and Alms of Religious Houses who, in despite of the Gospel Injunction, and to the Ruin of Industry, gave liberally, *to eat*, to those who (therefore) *will not work*.

57   Ibid., I, p. 100; II, p. 125.

58   Ibid., I, p. 134; II, p. 261.

59   Ibid., I, pp. 144–5. On Owen's notably ambivalent relations with capitalism, see Russell Dean, '"Pre-Trading Owenism" and Capitalism, 1817–1827', *History of European Ideas* 21: 353–66 (1995).

60   John Walsh, 'John Wesley and the Community of Goods', in Keith Robbins (ed.) *Protestant Evangelicalism: Ireland, Germany and America c.1750-c.1950* (Oxford, 1990), pp. 25–50; Southey, *Colloquies*, I, pp. 134–40, 143; II, p. 82. It was also an

ideal common to several radical groupings in the early nineteenth century, both religious and secular, on which see Gregory Claeys, *Machinery, Money and the Millennium: From Moral Economy to Socialism, 1815–60* (Cambridge, 1987), especially Chapter 1.

61 Southey, *Colloquies*, I, p. 148.
62 Ibid., II, p. 57.
63 Ibid., I, pp. 195–7.
64 Ibid., II, pp. 246–7.
65 Ibid., II, pp. 249–50.
66 Ibid., II, pp. 264, 36, 314. Cf. Bridget Hill, 'A Refuge from Men: The Idea of a Protestant Nunnery', *Past and Present* 117: 107–30 (1987).
67 Southey, *Colloquies*, II, p. 253.
68 T. B. Macaulay, 'Southey's Colloquies' (*The Edinburgh Review* [1830]), *The Works*, (London, 1898), VII, pp. 450–502, at p. 467.
69 Southey, *Colloquies*, I, p. 180.
70 Macaulay, 'Sadler's Law of Population', *Works*, VII, pp. 570–604. Sadler replied to the review in *A Refutation Of An Article In The Edinburgh Review* (London, 1830), to which Macaulay replied in his turn, 'Sadler's Refutation Refuted', *Works*, VIII, pp. 18–55.
71 Michael Thomas Sadler, *The Law of Population*, I, pp. vii, x, 6, 7, 9.
72 Ibid., I, pp. 11, 387. For further discussion, see *Memoirs of Sadler*, Chapter 7, and Winch, *Riches and Poverty*, pp. 389–91.
73 For a recent approach, see S. A. Skinner, 'The Social Thought of the Oxford Movement: With Specific Reference to "The British Critic" 1827–1843', Oxford MPhil thesis (1989). This work is currently being extended into a doctoral thesis by Mr Skinner.
74 Skinner considers Bosanquet's to be the 'most sustained and vitriolic assault on political economy' ever made in the pages of the *British Critic* ('The Social Thought of the Oxford Movement', p. 120).
75 Samuel Richard Bosanquet, 'Pauperism and Alms-giving' in *The British Critic* 28: 195–257 (1840), at pp. 195, 196, 203, 222–3, 227, 232.
76 Ibid., pp. 246, 247, 254–5.
77 Bosanquet, 'Private Alms and Poor-Law Relief', *The British Critic* 28: 441–70 (1840), at pp. 441, 442, 470.
78 Ibid., pp. 451–2.
79 Samuel Johnson, *The Idler* (Number 4, 6 May 1758), ed. W. J. Bate, J. M. Bullitt and L. F. Powell, *The Yale Edition of the Works of Samuel Johnson*, II (New Haven, 1963), pp. 12–16, at pp. 12–13. For a good discussion of Johnson and the intricacies of Christian charity, see Nicholas Hudson, *Samuel Johnson and Eighteenth-Century Thought*, (Oxford, 1988) Chapter 6.
80 Thomas Balguy, *Divine Benevolence Asserted; And Vindicated from the Objections of Ancient and Modern Sceptics* (London, 1781). Balguy's notions of property and happiness are of a rather utilitarian nature (cf. *Divine Benevolence*, pp. 50, 57). For Paley's recommendations of Balguy's work, see *Natural Theology: Or, Evidences of the Existence and Attributes of the Deity* (London, 1802), pp. 518, 526. For a more censorious view of clerical concerns in this area, see Deborah Valenze, 'Charity, Custom, and Humanity: Changing Attitudes Towards the Poor in the Eighteenth-Century', in Jane Garnett and Colin Matthew (eds) *Revival and Religion since 1700: Essays for John Walsh* (London, 1993), pp. 59–78. Smith was famously dismissive of 'benevolence' considered purely as an economic motive, on which see *Wealth of Nations*, I, pp. 26–7, and, more generally, Istvan Hont and Michael Ignatieff, 'Needs and Justice in the *Wealth of Nations*: An Introductory Essay', in *Wealth and Virtue: The Shaping of Political Economy in the Scottish Enlightenment* (Cambridge, 1983), pp. 1–44.
81 Bosanquet, 'The Age of Unbelief', *The British Critic* 31: 91–123 (1842), at p. 100. On

geology, mesmerism and phrenology, see Hilton, *Age of Atonement*, pp. 148–54, 299–301, 308–9; 306, 311, 325; 189–201.

82 Bosanquet, *A Letter to Lord John Russell on the Safety of the Nation* (London, 1848), pp. 9, 26–7. The later essays in *Principia* are concerned with the providential judgement England was to suffer as a result of its rampant commitment to capitalism. On Bosanquet's notable 'extremism', see Hilton, *Age of Atonement*, pp. 96–7, 215.

83 P. d'A. Jones, *The Christian Socialist Revival, 1877–1914* (Princeton, 1968); Edward Norman, *The Victorian Christian Socialists* (Cambridge, 1987); David M. Thompson, 'The Christian Socialist Revival in Britain: A Reappraisal', in Garnett and Matthew, *Revival and Religion*, pp. 273–95; Noel Thompson, *The Market and Its Critics* (London, 1988), Chapter 7; R. A. Soloway, *Prelates and People: Ecclesiastical Social Thought in England 1783–1852* (London, 1969); G. Kitson Clark, *Churchmen and the Condition of England 1832–1885: A Study in the Development of Social Ideas and Practice from the Old Regime to the Modern State* (London, 1973).

84 On evangelicalism and capitalism, see, besides Hilton, Jane Garnett, 'Aspects of the Relationship Between Protestant Ethics and Economic Activity in Mid Victorian England', Oxford DPhil dissertation (1986); Garnett, '"Gold and the Gospel": Systematic Beneficence in Mid-Nineteenth-Century England', in W. J. Shiels and Diana Wood (eds) *The Church and Wealth: Studies in Church History* 24 (Oxford, 1987), pp. 347–58; J. Garnett and A. C. Howe, 'Churchmen and Cotton Makers in Victorian England', in David J. Jeremy (ed.) *Business and Religion in Britain* (Aldershot, 1988), pp. 72–94; Garnett, 'Evangelicalism and Business in Mid-Victorian Britain', and Brian Dickey, '"Going about and doing good": Evangelicals and Poverty *c.* 1815–1870', in John Wolffe (ed.) *Evangelical Faith and Public Zeal: Evangelicals and Society in Britain 1780–1980* (London, 1995), pp. 59–80, 38–58.

85 Southey, *Colloquies*, I, p. 169.

2 From canon to cannon fire

Religion and economics, 1730–1850

Boyd Hilton

In pointing to so many Christian writers who contributed to the canon of political economy in the eighteenth and nineteenth centuries, Brian Young joins a growing band of historians who in the last decade or so have emphasised the interconnected histories of religious, economic and social thought. Of course, it would not have surprised social moralists in the inter-war period, such as Vigo Demant and Maurice Reckitt, to be told that Christian writers like Tucker, Paley and Chalmers had contributed to the development of so-called classical economics. It only became necessary to rediscover this truth as a result of developments in the 1960s and 1970s, when an increasingly technical approach to the history of political economy gave rise to detailed internalist accounts which seemed to ignore wider cultural debates altogether.

Dr Young surveys the field with characteristic subtlety and discrimination, and the only objection which will be taken here is rather to the tone of his remarks than to the argument. Like many scholars today, influenced perhaps by Jonathan Clark's vision of a 'long eighteenth century',[1] Young's account plays down the extent of the intellectual and cultural discontinuity caused by the American and (especially) French Revolutions. In tracing a canon of economic thought through the period 1730–1850, and in emphasising the similar preoccupations of different thinkers at different times, he possibly underestimates the changes of the late eighteenth century. As Young rightly observes, there was a 'stark division' between Law and Mandeville – 'a genuine binary affair' – and there was an equally stark division between Southey and Macaulay a hundred years later. Analytically it might be justifiable to relate the two controversies, but atmospherically it seems all wrong because, following the French Revolution, intellectual hatreds and anxieties had become so much greater than seems to be acknowledged in Young's casual phrase, 'a fissure began to widen'. In practice, 'binary affair' had become vicious polarity.

In Britain the single most important intellectual contribution to the new atmosphere was Robert Malthus's *Essay on the Principle of Population* (1798).[2] Malthusian ideas held a powerful sway in the first half of the nineteenth century, and it is only a slight exaggeration to say that the stance which one took on the Malthusian question was a predictor of all one's other beliefs. Dr Young claims that it is important 'not to minimise' the antagonism felt towards Malthus by many of his contemporaries, but his (in many ways commendable) willingness to emphasise 'subtleties' and 'nuances' undermines the impact of that pronouncement. So let it be stated again as baldly as possible: *the first half of the nineteenth century was different from most of the eighteenth*! Part of the difference was the way in which orthodox thought was infected by a profoundly anti-utopian sentiment, of which Malthusianism was the most obvious manifestation, and which effectively proscribed happiness as an object of human endeavour. Dismal economists like Ricardo argued that if the vast majority of the people earned more than they needed for subsistence, bang would go profits, in would come the stationary state, and everyone would suffer including themselves. Many evangelicals like Thomas Chalmers argued that if people were made happy – either by private charity or public welfare legislation – they would simply breed more children and end up hungrier and more miserable than before. Worse still, improvement in their earthly prospects would be detrimental to their spiritual prospects – a far cry from Tucker and most eighteenth-century thinkers who, as Brian Young shows, believed that one could book one's ticket to Heaven and help others at the same time, since self-love and social coincided. Chalmers's other-worldly philosophy was satirised by his Whig-Radical opponent G. P. Scrope as a doctrine of 'Evil, be thou our good!'[3] 'God smites those whom he most loves', is how Chalmers himself put it. In just such a spirit many contemporaries found spiritual solace in their temporal unhappiness, and embraced the 'dismal science' as yet another sign of God's tough love towards them.

Tonally at least, Young's essay plays down the tensions caused by such anti-utopian ideology. For example, he is right to present S. R. Bosanquet as a Christian who 'repudiated' political economy, including the Christian political economy of evangelicals like Sumner and Chalmers. However, 'repudiated' hardly does justice to the almost hysterical antagonism between Bosanquet's and Chalmers's philosophies. Young even identifies an area of agreement between the two by concentrating on an institutional issue: both men preferred private alms-giving to state relief and disliked the New Poor Law for that reason. But there all likeness ends between the pair. Chalmers wanted to minimise the amount of money which was given to the poor, whereas Bosanquet wanted to maximise it. Chalmers thought that the New Poor Law was too generous, but was better than the Old Poor Law which was more generous still, whereas Bosanquet thought it was much too mean. Finally, many of the phenomena which Bosanquet denounced as 'great evils' (such as the 'mercantile system',[4] capitalism, competition, the 'passion for liberty', and the 'desire for cheapness') were all indispensable to Chalmers's economic philosophy.

The only sentence in Young's essay which seems to be seriously misleading is his statement that 'the question of providentialism was where Bosanquet did share in a large part of the world of the evangelicals'. For evangelicals were bitterly divided among themselves, and nowhere more so than on the question of how providence operated. Young refers to Bosanquet's belief in providential judgement on capitalist Britain, and quotes his remark that 'the Tyre of trade shall repent of her fornications'. What he does not say is that Chalmers would never have used a phrase like that. This is not because he did not believe in providence (of course he did), nor because he was too squeamish to use such a phrase, but because he did not believe in Bosanquet's type of vengeful Old Testament God. Bosanquet's writings quote at inordinate length from Revelations, and are stuffed with references to 'the seventh seal', 'the image of the beast', 'the noisome and grievous sore', the 'last times of national degeneracy'. London was guilty of 'spiritual incest' and was now 'the Babylon of the Apocalypse'. There was no option but to await 'the advance of that final apostasy which shall precede the second coming of our Lord'.[5] In other words, Bosanquet was a *pre*-millennialist who believed (like Southey, incidentally) that *all* providence operated as special dispensation, whereas Chalmers was a *post*-millennialist, for whom the last times were still far distant, and for whom providence operated – except on very special occasions[6] – generally through the mechanisms of natural law.

It was those Christians (like Chalmers) who believed in the ordinary operation of general providence that plugged so easily into political economy, whereas believers in special providence (like Bosanquet) rejected it out of hand in favour of a 'paternal government' which would 'protect' the poor. This was no armchair skirmish, as is clear from Henry Drummond's howl of rage against Chalmers in 1829. Drummond, a pre-millennial Irvingite and conventionally regarded as an evangelical, described Chalmers as 'the most redoubted champion of Evangelical Liberalism',

> that spurious theology, commonly called Evangelicalism, which has pervaded the land; and which, wholly blind itself, has blinded the people to the great principle, that all power is held *of* Christ, and is to be used *for* Him: a principle, the observance of which in every rank of society, by King, magistrate, subject, husband, wife, child, master, servant, alone makes the Christian performance of those duties in any degree different from their performance by heathens. Where this is lost sight of, there is no principle at all; for the Evangelical doctrines destroy the old principle of proud and self-righteous disinterestedness, the foundation of those pagan virtues, patriotism, and chivalrous feeling, without supplying any other which can perform as noble deeds.[7]

Drummond's brand of evangelical Christian paternalism had much in common with stoic and civic humanist values. Whereas Chalmers saw Christ as a mediator whose sacrifice on the cross ensured the salvation of individual souls, Drummond saw him as a legislator aiming to improve the lot of society. Whereas Chalmers argued that Christ's Kingdom was not of this world, Drummond looked to the imminent resumption of Christ's reign on earth. Whereas Chalmers advocated the 'economy of the Gospel', Drummond held to the values of the Old rather than the New Testament. Whereas Chalmers argued that the Church and State should be separate – with the function of the Church being simply to 'prepare men for Heaven's exercises and for Heaven's joys' – Drummond argued that Church and State should be intimately blended in a theocratic government. Christ was born and crucified King of the Jews, and earthly kings were merely his vice-regents, ruling in his paternal image:

The abuse of a truth has no necessary connection with the truth itself: the delegation, as in the priesthood, and every office, and rite, and ceremony, and sacrament in the Church, belongs to the function, and not to him who discharges it; is equally applicable to all Sovereign authority, be it called imperial, regal, or consular. It is the denial of this principle which has now dissolved the only solid cement that can unite this or any other social fabric.

True religion was 'a system of bindings'. 'It is the denial of this principle which constitutes liberalism.' Liberalism was 'a system of letting loose all ties and bonds whatever, but that of selfish interest'.[8] Drummond's immediate target was Chalmers's support for Catholic emancipation. Emancipation was 'as great and flagrant a rebellion against Christ the King as any ever committed', and was sure to bring down civil war, famine, or pestilence. 'Surely it must be admitted, that wherever Christ is King there can be no free trade in creeds.'[9] But it was free trade generally, and indeed Chalmers's entire social philosophy, which Drummond had in his sights. By denying the principle that 'the comfort of the labouring class is the exclusively infallible test of all equitable government', Chalmers had furnished 'shallow heads with excuses for cold hearts': 'I am wholly opposed to "the Satanic School" of Scotch Political Economy, which looks to the creation and production of capital as the end, to the attainment of which the population is but the means.'[10]

Rather than thinking about a canon of political economy, which gives a somewhat consensual flavour to the first half of the nineteenth century, it is better to think in terms of polar opposites. It was a period in which almost every thoughtful person felt beleaguered, with ideological cannon to left of them, cannon to right of them, the valley of death in front of them, the terrible certainty of judgement hanging over them, and the possibility of agnosticism not yet open to them. Political economy was an important element in their religion, but it was subservient to that religion, which was still *all-important*.

NOTES

1 J. C. D. Clark, *English Society 1688–1832: Ideology, Social Structure and Political Practice during the Ancien Regime* (Cambridge, 1985).
2 Gertrude Himmelfarb, *The Idea of Poverty: England in the Early Industrial Age* (London and Boston, 1984), pp. 100–44.
3 [G. Poulett Scrope], 'Dr Chalmers on Political Economy', *Quarterly Review*, 48: 63 (1832).
4 Meaning not mercantilism but the commercial system.
5 S. R. Bosanquet, *Principia: A Series of Essays on the Principles of Evil Manifesting Themselves in these Last Times in Religion, Philosophy, and Politics* (1843), pp. 139, 331, and *passim*.
6 This is a point which the late David Nicholls unaccountably failed to understand in relation to Chalmers's support for state relief to victims of the Irish famine in 1847. Support for such relief did not signify any change in his theology at this time, since like all evangelical Christians Chalmers had always believed that God very occasionally suspended the operation of his own natural (or secondary) laws. All he said in 1847 was that on such occasions the ordinary rules of free trade should not apply. D. Nicholls,

God and Government in an 'Age of Reason' (1995), p. 226; B. Hilton, *The Age of Atonement* (Oxford, 1988), pp. 108–12.

7 H[enry] D[rummond], *A letter to Dr Chalmers, in Reply to his Speech in the Presbytery of Edinburgh* (London, 1829), pp. 1, 14.

8 Ibid., pp. 2–4, 21–3.

9 Ibid., pp. 10–11, 18–21.

10 Ibid., pp. 24–5.

Part II
Nonconformists and wealth

3   Methodism and wealth, 1740–1860

W. R. Ward

This theme has a strong Weberian flavour to it and as such is an illustration of the extraordinary element of fashion in styles of historiography. Four years ago I commented in a survey of the immense literature of German Pietism that work in this style went out of fashion after the Second World War, and that there had been no successors to the two admirable monographs on the relationship between faith and and economic organisation in old Herrnhut published there by Otto Uttendörfer in 1925 and 1926.[1] This is extremely odd in view of the fact that in German social history the dominance of Weber is greater than it has ever been, but it is repeated also in the history of Methodism over the last twenty-five years, notwithstanding that the two most substantial contributions to the beggarly bibliography on this theme have both been in the German language. It is not easy to suggest why this should have been so. The appalling intrusion of ecumenical politics into Methodist historiography had by this time spent itself, and the story was once again being told in its own terms. It is possible that the English-language practitioners of Methodist as well as other kinds of history believed that the doctrine of the *Protestant Ethic and the Spirit of Capitalism* was somehow exploded, and did not take the trouble to see how enormously German *Gesellschaftsgeschichte* had gained in comparison with our own by the theoretical stiffening provided by the rest of Weber's corpus. More directly, Methodist historiography benefited from two vigorous if often polemical inputs from modern British historiography at large, one from the standpoint of life-experience history and the other from those interested in recruiting movements. The one wished to study Methodism as a large-scale response to rapid social change and break-up, the other as a point of reference for popular politics and trade unionism. Though the one was dominated by the shade of E. P. Thompson, who did not mind sticking out his neck on eighteenth-century matters, most of the rest gave their minds to the nineteenth century when they had a movement of some size to deal with; and the recruiting men had no option but to do so. Meanwhile the sort of history which is continually produced as a by-product of the Church's life suffered from its usual failure to make contact with the interests of historians working from other standpoints. The flood of local histories grows no less; attempts in both America and Germany to build Wesley up into a significant school-historian continue, but neither are interested in Methodism and wealth. Perhaps significantly, the best of

Wesley's recent biographers, Henry Rack, who is not only a Primitive by origin but properly anxious to cut the Wesleyan totem down to size, has three or four excellent pages on this theme,[2] but they cut a small figure in a biography of 650 pages. Nor have changes in the Church's life helped. There is no mistaking the decline of the old social gospel interest; the new urban theology and romantically entitled Mission alongside the Poor are more interested in poverty than wealth and too dedicated to political correctness to contribute much to the understanding of either. The other recent clerical fashions, ecumenism, liturgical reform, and feminism have other targets in view. Still worse, the official *History of the Methodist Church of Great Britain*[3] intended as an ecumenical memorial to a religious tradition about to be swallowed up in a putative coming Great Church, by a combination of poor planning and extremely lax management which allowed more than half a generation to pass between the date for the receipt of contributions and actual publication, ended up as a set of tombstones to quite other things. Working historians had meanwhile turned to other interests.

It is not therefore as bizarre as it might otherwise seem that the first substantial contribution to the subject came from the old Czechoslovakia in the darkest days of Russian domination. Vilém Schneeberger's *Theologische Wurzeln des socialen Akzents bei John Wesley* (Zurich, 1974) was the work of a superintendent of the Evangelical–Methodist Church in Czechoslovakia, and was originally submitted as a dissertation to the Hus faculty in Prague in the Czech language. Apparently through Central European Methodist connexions it came to be published in Switzerland in the author's own German. The book thus not only represents an attempt to take Methodism back to something like its Moravian roots, but was a harbinger of much more in Central Europe. Methodism there was partly of British and partly of American origin; the paradox has been that the processes of assimilation in America which have led to the absorption of old German-language denominations into American Methodism have brought with them unions of central European Methodist communities of varied American and British provenance, and these unions in turn have led to a notable series of works of history and historical theology as the central European Methodists seek to explain to each other and the great Protestant establishments who they are and the hole of the pit from which they have been dug.

It is this, I think, as much as the political context in which the book was written which explains its odd features. The political context is nevertheless to be perceived. A book about Wesley's theology has no need to concern itself about a labour movement which formed long after his death; nevertheless Schneeberger begins with an argument that the ultimate breach between organised labour and Methodism goes back to Wesley himself, to his Toryism, his monarchism, his belief that authority descended from above, his loathing of democracy. Wesley was not merely not a revolutionary, he was not even a social reformer and did not seize the social need of his time with the same energy he devoted to other things. When after his death tension between exploiters and exploited sharpened, and the latter began to adopt the banners of atheism, there was nothing in Methodism to reconcile the two fronts.[4] All this has very little to do with Methodist history in the two centuries since Wesley's death, but is a recognisable sop to the government of the CSSR.

The substance of the book is equally odd but makes sense in the ecclesiastical context in which it is written. Fully three-quarters of the space is given up to an analysis of Wesley's theology in general and into this, disproportionate as it is to any 'theological roots of the social accent', the author put an enormous amount of work on both the sources and the secondary literature. The essence of the matter proves to be that Wesley builds his theology upon the two bearing pillars of faith and love; hope, the eschatological partner of Paul's trilogy is almost completely lacking, and when he preached on eschatological themes his utterances did not get into the standard sermons. The reason is that Wesley so emphasised love as to give it the character of a realised eschatology that he lost the eschatological dimension in the sense of the expectation of a future fulfilment. Faith and love are so related that love is the consequence of faith and is the quintessence of the Christian life; moreover, love is not a philosophical principle or the inward theme of the spiritual life, but always has a concrete form. Faith is not just fellowship with God but also with the neighbour without whom the Christian life is not possible.[5] It is in this sense that in an early sermon (and again in the preface to the *Hymns and Sacred Poems* (1739)) Wesley defines Christianity as 'essentially a social religion; . . . to turn it into a solitary religion is inded to destroy it'.[6] And although he seems not to have used the phrase again, the idea certainly underlay the astonishing number of measures of poor relief which he undertook, and the real ruthlessness with which he gave away all the money which came his way apart from what he needed for the income he had promised to settle on his brother Charles to enable him to marry into a South Wales gentry family. In short, though Schneeberger does not say so, Max Weber could hardly have chosen a worse example of the propensity of inner-worldly asceticism to lead to capital accumulation than John Wesley (whatever might be the case among his followers).[7] What is very odd is the other thing which Schneeberger does not say, i.e. whether Wesley had any more to say about wealth than that it should be lovingly given away in faithful imitation of the bounty of God. Indeed, in a private letter he subsequently admitted that his study stopped at the point where 'a study of Wesley's ethics ought to begin';[8] whether it was politically impracticable to say more I do not know.

Schneeberger did, however, provide a starting-point for the next central-European contribution explicitly entitled *Praxis und Prinzipien der Sozialethik John Wesleys* (1977) by Manfred Marquardt. So far as I know he is unrelated to Friedrich-Wilhelm Marquardt who at much the same time gained enormous notoriety but failed to obtain a doctorate for a thesis which maintained that the socialist commitment was the key to the understanding of the theology of Karl Barth.[9] Manfred's work formed a successful dissertation at Kiel, and the last time I came across him he was teaching at a Methodist seminary in Württemberg. It is a very useful book as it surveys in a systematic way the whole of the source material available in print and the whole of the secondary literature then available in the Federal Republic. System is indeed what is lacking in Wesley himself; his vast output consisted entirely of occasional writings, and his eclecticism meant that he was all the time putting his personal stamp upon the ideas of other men. He had, however, an economic ethic of his own, pungently summed up in the threefold formulary to 'gain all you can, save all you can, and give all you can'.[10] This clearly implied the lawfulness of striving for gain, and also the right to private property which is nowhere contested by Wesley. This may have owed a little to Wesley's desire to sidestep the charges of advocating community of goods, to which language which he drew from William Law, and his refusal to write off the post-Pentecostal community of goods in the primitive Church as simply an expedient for an unrepeatable occasion, offered some plausibility. Nor did Wesley require even the Methodist wealthy to divest themselves of their possessions, and he was sufficiently alive to the needs of his age to allow that money was required not only to purchase the necessities of life, but also for commercial and industrial investment. Indeed, the general tenor of Wesley's travel observations in his Journal is that economic progress was progress, and that nothing was worse than the chronic under-employment of the pre-industrial economy, notwithstanding that the Methodist multiplication of devotions required this surplus leisure, and was not easily combined with the discipline of factory employment.[11] Nevertheless Wesley beats the drum without restraint on the dangers of wealth, not least to Methodists, and he does not recommend getting and saving for economic ends; they were for fulfilling the will of God in concrete acts of love to neighbours. Luxury was unspeakable.

Finally there were the ends of social ethics themselves. They were the renewal of individual men and women, the renewal of society in so far as this could be accomplished by the influence of cells of men and women bent on perfection. But not every kind of social change was for the better. Democratic ordinances whether in church or state were to be rejected, as was also the way of independence from king and Parliament chosen by the American colonies. Here Wesley was not perhaps entirely consistent. In the 1770s he had been converted by Quaker connexions to the anti-slavery cause and fastened it to the early American Methodists with what speedily became embarrassing strictness. When denouncing slavery he had held that law could not override the legitimacy of natural rights; but this of course was precisely the justification which the American rebels claimed. Marquardt winds up his discussion by pointing to three weaknesses in Wesley's social ethics. His conservative view of the state practically exempted it from the renewal he was looking for everywhere else, and the 'no politics' rule imposed upon the preachers went beyond prudence to requiring a political intervention on their part on behalf of king and government. Then second, Wesley refused to contemplate structural alterations in the order of society, and, third, this may actually have been as well since he was no economist and had not much sense of causal connexions in politics. How just are these conclusions?

The thing which is lacking from Marquardt's analysis is any scheme of the progress of Christian social ethics against which to test Wesley's thought. There are in fact three stages in the process. The first is *alms*, in which the object is the sanctification of the giver; in the second stage, that of *charity*, the necessities of the recipient are acknowledged to constitute a claim upon the giver, and the intention is to relieve them; the third stage, that of *policy*, is arrived at with the recognition that it may be possible, by altering social arangements, effectively to remove the causes of distress instead of merely palliating their effects by charitable action. Where does Wesley stand on this grid? Clearly much of what went on in the Holy Club before Wesley's conversion falls under the first heading, and Wesley's refusal to take over his father's parish on the ground that Oxford was a much better theatre for sanctification, tells its own tale. Yet it is hard to believe that all the strenuous do-gooding was entirely unrelated to the perceived needs of others or that the extraordinarily impressive record of Methodism, in company with the evangelical movement as a whole, of innovative charitable enterprise had wholly to wait on Wesley's conversion. No doubt a great difference was made by Wesley's abandoning the cloistered groves of academe and acquiring a remark-ably extensive knowledge of the real world, but the difference could hardly have been total. The problems come with the third stage, that of policy, where the Christian record in the modern world is at its weakest. It would be easy to write Wesley off altogether, and to say that he had no conception of organised social change, notwithstanding the resolution of the first Conference 'to reform the nation and especially the Church'. His half-baked economics and lack of understanding not of political wrongs to be righted, but of political mechanisms by which a result might be achieved, all point in the same direction. But there are two considerations which must be urged on his behalf. Much of Wesley's work in prisons was of a charitable nature but he wrote a good deal on prison and penal reform that was clearly of an institutional kind, though he did not live to see much practical result of his efforts; and in the same way, by the time he took up with the anti-slavery cause in the 1770s the success of that cause implied major social engineering in some of the American colonies, and cannot be reduced to mere charity. The second consideration which must be urged on Wesley's behalf is that the whole political tradition in which he had been raised predisposed him against the sorts of policies involved in social engineering. Wesley came out of a Jacobite milieu with its implications of treason and revolution, but by the time of the 1745 his movement had a sufficient stake in the liberties grudgingly conceded by the Hanoverian system to ensure that he gave the required pledges of loyalty. In any case, by this time like so many of similar mind he had thrown in his lot with country party reform. The essence of country party reform was to redress the balance of the constitution against the government, on the assumption that England was basically a state of nature requiring little government, and that what had gone wrong was the encroachment of dirty government into spheres where it was not required. The Conference programme 'to reform the nation and especially the Church' meant in effect to get Walpolism out of both. Whether the conception of England as a state of nature was really compatible with Wesley's grasp of original sin or with the more active monarchical traditions of his remoter past is a question, but there is no doubt that it militated against the kind of policies which the rapid social change which followed Wesley's death made unavoidable.

Is any further light cast on his state of mind in this matter, by a rather splendid paper on 'John Wesley and the Community of Goods' kindly contributed by John Walsh to a Festschrift presented to me by the Ecclesiastical History Society.[12] John Walsh takes up the patristic background of Wesley's mind and is able to show that through this channel the primitive communism of the Book of Acts was powerfully reinforced not merely by the patristic scholarship which was one of the features of the Restoration Church but by his own unsystematic reading in the Fathers. From this treasury Wesley drew not merely inspiration but schemes for joint-stock relief of the poor and many other details. What distinguished Wesley from most of the other churchmen of his time, who were quite prepared to say that the Bible was the religion of Protestants, but that New Testament miracles and common property were simply God's desperate and unrepeatable devices to get the church off the ground, was that he was prepared to believe that the evidence of Acts, clearly taken seriously in the patristic evidence, had exemplary force, and this radical conviction was strengthened by the influence of William Law. The way the Holy Club bailed each other out was indeed very like the community of goods in the New Testament, though the background to it was the rather safe one of an endowed college existence. But by the time he had arrived at his threefold formulary in the sermon on 'The Use of Money' it was quite clear that when the Christian had gained all he could, and saved all he could, the injunction to give all he could, meant that he was to give away the lot barring a pittance to keep himself alive. Wesley, in short, here adhered to that central Christian mystical tradition, of which Tersteegen (two of whose hymns Wesley translated) was a distinguished Protestant exponent on the continent, and he justified it by a patristic reference suggesting that from the beginning there had been two orders of Christians. The first conformed innocently to the world, practising piety as the opportunity offered; the others aimed at Christian perfection, and of them nothing less was demanded than a constant 'course of self-denial'. Hence the need for the ruthless returning of money to the poor whom God had appointed to receive it. Wesley was reintroducing the Catholic distinction between life according to the rule and the second-class Christian life, but he was keeping both classes in the world. Thus even had not the country politics which Wesley adopted required the rolling back of the sphere of the state, there could be no question of using the state to redistribute wealth because that kind of process contributed nothing to the sacrifice which led towards perfection. In short, in original intention Wesley's attitude towards wealth never budged from the first rung on the ladder; it was a source for alms radically conceived. And in his less cheerful moments late in life he began to fear that even real Christianity was a self-defeating enterprise; true Christianity begot diligence and frugality; they begot riches, and riches undermined Christianity and were ruinous to the holy tempers he prized so highly.

Whether Wesley's followers agonised over the issue of wealth as much as he did is unlikely, but there are two lines of inquiry which might profitably be pursued. My old friend Geoffrey Milburn in the days of his service to Sunderland Poly was inveigled by David Jeremy into one of them, producing a useful paper on Methodist business men in the North-East, which included an equally useful biographical appendix.[13] This attempt to Namierise a regional class of Methodist business-men shows principally two things. One is the extraordinary range of businesses in which Methodists prospered in the North-East. Of course Methodists were relatively thick on the ground in the area when the economic upswing there began, and certainly they took advantage of a very wide range of the opportunities there were. Then, second, Methodist entrepreneurs very seldom became fabulously rich, and, though statistical comparisons are not to be had, seem to have been been more generous to good causes while their fortunes were being made than the average business man who preferred to make his pelf before splashing out. If this inference is correct Wesley's conscience left some mark on his followers. What the method does not easily account for is the sort of difference between those two neighbours in twentieth-century Hull, Joseph Rank who left a great sum in trust for Methodist causes, and Thomas Robinson Ferens whose biggest single benefaction was an endowment to University College, Hull, i.e. outside the connexion to which he belonged. In this sense he was a better disciple of Wesley than Rank.

The second line of enquiry might cast more light on the business *mentalité*. One of the puzzles is how businessmen reconciled their evangelical personal ethic of love with the impersonal market economics of their weekday commercial orthodoxy. Years ago I came across the books of the Union Chapel in Manchester which showed how it might be done, and though I have never found it, similar Methodist material should survive. At the Union Chapel (as in Methodist chapels) the bankruptcy of a member which involved failure to meet obligations was a *prima facie* ground for expulsion from membership. When a case arose, and they were numerous in the 1840s, two church officers were required to investigate. If they found the bankrupt culpable, expulsion would follow; but, if they found that he had been a victim of cirumstances outside his control, it followed that the congregation had a duty to assist, at a minimum with prayer but in practical ways also. These inquisitions show an attempt to contain the worst savageries of the free market by the exercise of love, an attempt to develop an economic casuistry, and show also that one of the reasons for Nonconformist business success was not a Weberian one, but the safety net which congregational discipline could build beneath a business. As far as I know neither the safety net nor the discipline existed in the Church of England.

NOTES

1 W. R. Ward, 'German Pietism, 1670–1750', *Journal of Ecclesiastical History* 44 (3): 479 (1993).
2 Henry D. Rack, *Reasonable Enthusiast: John Wesley and the Rise of Methodism* (London, 1989) pp. 365–7.
3 Ed, by E. G. Rupp, R. Davies and A. R. George (London, 1965–88).
4 Schneeberger, pp. 14–17.
5 Ibid. pp. 116, 139 143.
6 John Wesley, *Sermons on Several Occasions* (London, 1872) I, p. 329, Sermon 24.
7 Max Weber, *Economy and Society*, ed. G. Roth and C. Wittich (Berkeley, 1978) I, pp. 479, 527.

8   Manfred Marquardt, *Praxis und Prinzipien der Sozialethik John Wesleys* (Göttingen, 1977) p. 11.

9   Friedrich-Wilhelm Marquardt, *Theologie und Sozialismus. Das Beispiel Karl Barths* (Munich, 1972).

10   Condensed from Sermon 50 on 'The use of money', Wesley, *Sermons* II, pp. 140–53.

11   John Rylands Library, Methodist Church Archives. Joseph Entwisle to George Marsden, 30 November 1802.

12   In *Protestant Evangelicalism: Britain, Ireland, Germany and America, c.1750-c.1950*, edited by Keith Robbins (Oxford, 1990), pp. 25–50.

13   G. E. Milburn, 'Piety, Profit and Paternalism: Methodists in Business in the North-East of England, c.1760–1920', *Proceedings of the Wesley Historical Society* 44, 45–92: (1983) (reprinted by the Wesley Historical Society as a pamphlet under the same title, Banbury, 1984).

4 Late-Victorian and Edwardian Methodist businessmen and wealth

David J. Jeremy

INTRODUCTION

Picture the scene. The date: the morning of Tuesday, 31 July 1900. The place: the freshly decorated Wesleyan Methodist Chapel, Burslem, most northern of the smoke-laden Pottery towns. The occasion: the annual Conference of the Wesleyan Methodist Connexion.[1] In the first week of Conference 300 ministers and 300 laymen, representing the 410,000 members and 2,200 ministers of the denomination, met in Representative session; in the second week, 400 ministers met in Pastoral session.[2] On this second day of Conference in 1900 the morning's business was dominated by a report from the committee of the Twentieth Century Fund, presented by Mr Perks.

Robert Perks was a businessman and a politician, as well as a Wesleyan layman. The son of a Wesleyan minister and Conference President, he had reached the company boardroom by specialising as a railway solicitor and becoming a partner of Henry Fowler, later Baron Wolverhampton and the first Methodist to sit in the Cabinet and the House of Lords. Perks shrewdly married the daughter of a Wesleyan railway director, William Mewburn sen., and by 1900 sat on the boards of the Lancashire, Derbyshire & East Coast Railway Co. and of the Metropolitan District Railway Co. (as chairman in 1901 and deputy chairman in 1905). The latter built or electrified much of the deep-level tube railway system under London. MP for the Louth Division of Lincolnshire since 1892, Perks was a wily intriguer who served as matchmaker between traditionally conservative Wesleyans and the Liberal Party. Among Wesleyan laymen in Edwardian England, he was one of the most eminent.

The Twentieth Century Fund, echoing earlier national and *ad hoc* denominational funds,[3] was his idea. He had launched it at Conference two years earlier, in 1898, persuading his brother Wesleyans that 1 million guineas could be raised from a third of the 3 million adherents which he then claimed for Wesleyan Methodism in Britain. Of the sum to be raised, Perks had suggested, £250,000 would afford 'material assistance to the village chapel or mission room or school' in areas where there were no wealthy laymen. Another £100,000 would be placed in the Home Missionary Fund. This was a clear response to resurgent Anglicanism as well as to rampant urban deprivation.

Now, in July 1900, time for reaching the 1 million guineas target of the Wesleyan Twentieth Century Fund was fast running out. Standing before the Conference at Burslem, Perks, dressed in black adorned by a white orchid (the Queen's son, the Duke of Edinburgh, had just died), reported that some £733,000 was already promised. But, as was later recalled, 'the success of the Twentieth Century Fund trembled in the Balance'. Perks appealed to English Methodists to match the generosity of their American cousins who were raising £4 million for their fund, the Canadians who had raised 250,000 guineas for theirs, and the Irish (subscribers to the British effort) who had gone beyond their goal of 50,000 guineas. He knew that there were objections to the principle of 'one person, one guinea'. (One guinea was equivalent to the week's wages of an agricultural labourer and two-thirds of the week's wages of a skilled industrial worker.)[4] Perks 'declared that from the beginning he had recognised the fact that large sums would have to be given. Some thought the principle had been worked for all it was worth. This he doubted.' Another 250,000 guineas was needed by 31 December 1900 to reach the million mark. Given the seeming impossibility of meeting the target, Perks proposed that the deadline be stretched into the new century.

Then the Reverend Hugh Price Hughes, passionate leader of the Forward Movement and prophet of 'Social Christianity' (seeking the salvation of society as well as of individuals), rose to his feet. He pleaded with 'the men of means in the Conference, and throughout the Connexion'. Let them give 'not out of income, but out of capital'. In an atmosphere of high emotion sober commercial men tossed thrift and caution to the winds as, one after another, they stood up to announce a new or increased donation.

Joseph Rank, the miller, sitting under the gallery on the President's right, was first. As the *Methodist Recorder* reporter noted:

> Tall and strong, dressed with absolute plainness, he walked up the aisle and mounted the tribune. I could see that every nerve in the resolute face was quivering. . . . With deepest humility he acknowledged how God had blessed him, and told the Conference that he felt he must give as the Lord had given to him. He wanted to challenge the rich men in the Conference. He had already tried to do his duty in his own Church, and in his own District. In other words, though he did not explain this, he had promised 2,000 guineas in his own circuit at Grimsby, and in the Hull District Synod had added a sum of 5,000 guineas. He now promised . . . 10,000 more and added he should like to give the last 10,000 guineas to the Fund. Including the gifts in his own circuit and District, Mr Joseph Rank has now promised, conditionally on the whole amount being raised in the way he indicates, a total sum of 27,000 guineas.[5]

The Vanner brothers, bankers, added 5,000 guineas to the 5,000 guineas they had already promised.[6] Henry Holloway, the London contractor, telegraphed his brother Tom suggesting they make a sacrificial gift of £2,000. Next morning came the reply, 'But if it is to be sacrifice make it £5,000.' And it was £5,000 that the Holloway brothers gave. Thomas Robinson Ferens, general manager of Reckitt & Sons, the Hull and Quaker starch manufacturers, gave an additional thousand guineas. Perks himself gave over £10,000. In short, between them, just seven Wesleyan businessmen gave over £65,000, or 26 per cent, of the 250,000 guineas (£262,500) needed to reach the Twentieth Century Fund target. In the event, and partly owing to the supervention of the Boer War (1899–1901), the 1 million guineas (£1,050,000) was reached on the last day of 1901 when £1,073,682 had been received by the Fund's five treasurers.[7]

Apart from offering some interesting contrasts with our own millennial arrangements, this glimpse of late Victorian Methodist businessmen publicly distributing their wealth raises a number of questions, four of which will be briefly addressed here. First, who were the lay leaders among the Methodists? What proportion were businessmen and how significant were they as businessmen? Second, what part did religion have in their wealth creation? That is, did Weber or Marx, spiritual or material drives, best explain their careers? Third, just how dependent was the Wesleyan Methodist denomination on the benefactions of its big businessmen? Last, how was beneficence mobilised for church causes?

WHO WERE THE LAY LEADERS AMONG THE METHODISTS AT THE BEGINNING OF THE TWENTIETH CENTURY AND WHO WERE THE BUSINESSMEN AMONG THEM?

My focus is on the Wesleyans, largest of the Methodist denominations, but in a penultimate section some comparisons will be drawn with lay leaders in other denominations, Methodist and non-Methodist. Leadership I have equated with membership of at least five national church committees (the minimum number held by denominational treasurers). In 1907 (my benchmark date)[8] 1,671 national committee positions were open to Wesleyan laymen and these were held by 875 individuals. Of these 875, just seventy-six laymen (no women at this date) held five or more denominational committee posts. One (Robert Perks) occupied fifteen committee seats. Although they comprised only 8.7 per cent of the 875 leading Wesleyan lay people (a number were women) in the land, these seventy-six men held 31 per cent of available committee posts. Between them, they shouldered the secular burdens of the denomination and held the centre of lay power in the connexion. Who were they?

What were the occupational backgrounds of these Wesleyan 'workhorses'? Of the 76, 1 was a farmer; 2 were in mining; 29 in manufacturing; 2 in construction; 5 in transport; 8 in distribution; 6 in finance; 17 in the professions (12 of them in professions, like the law and engineering, likely to deal with business people); 2 in public administration; 1 a trade union official; and 3 of unknown occupation. Two characteristics of this group of seventy-six Wesleyan lay leaders are noteworthy. First, over 72 per cent of them were engaged in business in some form or other. Second, all apart from the three unknown and the two administrators, were owners or managers of their businesses. Owners out-numbered managers.

If their occupational patterns are compared to those of the occupied male workforce in the whole country, it seems that clusters of industries preponderated among these Wesleyan lay leaders. At an industry level Wesleyan lay leaders heavily over-represented chemicals–petroleum, textiles and shipping. They under-represented clothing, utilities, and road transport. The biographical and auto-biographical impressions they gave to denominational publications bring their features into focus. Let me mention a clutch of these businessmen.

In manufacturing Joseph Rank the flour miller was enjoying rapid business expansion following his early adoption of roller milling in the 1880s; in 1904 he made the critical move to the metropolis, from Hull. Thomas Barclay ran the manufacturing chemists, South & Barclay of Birmingham. James Calvert Coats was a London varnish manufacturer. Thomas Robinson Ferens was an MP as well as managing director of Reckitt & Sons Ltd. Sir George Smith headed Bickford, Smith & Co., patent fuse manufacturers of Truro.

The relatively large group from the textile industry included self-made Alfred Brookes, director and secretary of Tootal, Broadhurst & Co. Edward Aston was partner in Marshall & Aston, a major textile merchant house in Manchester. John Robert Barlow BA headed Barlow & Jones Ltd, expanding cotton spinners of Bolton and Manchester. Charles Heap at Rochdale was managing director of Samuel Heap & Sons Ltd, dyers and finishers. He had left the Wesleyan ministry and returned to the family firm on the early death of his father. The other cotton manufacturers were George Crossfield of Prestwich near Manchester and William Horrocks Rawson, of Wigan. John Broxap was a Manchester yarn agent. Norval Watson Helme, MP and prominent Freemason, headed a sizeable oil cloth (linoleum) manufacturing firm at Lancaster.

Thomas Barnsley ran John Barnsley & Son of Birmingham, contractors for the Corporation Buildings, the Council House, and the Union Club in the city. Henry Holloway's firm was another thriving business. Starting in 1882 he and his brother Thomas had expanded their small house-building firm into a leading London contractor. Their first big job, the Chatham Naval Barracks (worth £340,000), was completed in 1903; in 1907 they won the contract for the new General Post Office in St Martin's-le-Grand, the first large reinforced concrete building in London. By 1911 they were employing between 2,000 and 3,000 people.

Three men were shipowners: Williamson Lamplough, with his brother Edmund S. Lamplough, had a lucrative business in London as steamship owners and underwriters. Isaac A. Mack was a Liverpool shipowner. Walter Runciman MP had been in shipping in the North-East. After ten years as managing director of his father's firm, Moor Line (the second largest line in the region with thirty-six steamers in 1911), Runciman had just retired in order to devote himself to politics. Only two of the seventy-six were associated with railways. Charles Sherwood Dennis trained in the office of his father Henry Dennis, goods manager of the North Eastern Railway at Hull; he then joined the Great Western Railway but rejoined the NER in 1894 as district superintendent at Darlington; a year later he was appointed general manager of the Cambrian Railway Co., one of the smaller railway companies, a post he still held in 1907.

Eight of these seventy-six Wesleyan laymen were in distribution, though only four were the proverbial English shopkeepers and none was of the corner shop variety. Thomas Hudson Bainbridge, with his brother, had inherited his father's large department store, and its branches, in Newcastle-upon-Tyne. At his death in 1912 he had 'heavy and responsible interests' in several other undertakings including the Consett ironworks After his death he was hailed as 'a Methodist merchant prince'. John Rayner Batty, with two brothers, expanded his father's Manchester jewellery business (established in the 1840s) to Liverpool. Thomas Cole Jun. was a Sheffield draper. Alfred Jermyn in 1872 had purchased a drapery business in King's Lynn where he had finally settled after training with a Cambridge draper (the Wesleyan Robert Sayle) and a firm in London's West End; he employed 120 people in 1911. Those Wesleyans on the wholesale side of distribution operated in London's commodity markets. Alfred Booth, a son of the manse, was in the South African trade. George Wigram McArthur and his brothers inherited a well-known Australian merchant house from their father Alexander McArthur MP and their uncle William. Norman Thomas Carr Sargant, metal and colonial broker, inherited his father's business in Mincing Lane in the City. Digby Frederick Shillington, who hailed from Northern Ireland, was a tea merchant.

The seventy-six Wesleyan businessmen included four stockbrokers. William Mewburn Jun. and John Lees Barker belonged to the Manchester firm of Mewburn & Barker. John Gibbs and Sir Clarence Smith each had their own London stockbroking businesses. Insurance broker Albert Wellesley Bain had a growing business in Leeds. John Wesley Walker of Maidenhead chaired a building society.

So much for individuals. Second, how significant were these Wesleyan businessmen as businessmen? That is, how big were their businesses and how much political and/or commercial clout did they wield? Alfred Brookes, on the board of Tootal, Broadhurst & Co., and Thomas H. Bainbridge, on the board of Swan, Hunter, & Wigham Richardson, were the only members of this group of leading Wesleyans to sit on the boards of the 100 largest manufacturers (having over 3,000 employees) in the United Kingdom in 1907.

Of the seventy-six, twenty-nine were members of the Institute of Directors and between them held eighty-two directorships, accounting for almost the whole of the key Methodists' presence in British boardrooms (assuming these to be representative samples). Of the eighty-two directorships only twenty-one were associated with manufacturing. Preponderantly Wesleyan businessmen sat on the boards of distribution and financial services companies.

As for political influence, the dominance of Liberal interests in the highest counsels of Wesleyan Methodism is of course well known.[9] Eight of the seventy-six were or had been MPs: John Bamford-Slack (solicitor), William Howell Davies (Bristol leather merchant), Thomas R. Ferens, Norval Helme, Robert Perks, Walter Runciman and Sir Clarence Smith (stockbroker), all Liberals, and Arthur Henderson, Labour. Of the eight MPs, four were knighted by the end of 1907, only one of them (Sir John Bamford-Slack) by the victorious Liberals. (The others were Sir George Hayter Chubb, philanthropic safe and lock manufacturer, knighted 1885; Sir Clarence Smith, former Sheriff of London, knighted 1895; and Sir George Smith, County Council leader in Cornwall, knighted 1897.) Sir George Chubb, manufacturer, whose family safe business pivoted between

Wolverhampton and London, played an important political role. He was one of the few Nonconformist laymen with links to the Court – not with the Queen, who had little to do with Dissenters, but with the Duchess of Albany and later the Duchess's daughter Princess Alexander of Teck. As Perks jocularly remarked in an after-dinner speech, 'his friend, Sir George Hayter Chubb, never seemed happy unless he had titled friends around him'. In marshalling persons of influence, Perks had little to learn from him. As founder in 1898 of the Parliamentary Committee, Perks co-ordinated 200 Free Church MPs returned in the 1906 Liberal 'Landslide'.

WHAT PART DID RELIGION PLAY IN THEIR BUSINESS AND WEALTH CREATION?

As Weber might have asked, did these Wesleyan businessmen start their careers with some church involvement at the outset, religion motivating and paving their rising way as capitalists? Or, as Marx might see it, was church affiliation merely a later adjunct, ornament or tool, to their material success?

A definitive answer to this question is, as ever, hard, perhaps impossible, to give. I have no non-religious control group with which to compare them since this cohort lived in a predominantly religious age. Nor have modern historians yet constructed quantitative profiles of the national business community at specific points in time in the nineteenth and twentieth centuries. However, some pointers may be offered. First, the age structure of the group, ranging between the ages of 34 and 79 and averaging in the mid-fifties, suggests that the take-off of their careers coincided with two upward growth trends. One was that of the Victorian economy which continued to grow in terms of labour and capital productivity (though at a slowed rate) after 1873. The other was that of New Dissent and Methodism which enjoyed a second, if slower, period of nineteenth-century membership growth after 1850 lasting until the turn of the century.[10] In this sense the cohort's careers derived advantage, in part from the economic expansion, in part from religious vigour.

Evidence on social origins is incomplete. For 34 of them their father's occupation is known – 24 being sons of men in business, 3 sons of professionals, and 7 sons of Wesleyan ministers. Two of the seventy-six, Robert Perks and Sir Clarence Smith, were proud to be sons of previous presidents of the Wesleyan Conference. No hard conclusions about material or religious factors readily follow, except that nearly a tenth of the cohort were raised in Wesleyan manses where official church teaching on the creation of wealth was loaded against becoming rich.

Education suggests a stronger role for religion in shaping the cohort, though information on only fifty-three of the seventy-six is available. At least fifteen of the fifty-three went to one or other of four Methodist schools (Kingswood, Bath; Wesley College, Sheffield; Woodhouse Grove, Bradford; The Leys School, Cambridge); six attended Wesleyan elementary schools; the rest attended a mixture of grammar schools, private schools and forms of private education. Hence 40 per cent of the known cases in the cohort received a Wesleyan education.

That was important. Interestingly, it suggests either some relaxation of John Wesley's harsh instructions on child-rearing and education, or that they were not as inhibiting of high achievement in business as McClelland's psychometric techniques implied.[11] Perks left an unflattering recollection of religion at Kingswood: he remembered occasional revivals when classes and games were suspended for the day and boys were kept on their knees until they found 'peace' of soul. But his overall verdict chimes with, though by no means proves, Weber: 'Kingswood certainly turned out a body of hard-working, self-reliant, well-educated lads who knew that they had to face the struggles of life with courage. Most of us have done so.'[12]

Wesleyan networks were of perceptible if unmeasurable significance in promoting the careers of these businessmen. Of the seventy-six, education and kin networks arose from bonds of religion. For example five, William Butterworth (b. 1851), John Bamford-Slack (b. 1857), Charles Heap (b. 1845), Thomas Osborn (b. 1843), and Henry A. Smith (b. 1848), attended Wesley College, Sheffield, and together must have overlapped between the mid-1850s and late 1860s. Three, Alfred Booth (b. 1851), Robert Hartley (b. 1854), Sir Clarence Smith (b. 1849), were contemporaries at Woodhouse Grove School. Smith moved on to Kingswood where he might have met Robert Perks, who was his own age but who left in 1865. Marriage drew others in the cohort together. Both Perks and John Lees Barker married sisters of William Mewburn. Sir George Chubb's wife was the sister of Charles William Early, the Witney blanket maker. The latter's brother, Charles Vanner Early, married a sister of Thomas Cole, the Sheffield draper.

Certainly there were Wesleyan connections in business networks. One or two cases suggest their strength. Four of the twenty-nine sat on the Star Life Assurance Co. board (Chubb, chairman; Ferens, Mewburn and Sir Clarence Smith). Henry Holloway was a director of Albert E. Reed & Co., the paper manufacturers founded by fellow Wesleyan Albert E. Reed. If Perks is to be believed, he was instrumental in the takeover of the West Lancashire and the Liverpool, Southport & Preston Junction Railways (both in 1897) by the Lancashire & Yorkshire Railway. His object, he claimed, was to relieve his valuable business friend, and fellow Wesleyan, Edward Holden of Southport (and son of Sir Isaac Holden, the famous woolcomber) of a £400,000 loss-making investment.[13]

Location facilitated some networks. Where this happened, the bonds of a shared faith, 'the tie that binds our hearts in Christian love',[14] conceivably reinforced the networks. There was a marked concentration of Wesleyan businessmen in the London area. Out of the seventy-six, some twenty gave private addresses in London, ten lived within a 40-mile radius of London, and three more (Ferens, Helme and Howell Davies) would have been brought there regularly by parliamentary duties. Since 16 per cent of the population of England and Wales lived in London and Middlesex in 1911, the presence of 28 per cent of the Wesleyan workhorses there suggests an over-representation of a London mentality, if not London interests, in the counsels of Edwardian Wesleyan Methodism. (One reason for this over-representation was that the London Wesleyans provided most of the denomination's financial resources.) The other areas well represented were the

West Midlands, the North-West and Yorkshire, reflecting the geographical strengths of the denomination. Undoubtedly, at meetings of circuits, District synods and Conference, sacred–secular network links were renewed and modified.

Provincial business communities, a topic needing much more investigation than it has hitherto received, might well reveal church networks to have been important in the upward mobility of individuals like these Wesleyan laymen. Many of the seventy-six were civic and political leaders in their local communities. As noted, several sat in the Commons. At least twenty were JPs. Five were serving or recent mayors (Charles Heap of Rochdale, Isaac Mack of Bootle, William Middlebrook of Morley, William Horrocks Rawson of Accrington and John Wesley Walker of Maidenhead). Four were county councillors (Josiah Gunton, Norval Helme, Sir George Smith and William Henry Smith). Three were aldermen (John Wilcox Edge of Burslem, Sir George Smith of Cornwall and William Henry Smith of Shropshire). As Perks recalled of his election to the Louth seat in 1892, 'It may be said that Methodism has no politics. Theoretically that is true. But when the tug of political war comes, Methodist as a rule stands by Methodist. I trust it will always be so.'[15]

Of course denominational networks were not the only ones which propelled able and aspiring Edwardian businessmen upwards. For example, the high arcing career of Charles Cheers Wakefield, lubricating oil manufacturer, took him from Liverpool to London and thence through the livery companies, Masonic lodges, and a multitude of philanthropies in the City. Eventually he would sit alongside a fellow Methodist, Walter Runciman (President of the Board of Trade in the 1930s), in the ermine and scarlet robes of a viscount of the realm. Alternatively, the trade union movement was an important vehicle of upward social mobility. The solitary trade unionist among these seventy-six Wesleyans would in time become the most eminent layman of them all, with the exception of Runciman. Starting as an ironfounder's apprentice, Arthur Henderson eventually sat in the first two Labour Cabinets and distinguished himself in Labour Party annals for leading the revolt against Ramsay MacDonald in 1931.

One element is impossible to measure: their individual faith. However, of the seventy-six some twenty-five were active local preachers and this may be taken as meaning a stronger and more serious motivation and commitment than would be suggested by simple churchgoing or even church committee membership. Two (Bainbridge and Bamford-Slack) had published small volumes on the leadership of Class Meetings, titles which are listed in the *British Library Catalogue of Printed Books*. Unlisted in the *Catalogue* are Bainbridge's *Counsels to Young Christians* (c. 1875), which sold 250,000 copies, and his *Conscience and System in the Stewardship of Money*, which sold 100,000 copies,

If religion played a part in motivating or facilitating the business success and wealth accumulation of this cohort of Wesleyan lay leaders, it did so in the face of some ambivalence in church teaching. The official doctrines of Wesleyan Methodism were encapsulated in John Wesley's *Sermons*, the full title being *Sermons on Several Occasions, First Series, Consisting of Forty-four Discourses; to which Reference is Made in the Trust Deeds of the Methodist Chapels, as*

Constituting, with Mr Wesley's Notes on the New Testament, the Standard Doctrines of the Methodist Connexion (4th edn, 1787). This source of doctrinal authority was renewed by Conference throughout the nineteenth century, as it was in 1914.[16] What did Wesley teach about wealth? His XXIII Sermon, explicating Matthew 6: 19–23, that part of the Sermon on the Mount in which Christ warned against laying up corruptible treasures on earth, has two messages. To love riches is to gain hell-fire.[17] Most of the sermon dwells on this hazard. On the other hand, riches may be accumulated in order to meet social needs (to 'owe no man anything'); to supply personal physical necessities; to provide for one's children and family; and to create 'what is needful for the carrying on our worldly business, in such a measure and degree as is sufficient to answer the foregoing purposes' (social, personal, family needs).[18] If the obvious message of Wesley restrained the garnering of riches, it might be argued that that message also induced a cautious judgement and frugality which predisposed its adherents to capital accumulation. Certainly the literature commended with nigh- episcopal authority by John Wesley to his fellow Methodists urged a dedication to spiritual attainment and moral purity which would rigorously test the professional motivations and methods of entrepreneurs and managers in Methodist congregations.[19]

A collective profile of the leading Wesleyan Methodist laymen of 1907 therefore reveals a narrowly selected group: generally of mid- or late middle age; ascendant in business and capital; dominated by London perspectives; bonded by a Wesleyan education or, less frequently, marriage; and enjoying solid civic and political (usually Liberal) status. These were men rising within and between classes, despite any social handicap associated with their minority religious faith. How far religion motivated or facilitated their business success is impossible to measure. The inculcation of values appropriate to business, and the opportunity to enter additional networks and markets (church-related), suggest that Methodism could promote rather than hinder business success. However, probing individual careers and episodes with the approach of 'dense description', as pursued by Clifford Geertz[20] and the social anthropologists, may be as far as historians can presently go.

HOW DEPENDENT WAS WESLEYAN METHODISM ON THE BENEFACTIONS OF THEIR BIG BUSINESSMEN?

The short answer is that we do not know, simply because of the confidentiality surrounding most charitable giving. However, there are some clues which may suggest a minimalist picture. There is the evidence of the Twentieth Century Fund. When giving on the principle of 'one person, one guinea' dwindled in summer 1899, it was urged that the time had come for 'the rich men of the Connexion to save the situation'. The press reported various rumours: one, that a single family would subscribe £100,000; another, that three brothers had promised a similar sum.[21] We have seen the response of Wesleyan businessmen at the Conference in summer 1900. Just seven 'big' businessmen provided £65,000 of the £1.073 million that was eventually raised. Presumably other capitalist brethren anonymously donated more. We may safely guess that at least 10 per cent of the million guineas came from a relatively small number of Wesleyan businessmen.

Another indicator of the dependence of the denomination on wealthy laymen was their prominent financial participation in every church scheme that required money. Despite Wesley's strictures against riches, the Methodist clergy and poorer laity were glad that rich men of generous spirit were in their midst. One example from the first decade of the new century must suffice to illustrate the point. When an earthquake struck Jamaica in 1907, Conference made space for an appeal for money to help rebuild destroyed West Indian churches and some £5,000 was raised.

The denomination valued rich men. Sir Henry Lunn critically recalled how the Wesleyan pulpit of the 1870s glorified merchant princes. After such complacencies were disturbed by Hugh Price Hughes and his message of social Christianity, men of talent and wealth were still needed to support the voluntary missions and large mission halls projected by the radicals for the needs of the poor and the inner cities. Perks and Ferens were among the businessmen who donated £1,000 or more each to the building in 1912 of Kingsway Hall for the West London Mission founded by Hugh Price Hughes himself.

The richest Wesleyan layman in the three decades before Methodist Union in 1932 was Joseph Rank, the miller, whose generosity to the Methodist Church was continued by his son J. Arthur Rank, the film magnate.[22] Between 1921 and his death in 1943 Joseph Rank made recorded gifts of £3.5 million. In addition there were unrecorded sums. Since the income of the three main Methodist denominations before union (Wesleyans, Primitives, United Methodists) was £825,000, Rank's gifts were equivalent to four years of denominational income. The bulk of his known giving, £2.4 million, went to the Methodist Missionary Society.

HOW WAS BENEFICENCE MOBILISED FOR CHURCH CAUSES?

As Jane Garnett has shown[23] pious mid-Victorians adopted systematic alms-giving in proportion to their means and income. Giving was to be careful, regular, calculated, treated with the same prudent respect as commercial accounts. Indeed, the Charity Organisation Society warned against indiscriminate and impetuous beneficence. Among the Wesleyans spontaneous giving and the publicising of donations were familiar before the 1890s. The Vanners spontaneously gave over £2,000 to help launch the Wesleyan Thanksgiving Fund of 1878 and they and other large benefactors, like Sir Francis Lycett, John Beauchamp, T. Morgan Harvey, and Mr J. S. Budgett (who each gave £1,000 or more), were listed in a 507-page volume showing exactly who had given what (though some gifts were anonymous).[24] However, only since the Conference of 1878 were laymen allowed to join ministers in the management of church affairs in the Wesleyan denomination. Joseph Rank seized that chance to import a much more flamboyant approach to fund-raising in the denomination. When unexpected crises demanded an *ad hoc* donation, like the flagging Twentieth Century Fund, rich men had to be persuaded to give more than systematic methods allowed. Rank made charitable giving instantly public, dramatic and provocative. He realised he was contravening Christ's teaching, not to let the left hand know what the right was doing (Matthew 6: 3). He was stirred by the text about 'provoking one another to love and good works' (Hebrews 10: 24). Expressing these thoughts, he stood up in the annual Wesleyan Methodist Conference at Burslem in 1900 and challenged the rich men of Methodism. If fourteen of them would give 90,000 guineas to the Twentieth Century Fund he would add 10,000 guineas to the 7,000 he had already promised and would also give the last 10,000 guineas that were needed for the million mark. He disclaimed a spirit of pride but declared it would be a great joy to give his thousands of guineas and (by implication) see other rich men open their purses as well. Seven did so, giving over £65,000 between them.

A similar technique was again incited by Rank in 1907, to raise £5,000 for Methodist churches in Jamaica recently destroyed by an earthquake. Sir William Stephenson,[25] the Newcastle-upon-Tyne industrialist, former Vice-President of the Wesleyan Methodist Conference, and Newcastle District Treasurer for Foreign Missions, proposed a 'financial lovefeast'. The very use of the term lovefeast incited passionate generosity. It recalled not only Methodist revivalism but also the spontaneous, sharing *agape* spirit of the New Testament church.[26] Declaring that he had an unwritten power of attorney from Joseph Rank to pledge anything on his behalf for the Jamaica Fund, Stephenson announced that he and Rank would each give £500. In an atmosphere charged with emotion, one after another stood up to promise sums ranging from three guineas to £200. Now and again one donor would increase his gift to match another donor. Over 100 names and the size of their gifts were reported by the *Methodist Recorder*. Nearly thirty of them were ministers but many more were businessmen and it was the latter who subscribed the bulk of the £5,000 raised.[27]

Between the 1890s and the early 1930s Joseph Rank was happy to hand over large sums to the various church agencies appealing for help. However, in the 1930s he set up a Benevolent Fund in which he and his son, J. Arthur Rank, the film magnate, had a controlling interest. Why the change? His age (born in 1854, he was then an octogenarian) would have been a factor. There may have been some tax reason. However, a snippet of evidence suggests he had become disillusioned with the clerical stewardship of his money. On one application for the assistance of his Fund in 1939 he commented, 'Now I do not know why they should want Vestries for the Minister and an Office. I consider that one Vestry is quite sufficient.' On another application he observed,

> I am sorry to differ with some people, but I have seen too much money wasted in Methodism. I have had to work hard all my life and to deny myself of many things so that I might be in a position to do good, and I do not agree with wasting money to carry out the views of some people who do not mind how much they spend so long as they do not have to provide the money.

A largely-self-made man like Joseph Rank could not see why the standards of personal and business frugality which underlay his own business success should not be followed by the church which taught them.

COMPARISONS WITH OTHER DENOMINATIONS

Dependence on the laity and men in business in particular was not confined to the Wesleyans. In this section some comparisons are briefly drawn with other church groupings, first among other Nonconformists, and then with the Church of England.

Without the tithes and centuries-accumulated legacies of the Church of England, the Protestant Nonconformist sects heavily relied upon the resources of their laity, newer Dissenting sects more than older ones presumably. Methodist denominations other than Wesleyans also included high proportions of business-men in their national leaderships. Among thirty-three multiple national office-holders in the four other Methodist sects, twenty-six were in business in 1907.[28] Among other Nonconformists the proportion was lower if businessmen are defined as members of the Institute of Directors in 1907.[29] Such a narrow identifier understates the provincial if not the national significance of the Nonconformist businessman at the turn of the century. Congregationalists, in their provincial centres in the North West, Yorkshire, as well as London, produced imposing crops of business leaders among their national lay activists – Pilkington, Crosfield, Oldroyd, Spicer, names that conjured up dynasties among captains of industry.

However, Wesleyans were exceptional among the Nonconformist denomina-tions because they were strong across several 'power dimensions'. Outside Scotland they were the largest Nonconformist denomination, having 446,368 members and 2,445 ministers in 1907.[30] To size they added political weight. Among the Methodist sects they secured the largest number of MPs in the 1906 and 1910 elections. The Congregationalists had twice their number of Commons seats (73 compared to 35 Wesleyan ones) in 1906.[31] Wesleyans were prominent in the 1906 bloc of 191 Nonconformist MPs, of whom three-quarters were Liberal. Admittedly, the size and solidarity of this bloc, organised in 1898 as the Nonconformist Parliamentary Committee, were not as considerable as Robert Perks, its Wesleyan founder, pretended.[32] Yet to political power, if not as great as sometimes projected, the Wesleyans via Chubb could add a measure of standing at Court. This gave them a social status advantage ahead of most, perhaps all, other Nonconformist denominations. In society generally Wesleyan membership depended on middle-class support. So did that of the Congregationalists. Where Wesleyans had their greater advantage was in the absolute numbers of men who were both active in the service of their denomination and experienced in the ways of the world of business, as proprietors, directors, or managers. Of seventy-six laymen who in 1907 each held five or more national-level posts, twenty-nine were members of the Institute of Directors. Among the Congregationalists (whose church organisation was locally, rather than nationally, based) of 171 laymen holding 178 national denominational posts between them only 27 were in the Institute of Directors.[33] In other words, the structure and dynamic of lay leadership among the Wesleyans captured energetic businessmen for national roles far more effectively than any of the other Nonconformist denominations, in this period. Another study is needed to see whether lay leaders in other denominations matched the Wesleyans in charitable giving, especially in their quest for innovatory techniques and purgative generosity practised collectively and publicly. The impression is that individuals here and there (e.g., Sir William Hartley among the Primitive Methodists or Sir Albert Spicer among the Congregationalists) gave to their churches, both local and national, on a scale exceedingly generous in terms of time and money.[34]

How dependent was the Church of England on businessmen in comparison? Scope for the laity in the Church was relatively limited. The twelve 'eminent laymen' who sat on the Ecclesiastical Commission at the beginning of the century were mostly peers, national politicians, and landowners, not provincial industrialists.[35] The annual Church Congress did see an occasional industrialist make a speech but their thin attendance evoked rebuke from the Archbishop of York in 1912.[36] A survey of the 381 laymen who sat in the two Houses of Laymen (for the two dioceses of Canterbury and York) in 1907 showed that 107 of them held 246 directorships between them.[37] However, they had little influence inside their church before the First World War. In 1911 the obituary of one of them, Sir Henry Bemrose, Tory MP for Derby, head of the family printing business, Evangelical churchman, and freemason, recorded a situation that was probably true of others:

> Had the accidents of birth placed Sir Henry within the Presbyterian, or Congregational, or Wesleyan Churches it is certain he would have exercised a commanding influence in any one of these respective communions, where laymen are accorded their rightful position in the management of affairs. But in the Established Church, as at present constituted, the layman, however talented and devoted, is practically powerless.[38]

CONCLUSION

Rich men, mostly in business and taking their duties of Christian stewardship seriously, have invariably been patrons of emergent revitalising movements in the history of the church[39] and the Wesleyan Methodists were no different. Close inspection of their case as they came to denominational maturity shows that it is easier to identify the laymen involved than to unravel motivations and mechanisms behind either the accumulation of wealth or its distribution in the church. Five features stand out in the behaviour of late Victorian–Edwardian Wesleyan businessmen and their wealth. First, as a group these men were mostly self-made and still moving upward in their careers. None was super-wealthy, like the merchant bankers of their day, though one or two like the Ranks would become super-rich. Second, some of their largest gifts to the church were made in a highly emotional atmosphere at the annual Conference of the Connexion. In this setting there was an element of cheerful competition in publicly pledging very considerable sums, on top of whatever they gave to the church week by week. Third, a tiny number of individuals, like Robert Perks and Joseph Rank, played a key role as mobilisers and exemplars in surrendering gold for the purposes of the gospel. Fourth, over time the values of the business boardroom, which rich businessmen inevitably introduced to the church, proved uncomfortable in the more idealist realm of denominational headquarters or the local church vestry. Last, compared to all other denominations before the First World War, the Wesleyans were the most successful in harnessing the talents, time and wealth of their dedicated lay people in business to the work and good works of the denomination.

ACKNOWLEDGEMENT

I am grateful to Professor Patrick O'Brien for commenting on this chapter prior to publication. I am glad also to acknowledge the continued research support given to me by my university, The Manchester Metropolitan University.

NOTES

1   *Methodist Recorder*, 2 August 1900.
2   *Minutes of Conference*, 1899, 1900; Robert Currie *et al.*, *Churches and Churchgoers* (Oxford, 1977).
3   The Centenary Fund of 1839 raised £250,000; the Jubilee Fund of 1863, £200,000; and the Thanksgiving Fund of 1878, £300,000. These figures can be multiplied by at least 40 to translate into 1997 values.
4   John Burnett, *A History of the Cost of Living* (Harmondsworth, 1969), pp. 248–52.
5   *Methodist Recorder*, 2 August 1900.
6   For the Vanners, see S. D. Chapman, 'Vanners in the English Silk Industry', *Textile History* 23, no 1 (1992). In memory of John Vanner (1800–1866) three of his sons, all members of the City Road Chapel (John Wesley's pulpit), gave £2,100 to the Wesleyan Thanksgiving Fund of 1878. This and John Beauchamp's £2,000, the largest single donations among a multitude recorded and later published in book form, helped to launch the Fund at a special meeting of Wesleyan ministers and laymen on 29 October 1878: *Report of the Wesleyan Methodist Thanksgiving Fund 1878–1883* (London, 1883) pp. xi, xvii, 3. Three of the six sons of John Vanner married three daughters of the Early family, blanket makers of Witney, Oxfordshire. They included James Engelbert Vanner (1834–1906), silk manufacturer, insurance underwriter, and director of the City Bank which merged with the Midland Bank in 1898. The merger took Vanner (a leading City Bank director) onto the board of the Midland Bank (then named the London, City & Midland Bank) under the leadership of Edward (later Sir Edward) Holden, its managing director and the most dynamic clearing banker of his day. Holden was also a Wesleyan Methodist. See Alfred Plummer and Richard E. Early, *The Blanket Makers, 1669–1969: A History of Charles Early & Marriott (Witney) Ltd* (New York, 1969) and A. R. Holmes and Edwin Green, *Midland: 150 Years of Banking Business* (London, 1986). Information from Edwin Green.
7   Denis Crane, *The Life and Story of Sir Robert W. Perks* (London, 1909) p. 152.
8   See David J. Jeremy, *Capitalists and Christians: Business Leaders and the Churches in Britain, 1900–1960* (Oxford, 1990) Chapter 8, from which most of this chapter is derived.
9   See Stephen Koss, *Nonconformity in Modern British Politics* (London, 1975); David W. Bebbington, *The Nonconformist Conscience: Chapel and Politics, 1870–1914* (London, 1982).
10   R. C. O. Matthews *et al.*, *British Economic Growth, 1856–1973* (Oxford, 1982), pp. 541–3; Alan D. Gilbert, *Religion and Society in Industrial England: Church, Chapel and Social Change, 1740–1914* (London, 1976).

11 Michael W. Flinn, 'Social Theory and the Industrial Revolution', in Tom Burns and S. B. Saul (eds), *Social Theory and Economic Change* (London, 1967, repr. 1972).

12 Sir Robert Perks, *Sir Robert William Perks, Baronet* (London, 1936), pp. 16, 20.

13 Ibid., pp. 93, 115.

14 Quote from the much-sung hymn 'Blest be the tie that binds' by John Fawcett (1740–1817) composed c. 1772 when he was Baptist minister at Bradford, Yorkshire.

15 Perks, *Sir Robert William Perks*, p. 115.

16 *Minutes of Conference* 1914, p. 373.

17 Wesley, *Forty-four Sermons*, Sermon xxiii, para 13.

18 *Ibid.*, para 11.

19 Isabel Rivers, 'Dissenting and Methodist Books of Practical Divinity', in Isabel Rivers (ed.) *Books and Their Readers in Eighteenth-Century England* (Leicester, 1982).

20 Clifford Geertz, *The Interpretation of Cultures* (London, 1973).

21 Crane, *Perks*, p. 150.

22 Jonathan Brown, 'Joseph Rank', in David J. Jeremy and Christine Shaw (eds) *Dictionary of Business Biography* (6 vols, London, 1984–86) (*DBB*); Roger Manville and Joseph Rank, 'Joseph Arthur Rank', in *DBB*.

23 Jane Garnett, '"Gold and the Gospel": Systematic Beneficence in Mid-Nineteenth-Century England', in W. J. Shiels and Diana Wood (eds), *The Church and Wealth* (Oxford, 1987).

24 See note 6.

25 R. W. Rennison, 'Sir William Haswell Stephenson', *DBB*.

26 Frank Baker, *Methodism and the Love-Feast* (London, 1957); Acts 2: 43–7.

27 *Methodist Recorder*, 25 July 1907.

28 Jeremy, *Capitalists and Christians*, p. 324.

29 Ibid., p. 360.

30 Currie *et al.*, *Churches*, pp. 143, 205.

31 Koss, *Nonconformity*, p. 228.

32 Ibid., 77–8.

33 Jeremy, *Capitalists and Christians*, pp. 303, 360.

34 Ibid., pp. 324–35, 355–93.

35 Information in letter from Mr D. A. Armstrong, Records Officer at the Church Commissioners, to author, 28 February 1989.

36 Jeremy, *Capitalists and Christians*, p. 141.

37 Ibid., p. 249.

38 *Derby Daily Telegraph*, 5 May 1911, quoted in Jeremy, *Capitalists and Christians*, p. 259.

39 See numerous essays in Shiels and Wood (eds), *The Church and Wealth*.

5   The Wiener thesis vindicated

The onslaught of 1994 upon the reputation of John Rylands of Manchester

Douglas A. Farnie

> False facts are highly injurious to the progress of science, for they often endure long; but false views, if supported by some evidence, do little harm, for everyone takes a salutary pleasure in proving their falseness.
>
> Darwin, *The Descent of Man*[1]

In 1981 Martin J. Wiener identified an entrenched sentiment of hostility to business in British culture as one cause of the economic decline of the United Kingdom. His prize-winning book was very extensively reviewed and attracted the attention of scholars well beyond the ranks of economic historians.[2] In that respect it may be compared with two other works, also distinguished for their provocative and revisionist interpretation of history, R. W. Fogel and S. L. Engerman, *Time on the Cross: The Economics of American Negro Slavery* (1974) and Alan McFarlane, *The Origins of English Individualism* (1978).[3] It is important to emphasise the crux of Wiener's argument. That thesis focused upon the low status ascribed to businessmen in British society. Such status became apparent in an attitude of, at best, ambiguity towards modern industrial society and, at worst, downright hostility towards business activity. This chapter examines this central ethos rather than its peripheral manifestation in any tendency towards the 'gentrification' of the industrialist. In 1994 a bitter dispute about the reputation of a leading merchant of Victorian Manchester flared up and served to reveal the vitality of the anti-business ethos in contemporary Britain. The name of that businessman first became famous as that of the defendant in *Rylands* v. *Fletcher* (1868), a leading case in the law of tort,[4] and then as that bestowed upon a memorial library. The name still remains more familiar than those details of his life which were to give rise to controversy a century after his death. His widow's purchase of the Spencer Library in 1892 and her inauguration in 1899 of the John Rylands Library first imprinted the name upon the national consciousness. It was, however, only in the 1980s that his name achieved mention in histories of the cotton industry.[5] The reasons for such a low posthumous profile must remain a matter for speculation. One reason may be that John Rylands was a latecomer, maturing in business after the close of the classic period of the Industrial Revolution. Another may lie in the bias of historiography towards spinning firms, whereas John Rylands concentrated upon manufacture and marketing. A third reason may be that his greatest achievements were made within the humdrum sphere of the domestic market rather than in that of the exotic export trade. A fourth reason must lie in the simple absence of source material. Only in 1984 were the archives of the firm placed upon deposit in Manchester.[6]

THE CHARACTER AND FAITH OF JOHN RYLANDS

John Rylands was born in 1801, the youngest child of Joseph Rylands (1767–1847) and Elizabeth Pilkington (1761–1829). His father and grandfather were both handloom manufacturers in the village of Parr, near St Helens. He himself became a merchant–manufacturer and excelled all other Manchester merchants in the magnitude of his achievements. In 1888 he died at Longford Hall in Stretford to the west of Manchester, leaving an estate of £2.6 million. Those qualities which virtually guaranteed his success comprised good health, innate ability, a code of values and self-confidence. His good health remained a tribute to an excellent

Plate 5.1 John Rylands (1801–88) in 1869

Source: John Rylands University Library of Manchester

upbringing since at birth he had been the most delicate of infants, having been born when his mother was aged 40. In maturity his remarkable stamina enabled him to work sixteen hours a day for seventy years. His untiring diligence was best epitomised in the title of the biography of a Congregational minister of Salford, *Ever Working, Never Resting: A Memoir of the Revd. John Legge Poore* (1874) by John Corbin. His mental and physical powers verged upon the superhuman and were inherited through his mother from the Pilkingtons. His mother's nephew, Richard Pilkington (1795–1869) became a glass manufacturer in St Helens in 1826. A true mastermind, John Rylands developed a pronounced ability to read character, a superb capacity for organisation and a conspicuous mathematical faculty. His values derived from his education and his religious convictions. They centred on absolute integrity of conduct and were reflected in a profound belief in truth, justice, honesty, purity and 'whatsoever things are of good report'. His way of life, moulded by such a creed and suffused by a deep humility, imbued him with immense moral authority, inspiring his associates with a profound and abiding loyalty. 'You are respected most by those who know you best.'[7]

His self-confidence stemmed from his mother's inculcation of the sublime principles of 'pure and undefiled religion'. In this respect John Rylands may well appear as the ideal type of entrepreneur inspired by other-worldly ideals, such as Max Weber, the atheist son of Lutheran parents, first discussed in 1904. Here it may be necessary to plead for the reading and even more for the understanding of Max Weber. In England his work has for far too long been misunderstood and misrepresented, especially by the Anglican Socialist Tawney in his lectures in 1922. This misunderstanding survived the translation into English in 1930 of *The Protestant Ethic and the Spirit of Capitalism* and even the efforts at intellectual rehabilitation made by Gordon Marshall in his pioneering works of 1980–82.[8] What fascinated Weber was 'the tremendous cosmos of the modern economic order'. He assumed that such a cosmos could best be interpreted in terms of the creative power of the economic ethic of a world religion. The core of his thesis seems to lie in two separate concepts. First, he distinguished between the ideal aspired to by a religion and the actual results of its influence upon the lives of its adherents. Second, he distinguished between church and sect and emphasised the capacity of a sect, as a voluntary association of believers, to maintain high moral standards amongst its members, a capacity forever denied to the church, as a compulsory and comprehensive association. Such methodical and moral behaviour might prove so conducive to success in business that Protestant sects found an inevitable 'elective affinity' with the all-transforming spirit of capitalism. The relevance of this thesis to the career of John Rylands was examined in 1984 by Kazuhiko Kondo.[9] That particular theme may well evoke further study in the future. Here it may suffice simply to make three suggestions. First, denominational history offers a veritable minefield to the unwary intruder, dominated as it seems to be by a profound teleological bias as well as the inevitable 'theological hatred'. Second, the Lancashire cotton industry seems to have differed from the rest of the business world in Britain in so far as more than half of the leading twenty firms in 1888 were controlled by partners bred in the Nonconformist tradition. Third, it seems impossible to establish clear links between the successive denominational affiliations of John Rylands and the different phases of his business career. What seems undeniable is the fact that from 1830 his firm prospered as never before. He 'accepted his work and calling as divine'[10], made religion and commerce his dominant interests and held fast to the belief that 'all things work together for good'. His religious history partook of the nature of a pilgrimage, during which his faith became ever deeper and wider. For the first forty years of life he remained loyal to the Nonconformist tradition, defined in 1775 by Burke in reference to the creed of the descendants of the Pilgrim Fathers as 'the dissidence of dissent, and the protestantism of the Protestant religion'. Such a creed entailed separation from the body of the nation and from the national church. It nevertheless imbued Dissenters with immense confidence since they could draw for support upon the highest authority. 'Where two or three are gathered together in my name, there am I in the midst of them.'

Reared in the Congregational tradition of the Pilkingtons and the Rylandses, John Rylands remained largely conventional in his faith until 1829. The death of his revered mother then compelled him to review his life in the light of eternity and forced him to change his ways. He clearly recognised that for the first twelve years of his business career he had attached too much importance to the acquisition of wealth. In 1829 he realised that he would pass through the world but once and determined to act upon that perception. He resolved thenceforth to live for the good of others as well as his own. The outward sign of his conversion lay in his adoption of the views of the Baptists. In 1830 at the age of 29 he first made a public profession of his faith in Christ and was baptised at the York Street Chapel in Manchester of John Birt (1787–1862). He remained a member of that chapel, serving from 1834 as a deacon, until 1842 when Birt ceased to be pastor there. Thereafter he returned to the Congregational fold. He remained, however, a Congregationalist with a difference, retaining a strong affinity for the Baptist faith as the most dynamic 'cause' in all Christendom. Increasingly from the 1850s onwards he was drawn towards a non-sectarian form of Christian belief. Such a form was embodied in the Union Chapel, established under his patronage in Stretford in 1865.

All of his efforts to lead a truly Christian life never afflicted him with doubt or despair but always reinforced an abiding self-confidence. Even during his schooldays he had been sure enough of his own capacity to engage in profitable barter transactions. At the very outset of his career he declined to join his fellow commercial travellers in an evening of carousing. He required all his confidence in order to survive the first week of business in Manchester in 1822, a week which passed by without him receiving a single order. On the eighth day he received his first order and thereafter never looked back. Successive crises in his domestic life served only 'to stir up the very depths of his soul'[11] inspiring him to meet each new challenge 'with unappalled and unblenched eye' and enabling him to turn every difficulty to ultimate advantage. From Bunyan's Mr Greatheart he adopted the maxim 'Watch and Strive'. From William Carey, the Baptist missionary of Serampore, Calcutta, he borrowed the motto 'Attempt great things and expect great things.'

JOHN RYLANDS AS A MANCHESTER MERCHANT

No other businessman approaches so closely to the ideal type of self-made man nurtured by 'Cottonopolis' during its golden age as John Rylands. No other firm became so much the lengthened shadow of one man as did that of Rylands & Sons. John Rylands preferred to regard himself as a manufacturer and professed scorn for the pure merchant. On his wife's death certificate of 1843 he was described as 'millowner' and on his own death certificate in 1888 as 'cotton manufacturer and general merchant'. He was, however, simply styled 'merchant' on three certificates issued in 1848 and 1875. In fact he proved to be a born merchant who delighted in buying and selling well. In his marketing skills he came to excel all of his local contemporaries. He did so by responding swiftly to emerging opportunities and by maintaining total secrecy about his operations, especially in relation to prices. His quickness of perception and immense fertility of resource enabled him to adapt rapidly to changing conditions of trade. He remained ever ready to make innovations, abandoning traditional practices with zest whilst always providing for the unknown and the uncertain. Freedom from dependence upon the constraining opinion of any secular peer-group enabled him to accomplish a notable task of 'creative destruction' within the Manchester trade. He concentrated his innovations largely within the sphere of marketing. Thus in 1822 he transferred the main market of the firm from the Chester Fair to Manchester where, as a country manufacturer, he entered into competition with the established wholesalers. During the midday 'dinner hour' he kept the doors of his warehouse open, in defiance of existing custom. From 1829 he shattered the monopoly maintained by the four or five linen houses of the city by undertaking the sale of Scotch and Irish linen. In a most unusual step for a Manchester merchant he opened a warehouse in London in 1849. In 1864 he pioneered the local development of the ready-made clothing trade and extended that branch of the firm's operations to Crewe from 1872 and to London from 1874. From 1870 onwards he extended his interests more fully into the finishing trades, especially into bleaching, in order to overcome a boycott imposed by the trade, and built up the largest bleach works in Europe. From 1874 onwards he extended operations abroad in a most unusual venture for an established home-trade house but in a most determined manner, using 'the sword of cheapness' as an offensive weapon. He despatched travellers to overseas colonies when the wholesale colonial houses of London imposed a boycott of all English manufacturers and merchants who had presumed to serve colonial drapers directly. In 1877 the firm began to win awards at colonial and foreign exhibitions. No other Manchester firm undertook such an expansion of overseas operations. When his own mills could not supply the goods the warehouses sold, John Rylands resorted without hesitation to out-sourcing on a large scale. He seemed to thrive upon competition, cared naught for the offence given to established interests and preferred to share the benefits of his initiative with the consuming public. He may well have made, as he himself professed, more mistakes than any man in Manchester but he consistently profited from his own errors of judgement, finding experience to be cheap at any price.

Since 1843 John Rylands had been the supreme governor of the firm of Rylands & Sons after his father agreed to dissolve the family partnership formed in 1819 and, thereafter, he remained the firm's mainspring and prime mover. He retained absolute power as Governor when the firm became a limited company in 1873. With such authority he proved able to realise his abiding vision, the creation of a great and viable firm which would excel all others in capacity and standing. By 1850 he had indeed become the largest wholesaler of textiles in Manchester. Business became for him an all-consuming passion. His imagination remained large and vital, combining a comprehensive view of an expanding field of operations with a minute care for detail. In administration he insisted upon the paramount necessity for the rigorous control of costs and for constant economy in the use of capital. Each department of the firm was compelled to stand upon its own feet and was denied any expectation of subsidy from another. John Rylands loved arithmetic, the compilation of statistical tables of discount, interest, production and cloth-prices, and the costing of labour-saving appliances. Such an armoury of information served him well in the daily campaign for orders. As a keen observer of men and a dedicated listener, he revealed exceptional judgement in his selection of managers, who proved efficient and loyal in the highest degree.

The great expansion of his mercantile operations seems to have taken place during the 1840s and 1850s, increasing the number of departments eightfold from 4 in 1840 to 33 in 1865. During the 1870s another wave of expansion, especially in London, raised the number of departments from 39 in 1875 to 42 in 1880. The firm developed certain branches of trade hitherto neglected in Manchester and extended its stocks over the whole range of dry goods, including smallwares, haberdashery, millinery, furs, mantles, boots and shoes, umbrellas, oilcloth and carpets as well as all types of textiles. Thus it spread its overhead costs by increasing the range of articles wherein it dealt. It also enabled its principal customers in the drapers of the United Kingdom to secure all of their needs through a single account. The essential link with those drapers was provided by the firm's travellers, who increased in number from 4 in 1840 to 19 in 1865 and to 70 in 1889.

From 1865 the firm also became the leading manufacturing firm in the cotton industry when it first surpassed Horrockses of Preston in capacity. The number of its factories had increased slowly from 1 in 1825 to 3 in 1854 but then rose sharply to 6 in 1864, to 12 in 1872 and to 16 in 1874. Usually it acquired existing mills cheaply and often persuaded vendors to lend the purchase price back, against the security of a mortgage upon the property concerned. In productive capacity the firm remained primarily a manufacturer. The 200,000 spindles it operated in four mills were exceeded in number by eight other firms. Its massed 5,000 power looms nevertheless surpassed those of its nearest rivals, such as Joshua Hoyle of Bacup with 4,831, T. & W. Sidebottom of Glossop with 4,700 and Horrockses with 4,405.

The achievements of John Rylands in business remained most unusual in so far as the original staple product of the firm was linen, it lacked connections in either Manchester or London, its operations were concentrated within the home trade rather than in export markets and it had no patent monopoly or any other basis for the control of a niche market. Making a fortune in the cotton industry was never easy because the trade remained forever free from any barriers to entry. The Manchester market became in its operation a model of perfect competition and a positive slaughter-house where the turnover of firms remained very high. Indeed, competition became more intense than ever during the period when John Rylands flourished. It was nevertheless to his warehouse that the representatives of the economic world increasingly beat a path and thrust money into his hands in exchange for his wares. Thus he made his money in free, fair and open competition with other merchants. He became rich simply by producing goods of high quality and by selling them cheaply, always giving full value for money. Absolute probity remained the central value of his business strategy. He never indulged in conspicuous corporate consumption and never resorted to advertising, professing only contempt for mere publicity. In the absence of such methods the firm won a special reputation for the high quality of its Dacca calicoes so that its trademarks became assets of steadily increasing value. John Rylands earned recognition as 'the leading merchant of a city famed for its merchant princes'.[12] Rylands & Sons was singled out as 'the recognized and undisputed head and leader of the cotton trade', as 'the monarchs of the cotton industry of England'[13] and as 'perhaps the largest and most important manufacturing and mercantile undertaking in the whole world'[14]. The global interests developed during the 1870s confirmed its status as 'the greatest commercial house of any generation'[15] and as an enterprise without equal in either the Old World or the New. It may not be regarded in any respect as a representative cotton manufacturing firm. It was set apart from all others by its immense size and by its high degree of vertical integration, especially through the combination of spinning with weaving, finishing and marketing. Its range of ancillary activities extended to coal mining and farming from 1839, the manufacture of clothing and sewing thread from 1864, the production of oil cloth from 1874 and the leasing of warehouse space to other merchants from 1870. In the extent of its operations the nearest parallel seemed to lie only in the most flourishing days of the East India Company.[16]

So extensive had the cotton industry become that Rylands & Sons controlled only 0.5 per cent of the industry's spindles and only 0.8 per cent of its looms. Enlightening comparisons with the other home trade houses of Manchester may be made in respect of its mercantile operations, the number of its departments and employees and the extent of total turnover. In 1865 the 33 departments of the firm outnumbered the 21 departments of Henry Bannerman & Sons and the 15 departments of J. P. & E. Westhead. The 600 hands employed in the Manchester warehouse were three times the 200 employed by S. & J. Watts, who had opened their palatial warehouse in 1856, and were four times the 150 employed by Westhead's. The annual turnover of £1.5 million was half as much again as that of Westhead's. All told, its employees numbered 4,500 in 1865 whilst another

Plate 5.2 The Manchester warehouse of Rylands & Son built between 1928 and 1932 (1944)

Source: The City Engineer's Department of the Corporation of Manchester

6,500 were employed indirectly through outsourcing upon its orders. By 1875 the number of its employees had more than doubled to 12,000. Between 1865 and 1885 its customers doubled in number to 20,000, as did total turnover, to £3 million. The vast bulk of its capital of £2 million on incorporation in 1873 represented commercial rather than industrial assets. That capital was twice that of its nearest rival, Tootal's, which was incorporated in 1888, and equalled that of the London warehousemen, Cooke, Son & Co.[17]

The interests of John Rylands were not restricted to his own firm. When confidential information reached the City of London that he was worth between £2 and 3 million he was invited in 1878 to accept office as Sheriff of London. That position would have made him eligible, had he accepted, to become Lord Mayor of London. He was almost certainly the first provincial merchant to be so honoured. In 1882 he attended the initial meeting of Lancashire notables which launched the scheme for the Manchester Ship Canal. At first he was sceptical but he reconsidered and became the largest shareholder in the Ship Canal Company in 1885. His support was greatly valued by his fellow directors because it proved vital to the project at the most critical period in its history and so rescued it from financial disaster. This was inspired more by a sense of the public interest than by any desire for private profit. The company paid no dividend to its ordinary shareholders until 1915, some twenty years after the new waterway had been opened.

No criticism of John Rylands was ever voiced, despite the repeated eruption between 1841 and 1883 of metropolitan hostility to Manchester and to its new school of political economy. On his death he was crowned with new laurels, as 'The Cotton King' and 'the greatest merchant prince the world has ever seen'.[18]

Between 1830 and 1895 ten millionaires died, having made their fortunes in the cotton industry. The first of the deceased millionaires from Lancashire were Thomas Fielden (1791–1869) of Todmorden and Edward R. Langworthy (1796–1874) of Salford.[19] John Rylands himself had become a millionaire in the 1850s and a multi-millionaire in the 1870s, from the profits of commerce rather than of manufacture. The size of his final estate may usefully by measured against earlier fortunes and in terms of their proportion to GNP. The fortune of £1.5 million of Sir Robert Peel (1750–1830) was the equivalent of 0.44 per cent of GNP. The £3.25 million left by Richard Arkwright (1755–1843) equalled 0.7 per cent of GNP while the £4–6 million left by the London warehouseman, James Morrison (1789–1857) equalled 0.8 per cent of GNP. The estate of John Rylands was five times the fortune left in 1792 by Richard Arkwright and the largest left by any Lancashire manufacturer till then. It represented 0.19 per cent of GNP in 1888, the same proportion as the larger estate left by his widow in 1908, by which date GNP had quadrupled since 1831. The most effective comparison remains that with the estate of £26,829 bequeathed by his own father in 1847, an estate which formed a mere one-hundredth of that left forty years later by his youngest son.

The relative success of John Rylands may be estimated by the expansion of his firm and by its financial performance, measured in both returns on capital and in dividends. Rylands & Sons never passed a year without making a profit in a trade noted for the regularity and amplitude of its fluctuations. Its continuing success during the 1880s contrasted sharply with the declining fortunes of other home-trade houses.[20] Another measure of the proprietor's calibre may be found in the absence of any comparable successor and in the decision by the directors to place the chairmanship in commission, so that three directors served as chairman in annual rotation during the years 1889–99. The changing fortunes of the firm also testified to the immense loss suffered with the demise of an incomparable Governor. Competition increased sharply from Horrockses from 1887 and during the 1890s from J. & P. Coats of Paisley as well as from I. & R. Morley of London, which first surpassed Rylands & Sons in annual sales-volume.[21] From 1896 J. & P. Coats surpassed it in total capital, establishing primacy amongst the textile firms in the United Kingdom. During 1897–1900 seven large-scale amalgamations were established, in order to curb the influence of competition, especially in the finishing trades. In 1905 Rylands & Sons, with a capital of £4.16 million ranked as the twenty-first amongst the industrial companies of the United Kingdom and as the fifth largest textile firm, after J. & P. Coats, the Calico Printers' Association, the Fine Cotton Spinners' Association and the Bleachers' Association.[22] The foundations of the enterprise had been laid so securely that for a business firm it enjoyed an unusually long life span, preserving its independence until 1953 and remaining on the Registry of Companies until 1989. 'The authoritative history of the Manchester merchant has yet to be compiled. When it is, the name of Rylands will appear large on its pages.'[23]

JOHN RYLANDS AS AN EMPLOYER OF LABOUR

In the twentieth century interested observers invariably ask how John Rylands treated his workers. In the first place it must be conceded that the firm did not pay high wages to its mill-hands and that its wages policy precipitated strikes on four occasions, in 1849, 1869, 1870 and 1882. It is also true that the proprietor's elder brother, Joseph Rylands (1796–1853), as manager of the Hull Flax and Cotton Mill Company, was denounced in 1853 by his own workfolk during a strike as a 'tyrant'. It should, however, be borne in mind that other millowners paid low wages but none accumulated a fortune comparable to that of John Rylands. Moreover, mill-hands were in general unskilled machine-minders and had been liberated from the burden of manual labour. Their contribution remained of ancillary significance and did not create the wealth of their employer. Value was added to the product by a succession of mechanical processes, culminating in finishing. The marketing of the finished product always remained the firm's most important function. Warehousemen earned more than mill-hands because they served the firm's customers directly and contributed more to its prosperity through the quality of their service. It is therefore misleading to describe John Rylands as a tight-fisted millowner who made a fortune by exploiting his employees. Such an interpretation might well be in fact the very reverse of the truth.

In creating a vast industrial empire John Rylands performed a considerable social service by giving secure employment for so long to so many. Thus, during the depression of 1847 he avoided running his mills on short time, in the interests of the workfolk. When the Manchester warehouse was burned down in 1854 he immediately leased alternative premises in order to carry on business without interruption. It is true that he did not run his mills full-time during the Cotton Famine of 1861–65: out of 2,000 millowners only a dozen, mostly Dissenters, did so. However, he did build the magnificent palace of the Gidlow Mill at Wigan (1863–65). That model factory was fireproofed throughout in order to safeguard the lives of the mill-hands as well as the interests of the proprietors. It was probably the most expensive mill ever built, in proportion to its capacity. It earned the praise of Lord Stanley as 'a pleasure to the eye to rest on, so well has architectural effect been studied in its construction'.[24]

When the firm was incorporated as a limited company in 1873 John Rylands deliberately extended the privilege of shareholding to 454 of the principal employees (buyers, travellers, managers) and clients of the firm. The new shareholders greatly appreciated the gift of a beneficial interest in Rylands & Sons Ltd. Such industrial partnerships had been legalised in 1862. Few other manufacturers took their employees into partnership under such unusual conditions and those that did often failed. The industrial partnership created by John Rylands, remained, however, a significant if unobtrusive success.

The profit ratio of the firm remained consistently low and averaged only 3.6 per cent per annum in 1873–88. Its high returns were generated by a swelling turnover. The constant aim was to 'make only two per cent on our returns five times a year'.[25] John Rylands paid no fees to the directors and deliberately restricted the dividends paid to shareholders, of whom he himself remained the largest one. Dividends averaged 10 per cent (1873–76), declining thereafter to 5.6 per cent (1877–88). John Rylands preferred to plough profits back into the business. He built up a large reserve fund in order to safeguard the firm against unforeseen fluctuations in the volume of trade. Thus he extended the size of the workforce until by 1888 he employed some 12,000 and so indirectly supported some 40,000 persons, assuming an average of three persons per household. By supplying secure and gainful employment with a firm of the highest standing, he also enhanced the confidence and self-respect of all employees. In a typically bold initiative he favoured the employment of women as mule spinners, despite opposition from the spinners' union, and so extended opportunities for employment within the most highly paid of occupations. He also provided further subsistence through example and instruction. The firm became a virtual business school wherein other merchants were trained. Thus, indirectly, it extended employment outside its own confines.

On his death the organ of the unions published a full obituary of 'the Wellington of commerce' without a single word of criticism.[26] Within the firm itself widespread support was given to the Rylands Memorial Club which was established in 1889. Perhaps John Rylands overemphasised the role of the firm as an agent of social service since he not only retained seventeen mills and factories in full operation but also developed on a large scale the policy of outsourcing. By 1888 67 per cent of the firm's sales of textiles were sales of outside makes. The directors sold off three mills in 1888–89 and three more in 1902 but retained in production the main works in the belief that 'the Mills must be kept going'.[27] The reduction in the number of employees by 25 per cent from 12,000 to 9,000 in 1905 revealed the extent to which the firm had feather-bedded its hands and disturbed the balance between production and sales by overmanning at its mills. Gorton Mills were not closed until 1921 and the Gidlow Works only in 1957.

JOHN RYLANDS AS A PHILANTHROPIST

The whole life of John Rylands was one of toil, trial, tribulation, and tragedy, moulding a character which remained self-confident and self-controlled but resilient and earnest in the highest degree. He suffered the successive loss of three sons, of four daughters, of his first wife after eighteen years of marriage and of his second wife after twenty-seven such years. Two bereavements in particular caused him intense grief and sorrow, the death of his mother in 1829 and the death of his son and heir in 1861. Comfort he found in the realm of religion and especially in the words of the New Testament, 'My peace I give unto you.' In his new guise as a Christian capitalist John Rylands proved that he knew how to use wealth as well as how to acquire it. A profound believer in the value of education, he provided a mill-school and a library in his factories and, where necessary, a chapel or provision-stores. That policy he inaugurated at Ainsworth in 1839 and carried further at Gorton in 1845, maintaining a non-denominational approach to education and building a clutch of cottages in order to house the workfolk. In 1846 he earned the praise of the Inspector of Factories, Leonard Horner, for the provision of such liberal facilities for the education of his workfolk.[28] He also earned the public thanks of the hands in 1849 for his strict compliance with the Ten Hours' Act of 1847. After leasing the Heapey Bleach Works near Chorley in 1870 he established a mill-school and an institute, similar to those founded by Henry Lee, Hugh Mason and W. H. Houldsworth. He also maintained a large lending library in the Bolton mills which he bought in 1875.

From 1855 he extended the sphere of his good works into the wider community. He did not, however, bestow charity in conventional ways or for conventional reasons. In 1855 he became a life member of the Manchester and Salford Asylum for Female Penitents which had been established in 1822. He served the asylum first as a house steward for ten years and then from 1871 as Treasurer, in succession to Elkanah Armitage (1794–1876). In 1864 he established in Green-heys a female orphan asylum and in 1866 enlarged the accommodation in order to provide for fifty girls. As patrons of the new Rylands Home and Orphanage he secured the services of two Lancashire MPs, the merchant Benjamin Whitworth (1816–93) and the calico printer, F. W. Grafton (1816–90). Then in 1865 together with his wife, Martha, and William Woodward (1798–1870), a wealthy provision merchant and a deacon of Cavendish Congregational Chapel and his wife, Rose Anna, he co-founded the Servants' Home and Free Registry, in order to provide respectable servants with temporary board and lodging and to maintain a registry for the benefit of both servants and employers. He supported the establishment in 1869 of the Manchester and Salford Boys and Girls Refuges and Homes, the foundation in 1871 of the Manchester Religious Institute and the resuscitation in 1871 of the local branch of the YMCA. He headed the list of Manchester subscribers towards the cost of the City Temple which opened in London in 1874 as 'the most costly Nonconformist chapel ever built in England'.[29] From 1875 he became a leading benefactor to the township of Stretford by providing a whole series of public facilities, almshouses for aged gentlewomen in 1877, a town hall in 1878 (enlarged in 1886), a free library and coffee-house in 1883, the Longford Institute in 1886 and public baths in 1887. In 1881 he also provided at Ryde in the Isle of Wight a large rest home for ministers of slender means. His philanthropy was not restrained by national frontiers. From 1866 he became very interested in Italy and learned Italian. He sponsored the distribution of the New Testament in Italian and hoped for the conversion of the people to the Protestant faith. 'Attempt great things, and expect great things'! He proved a liberal benefactor to the poor of Rome, established an orphanage there and in 1880 was made a Knight of the Order of the Crown of Italy by King Umberto I. The cause of education exerted upon him a life-long appeal. He harboured an intense dislike and dread of unwholesome literature and made the Bible into an object of constant study. His scriptural interests were reinforced by his love of tracts and hymns. He remained a zealous supporter of the Religious Tract Society. In turn, that predilection for 'winged words' of edification led him to compile a paragraph Bible. The three successive editions of the Rylands Bible (1863, 1878, 1886) sought to restore the Scriptures to the individual reader by facilitating reference to their 5,810 paragraphs. The translations of the New Testament into Italian (1867) and into French (1869) sought to spread abroad a non-sectarian version of the Gospel. Four hymn books, culminating in *Hymns of the Church Universal* (1885) sought to recreate the inner unity and hidden harmony of the churches of Christendom which could not find embodiment in their creed. Appropriately enough, the best-informed memoirs of John Rylands were penned by the two divines who had led him out of the slough of sectarianism, the Baptist Dr Samuel G. Green (1820–1905) and the Congregationalist Dr Joseph Parker (1830–1912).

Throughout his life he bore in mind the successive losses he had himself sustained. He therefore made special provision for the bereaved, for the orphan, for the widow and for the aged poor. He maintained a large number of pensioners and therein, as in so much else, set the noble example followed by his widow. 'He was always ready to stand up and fight for the weak.'[30]

He agreed with Bunyan that 'the soul of Religion is the Practick part' and cared naught for theological disputation. He simply strove to exemplify in his own life the highest ideals of the Christian. If he became a 'mover and shaker' then he acted unobtrusively out of the public eye. Many of his largest benefactions he kept secret, in accordance with the precepts of the New Testament. Thus the full extent of his philanthropic activity still remains unknown. Only in his 17-page will did some indication emerge of his extensive charitable interests and only in 1894 was a memorial statue completed to the satisfaction of his widow and his closest associates, revealing to all observers the features of a 'philanthropist . . . touched with a spiritual fineness'.[31]

THE WILLS OF JOHN RYLANDS AND ENRIQUETA AUGUSTINA RYLANDS

John Rylands left an estate of £2,574,922, on which stamp duty of £77,226 or 3 per cent was paid. In his will he bequeathed £75,000 to 28 relatives and friends, £132,300 to 301 employees and £157,000 to 44 charities; £38,000 was left to six named directors of the firm; £90,800 was left to 292 other employees, as the co-creators of the firm's prosperity. That large group included 106 salesmen, 46 buyers, 45 travellers, 40 book-keepers and 22 foremen: it also comprised 2 saleswomen and 1 forewoman. Twelve of the sixteen friends were either clergymen or their relatives. Two-thirds of all the charitable legacies were devoted to educational causes, especially that of religious education. The five largest bequests of £10,000 each were made to the Baptist College, the Congregational Chapel Building Society, the Religious Tract Society, Owens College and the Manchester Warehousemen and Clerks Orphan Schools (see Table 5.1). John

Table 5.1 Charitable legacies of John Rylands (d. 1888) and of Mrs Rylands (d. 1908)

| | John Rylands | | Mrs Rylands | |
	Number	Amount (£)	Number	Amount (£)
Religious education	11	55,000	7	44,000
Missions	7	24,000	7	28,000
Aged ministers	7	21,500	3	15,000
Education	2	20,000	4	295,000
Hospitals	5	21,000	10	27,000
Orphanages and youth societies	8	13,000	13	22,000
Women's welfare			7	21,500
Total		154,500		452,500

Rylands doubled the value of his legacies by bequeathing them in the form of shares in the firm. Their market value doubled (1890–1907) while dividends averaged 12.5 per cent (1895–1907) or treble the return upon consols. The bulk of the estate, £2,210,622 or 86 per cent of the total, was inherited by his widow and executor, who became the principal shareholder in Manchester's two leading firms, Rylands & Sons Ltd and the Manchester Ship Canal Company.

Enriqueta Augustina Rylands (1843–1908) had been married for thirteen years when she was widowed. She closely resembled her husband in her formidable abilities, in her strength of will and in her philanthropic disposition. She followed his example in devoting her own time as much as her wealth to good causes. She always avoided dispensing charity simply by means of a cheque and consistently preserved anonymity in her donations. She decided to commemorate her husband in the most appropriate manner, to associate his name forever with his own ideals and in particular to reflect his profound commitment to the study of the Bible. She invested a million pounds in the John Rylands Library, in its land, its building, its books and its manuscripts. The creative employment of her wealth provided a contrast to the philanthropic sterility of the London textile merchant, Alfred Morrison (1821–1897).[32]

On her death in 1908 her estate of £3,607,056 paid death duties of £650,000 or 18 per cent. She left £196,573 to 21 friends, £1,820,520 to 27 relatives and, to the astonishment of the press, £448,000 to 52 charities, or treble the amount bequeathed by her husband. Her legacies included gifts to eighteen of the same institutions favoured by her husband (see Table 5.2). They nevertheless differed significantly from those of John Rylands. They were much more generous to relatives than he had been. Only one-fifth of her bequests may be classed as religious, in contrast to the 65 per cent of those of her husband. She devoted less to religious education and little more to the cause of missions. In her legacies to hospitals she proved more liberal, especially to those which had offered her some relief from her chronic rheumatism. She was especially generous in her gifts to ragged schools and to women's charities. Above all, she favoured education and made her largest bequests to the John Rylands Library (£200,000) and to the University of Manchester (£75,000).

Plate 5.3 Enriqueta Augustina Rylands (1843–1908) in 1875

Source: *The Christian*, 13 February 1908

Table 5.2 Bequests common to the wills of both John Rylands and Mrs Rylands (£000)

Religious	J.R.	E.A.R.	Secular	J.R.	E.A.R.
Religious Tract Society	10	5	Owens College	10	25
London Missionary Society	5	5	Manchester Warehousemen		
Baptist Missionary Society	5	2	Orphan Schools	10	20
Lancashire Congregational			Manchester Royal Eye Hospital	5	2
Union	5	10	Manchester Asylum for Females	5	2
Baptist College	10	5	Manchester and Salford		
Lancashire and Cheshire			District Provident Society	0.5	1
Congregational Chapel			Manchester and Salford Boys		
Building Society	10	5	and Girls Refuges and Homes	1	5
London City Mission	5	3	Hazelwood Home of Rest for		
Manchester City Mission	5	5	Commercial Young Men at Ryde	0.5	0.5
Manchester YMCA	3	2	Gardeners' Royal Benevolent		
Wesleyan Missionary Society	2	3	Society	0.5	3
TOTAL	60	45		32.5	58.5

People who were at one time included to cavil with the form taken by the tribute to her husband's memory have come to understand the value which accrues to the community by her departure from the beaten track of charity. She converted a beautiful ideal into a still more beautiful deed.[33]

The history of the library remains one of the great success stories in the cultural history of the twentieth century. It still stands as an enduring monument to a notable partnership in charitable endeavour.

THE ONSLAUGHT ON THE REPUTATION OF JOHN RYLANDS MOUNTED DURING THE LONGFORD HALL INQUIRY OF 1994

The first and isolated example of an unfavourable view of John Rylands dates from the year 1929 when W. F. M. Weston-Webb (1851–1937) published his autobiography. Therein he touched upon his twenty-seven months of employment by the firm of Rylands & Sons (1868–71) and also mentioned the excellent letter of reference penned by the proprietor on his dismissal. Weston-Webb's verdict on John Rylands was based upon a brief but superficial acquaintance. It was wholly negative and lacked any redeeming feature.

> I was told that he was very mean, and he looked it – that wee man with white hair and a shrivelled-up face. He was mean enough at any rate to bring grapes and fruit with him in his carriage from his gardens every day and send them to the market.[34]

John Rylands was compared with the New York department-store owner, A. T. Stewart (1803–76). 'They were men of about the same age. Neither knew how to enjoy the wealth he had amassed; their only interest was in acquiring it.'[35] Weston-Webb may well have been inspired by a festering sense of the injustice of his dismissal in 1871. John Rylands's most unusual practice in selling the produce from his estate helped to keep nineteen gardeners in gainful employment at Longford Hall. For fifty-five years after 1929 the reputation of John Rylands remained unsullied until controversy suddenly flared up in 1984, when the local authority decided to demolish his former home.

Longford Hall (see Plate 5.4) had been built by John Rylands and had served as his residence for thirty-two years from 1857. In 1911 the hall was bought by Stretford Urban District Council at the bargain price of one-third of the market value. In 1974 the ancient township of Stretford, together with nine other districts was absorbed into a new and artificial unit of local government, the Metropolitan Borough of Trafford. Longford Hall was regarded by some as 'the jewel in Trafford's crown'[36] but its condition began to deteriorate and it was closed down in 1983. A local charitable trust was established to ensure its preservation. On 17 June 1988 the Department of National Heritage listed the hall as a grade II building on the grounds of its architectural quality and its historical significance as the residence of John Rylands. Trafford was deeply dismayed by the listing of the building and did not believe that such a classification was justified. The leader of the council dismissed the hall as 'an ugly, jerry-built building'.[37] In 1992 Trafford reaffirmed its determination to demolish the hall. The reputation of John Rylands remained, however, a serious obstacle to its plans and it therefore hired a Bradford consultant to offer an expert opinion. Mr John Headland Ayers was a 62-year-old architect and the author of two studies of the architecture of Bradford. He submitted his report on the hall to Trafford on 26 March 1992, devoting three out of twenty-four pages to John Rylands.[38] Those ten paragraphs contained a series of allegations, all of which minimised Rylands' historical significance. According to Mr Ayers, he played little part in public life and his only achievement was to accumulate wealth. He did not invent or develop new machinery. He did not initiate new or innovative methods. He was not exceptional in his treatment of his workers. 'His philanthropic activities were not in any way exceptional.' He did not devote time or energy to the benefit either of the textile trade as a whole or of the City of Manchester. 'He was not, in my view, a great man, in an era which produced many great men.' 'He was not a great Victorian.' That series of judgements comprises the gravest indictment of John Rylands ever penned. The sheer number of criticisms was without any precedent. They emphatically rejected the traditional view of their subject. In effect Mr Ayers had thoroughly belittled the repute of one of Stretford's most notable past residents. His judgement was

Plate 5.4 Longford Hall, Stretford, in 1933

Source: The Trafford Local Studies Library, Sale

welcomed as authoritative by the officers and councillors of Trafford. The real issue at stake remained not the reputation of John Rylands but the fate of Longford Hall. In order to clear the way for the demolition of the hall it was necessary to remove the obstacle presented by its association with the original proprietor and to repudiate any claim that he had ever been admitted to the national pantheon. Such an Orwellian revision of history would deprive Stretford of a notable historical association. Stretford could indeed boast of an association with at least six figures of national repute. On the other hand, the remainder of Trafford could summon up only a single figure, that of the physicist J. P. Joule (1818–89). What mattered here was the whole thrust of Mr Ayers's arguments and not their foundations. In fact, his assertions lacked any solid empirical basis. They were founded upon only two sources, neither of which supported the specific allegations he had made.

In order to appease local critics of Trafford Council, the Department of the Environment decided on 24 November 1993 that a local inquiry should be held into the issue. Trafford arranged to hold the inquiry outside the district of Longford and indeed outside the borough of Stretford itself. Mr T. D. Bingham, an architect from Ashford in Kent presided over the inquiry which lasted for nine days from 26 April 1994. English Heritage submitted its own opinion to the inquiry, ranking John Rylands as 'an outstanding historical figure'.

> There should be no doubt about the significance, locally, nationally and perhaps internationally, of John Rylands. His business acumen and methods made him the outstanding figure in the cotton textile industry and trade in the second half of the nineteenth century. There could be no better figure to commemorate as a representative of Manchester business at a time when the city reached an unparalleled height of commercial prosperity.[39]

Inspector Bingham submitted his report on 3 August 1994; he discounted the views of English Heritage and accepted the judgement of Mr Ayers upon John Rylands. 'He was not a great Victorian, with his only achievement of note being the attainment of great wealth . . . John Rylands cannot be seen to have been a great man, certainly not one of national repute.'

> He was undeniably a man of local fame, and possibly of regional renown. I do not agree, partly in view of his reclusive nature, that he had a national reputation or that such a reputation has been recognised posthumously. He cannot be compared to contemporary figures with an undeniable national reputation.[40]

The inspector even suggested that a recent biographer had portrayed John Rylands as a person 'of insignificance in most respects', an assertion which the biographer in question found to be incomprehensible.[41]

Such a verdict upon John Rylands was eccentric and partial. Messrs Ayers and Bingham, as architects, were competent to pass judgement upon Longford Hall as a building. They were out of their depth, however, when they aspired to assess the significance of the hall's proprietor. They ignored the extent of the philanthropic activity of John Rylands and focused narrowly upon wealth-creation as his sole achievement. In so doing they neglected the beneficial aspects of such creative action and implied that the mere generation of wealth was of little value to society. Their verdict seems to have reflected an entrenched and elitist hostility to business, such as Wiener had identified in 1981, and such as Rubinstein had suggested in 1986 might well be universal in extent. 'It is probably no exaggeration to say that all of Western high culture in its ideological substance over the past 150 years has consisted of attacks upon capitalism.'[42] Mr Bingham's report was accepted on 5 December 1994 by the Secretary of State for the Environment. No appeal was made against the decision. Trafford was authorised to demolish the hall and duly complied, having taken twelve years to overcome the local opposition.

In order to set the verdict rendered in 1994 in perspective it will help to invoke one objective assessment which was strangely neglected by both Mr Ayers and Mr Bingham. Such an assessment had been made by Charles W. Sutton (1848–1920), the City Librarian of Manchester in his article in the *Dictionary of National Biography (DNB)* (1897), confirming the dictum penned by St Augustine in his work *Contra Epistolam Parmeniani* (AD 400), 'the verdict of the world is conclusive'. Inclusion amongst the original 31,000 entries in the *DNB* may be accepted as an objective test of national status. The failure by Messrs Ayers and Bingham even to mention, let alone to consider, Sutton's article constitutes their gravest act of omission and the fatal flaw in their case against John Rylands. Only one out of every 5,000 persons was honoured by inclusion in the *DNB*. The bias of the editors did not favour either businessmen or provincials. The selection of John Rylands may therefore be considered a valid test of true stature, especially since the competition from his contemporaries born during the golden age of 1751–1800 was intense. A summary account of his life was also included in the *Concise Dictionary of National Biography* (1903), in three other biographical dictionaries published by Chambers (1897), Boase (1901) and Webster (1943), in a Congregational roll of honour[43] and in two bio-bibliographies, Hyamson's *Dictionary of Universal Biography* (1916) and the *British Biographical Index* (1990). An entry in the authoritative eleventh edition of the *Encyclopaedia Britannica* (1911) ranks as another testimony to his stature.[44] During the decade of controversy, British Rail named a Pullman locomotive after him in 1988. The debate of 1994 over his reputation had nevertheless revealed the extent to which an anti-business ethos had survived the immense change in the climate of opinion since 1979.

In 1996 the continuing relevance of the Wiener thesis was vividly demonstrated upon at least three occasions. First, a National Opinion Poll taken on 12 December 1996 revealed that few business people had made any impact at all upon public consciousness. The nation in general remained unaware of the identity of the top managers of UK plc. Only two names, those of Richard Branson and Anita Roddick, had proved familiar to a representative sample of adults and had done so because of their coverage in the media.[45] Such a condition of passive ignorance was, however, far surpassed in significance by the formal rejection by the intellectual elite of the nation of the offer of £20 million for the establishment of a Business School in the University of Oxford. Finally, the centenary of the death of William Morris (1834–96) was celebrated in a whole host of laudatory and well-publicised exhibitions. The other William Morris (1877–1963), who became Lord Nuffield, was wholly overshadowed by his namesake, the Victorian socialist. The disparity in the posthumous reputation of the two William Morrises had been stressed by both Neil McKendrick in 1976 and Martin Wiener in 1981.[46] In 1996 that contrast was intensified by the publication of a scholarly but revisionist interpretation, blaming Nuffield for creating an essentially destructive managerial culture which in turn contributed to the collapse of the British car industry during the 1970s.[47]

The prospects for the future image of British businessmen were not, however, wholly bleak. In 1999 the centenary of the inauguration of the John Rylands Library would undoubtedly enhance the reputation of the man whom Dr Andrew Fairbairn had described as 'a modest merchant, a dutiful citizen and a humble lover of letters'.[48] Moreover, in 2004 will appear what Nigel Nicolson has called 'this ultimate Valhalla, this repository of our national greatness'[49] in the form of the *New Dictionary of National Biography*. One of its 60,000 entries will amplify Charles Sutton's biography of 1897 and will include the following judgement.

> John Rylands approximates closely to the ideal type of capitalist studied by both Max Weber (1904) and J. A. Schumpeter (1911): he remains a striking example of the innovating entrepreneur inspired by a profound belief in the truths of Christianity, especially as expounded in the New Testament, and in their essential relevance to daily life.

NOTES

1 Charles Darwin, *The Descent of Man* (London, 1871), II, p. 420.
2 M. J. Wiener, *English Culture and the Decline of the Industrial Spirit, 1850–1980* (Cambridge, 1981).
3 R. W. Fogel and S. L. Engerman, *Time on the Cross: The Economics of American Negro Slavery* (Boston, 1974) and Alan McFarlane, *The Origins of English Individualism* (Oxford, 1978).
4 A. W. B. Simpson, 'Legal Liability for Bursting Reservoirs: the Historical Context of Rylands v. Fletcher', *The Journal of Legal Studies*, 13(2): 209–64 (1984).
5 A. C. Howe, *The Cotton Masters 1830–1860* (Oxford, 1984).
6 *Archive of Rylands & Sons Ltd 1742–1969, catalogued by Sarah Smith* (John Rylands University Library of Manchester, 1996, 26pp.).
7 S. G. Green, *In Memoriam John Rylands born February 7, 1801, died December 11, 1888* (Chilworth, 1889), p. 31.
8 Max Weber, *The Protestant Ethic and the Spirit of Capitalism* (transl. Talcott Parsons, 1930; repr. London, 1968). Gordon Marshall, *Presbyteries and Profits. Calvinism and the Development of Capitalism in Scotland, 1650–1707* (Oxford, 1980).
9 Kazuhiko Kondo, 'John Rylands and the Protestant Ethic and the Spirit of Capitalism' (in Japanese), *Shiso* [*Thought*], 714: 24–43 (1983).
10 S. G. Green, p. 54.

11 *Manchester City News*, 1 April 1865, p. 3i.
12 *Momus*, 15 May 1879, p. 81.
13 *Manchester of Today. An Epitome of Results* (London, 1888), p. 79
14 *Momus*, 15 May 1879, p. 81
15 Lawrence Cowen, *Commerce*, 5 July 1893, p. 17.
16 *British Trade Journal*, 1 April 1887, p. 277
17 S. D. Chapman, 'The Decline and Rise of Textile Merchanting', *Business History*, 32 (4): 171–90, October 1990.
18 *The Young Man*, April 1893, p. 111. *Commerce*, 5 July 1893, p. 17.
19 W. D. Rubinstein 'British Millionaires, 1809–1949', *Bulletin of the Institute of Historical Research*, xlvii: 116–28 (1974).
20 *Manchester City News*, 13 October 1888, p. 5iv.
21 S. D. Chapman, p. 174.
22 P. L. Payne, 'The Emergence of the Large-Scale Company in Great Britain, 1870–1914', *Economic History Review*, second series, XX(3): 519–42, December 1967.
23 T. S. Ashton, 'Rylands & Sons Ltd. (1823)', *Manchester Guardian Commercial*, 5 May 1934, p. 9.
24 *Manchester City News*, 15 April 1865, p. 3i.
25 John Rylands Library, Archives of Rylands & Sons Ltd., General Meetings Minute Book, i, 20, 9 December 1875.
26 *Cotton Factory Times*, 14 December 1888, p. 7iii–iv.
27 Archives of Rylands & Sons Ltd., Minutes of the Board of Directors, iv, 376, 16 June 1906.
28 Leonard Horner, *Reports of the Inspectors of Factories*, 31 October 1846, p. 7.
29 G. H. Pike, *Dr Parker and His Friends* (London,1904), p. 90.
30 S. G. Green, p. 8.
31 C. E. Montague, *A Hind Let Loose* (London, 1910), pp. 4–5.
32 *Northern Finance and Trade*, 20 April 1898, p. 316.
33 *Manchester Courier*, 5 February 1908, p. 6iii.
34 W. F. M. Weston-Webb, *The Autobiography of a British Yarn Merchant*, (London, 1929), p. 52.
35 Ibid., p. 61.
36 Philip Tudor, *The Messenger* (Stretford), 1 October 1993, p. 6vi.
37 Frank H. Eadie in a letter to N.R. Mann, 28 December 1989.
38 J. H. Ayers, 'The Architectural and Historical Interest of Longford Hall', a report of twenty-four pages submitted to Trafford Borough Council on 26 March 1992. D. A. Farnie, 'John Rylands of Longford Hall: A Comment upon the Report by Mr J. Ayers with Particular Reference to the Three Pages (pp. 6–9) Relating to John Rylands', a 24-page manuscript, 29 June 1992.
39 English Heritage, 'Longford Hall, Stretford', a statement to Trafford Metropolitan Borough Council from Frank Kelsall of Conservation Group North, 22 April 1994.
40 A. J. Bingham, 'Application under Regulation 13 of the Planning (Listed Buildings and Conservation Areas) Regulations 1990 by the Trafford Metropolitan Borough Council', a report of sixty-five pages submitted to the Secretary of State for the Environment on 3 August 1994, 3.61; 8.18.
41 D. A. Farnie, *John Rylands of Manchester* (John Rylands University Library of Manchester, 1993); Bingham (1994), 3.58.
42 W. D. Rubinstein, 'Cultural Explanations for Britain's Economic Decline: How True?', in B. Collins and K. Robbins (eds), *British Culture and Economic Decline* (London, 1990), p. 78.
43 A. Peel, *A Hundred Eminent Congregationalists, 1530–1924* (London, 1927); A. Peel, *The Congregational Two Hundred, 1530–1948* (London, 1948).

44 *Encyclopaedia Britannica* (1911), vol. 23, 950 (Cambridge, 11th edition).
45 *Sunday Times Business*, 29 December 1996.
46 Wiener, pp. 133, 151.
47 R. A. Church, 'Deconstructing Nuffield: The Evolution of Managerial Culture in the British Motor Industry', *Economic History Review*, XLIX(3): 561–83, August 1996.
48 *Manchester Guardian*, 7 October 1899, p. 7i.
49 *Spectator*, 10 December 1994, p. 57.

6 Max Weber, religion and the work ethic

Patrick K. O'Brien

This chapter seeks to survey critically but ultimately to reaffirm the scepticism that is now widely shared among many economists and economic historians towards notions (bequeathed to history and social science by Max Weber) that verifiable connexions can be traced between the varieties of Christianity that emerged after the Reformation and the relative rates of economic growth achieved by regional and national economies in Europe between, say, 1517 (when Luther nailed his ninety-five theses to that door of the church in Wittenburg) and the outbreak of the First World War.

Weber's seminal and qualified theses have been repeated and popularised since their publication at the beginning of the century but I wish to deal with Weberian correlations between religion and work, as it often appears in a more text book form, because it is still widely believed that long-run connexions between religion and economic growth can be specified and validated in ways that can and should continue to motivate historical research and generalisation.

Nothing in my polemic seeks to deny that most, if not all, the businessmen mentioned in the chapters in this book possessed entrepreneurial flair and drives, that they worked much harder than others, or finally that these observed human proclivities can be somehow related to the religious beliefs that they as individuals espoused. What I am concerned to elaborate upon are the conceptual and empirical conditions that are required to transform biographical observations about people as businessmen and workers into more widespread attributes of communities and local and national cultures that might plausibly have effected the observed pace and pattern of macro economic growth as it has occurred in different parts of Europe since the Reformation. I propose to address one familiar but major hypothesis inspired by Weber; namely, that European societies well endowed with a workforce and/or businessmen imbibed with a 'work ethic' shared a set of transcendental and Protestant beliefs and that these distinctive resources turned out to be of discernible (and preferably quantifiable) significance for long-run economic progress of local, regional and national economies.

Outward manifestations of a presumed inner, but not directly observable compulsion to work long and hard, have often been traced in the lives of prophets and princes, saints and senators, artists and artisans, warriors and wives, and even among humble labourers in the vineyards of history. This has been carefully and convincingly delineated in several chapters included in this collection. For the 'concept' to transcend biography that compulsion must either be widely distributed across a nation's workforce or reposited in individuals (scientists, entrepreneurs, craftsmen, merchants, bankers) who somehow became role models for entire sub-groups of a population and whose contribution to material progress can be regarded (*pace* John Rylands) as significant.

Furthermore, and if such a thing exists and changes across time and place, a work ethic must be carefully specified in order to circumvent statistically validated explanations for hard work or individual effort drawn from the corpus of economics. That discipline has after all devoted more time and thought than other social sciences to labour as a factor of production. Since Adam Smith, classical and neo-classical theories of labour supply (including the intensity of effort devoted to any productive activity) are cast primarily in terms of incentives. Such incentives are usually, but not necessarily, pecuniary in form because in theory, the rewards for labour could include status, approbation, even fame. They are, however, treated as logically extrinsic to the work itself and accepted as a sufficient explanation for the volume and intensity of human effort. Economics, or rather the economics of business organisation, has, moreover, also recognised that different institutional frameworks for production also affect the quantity, quality and effort that people put into their jobs. Self and family systems of employment have historically been regarded as the most efficacious organisations both for increasing the participation rates and for extracting optimal work loads from a nation's population of potentially employable men, women and children. For example, and in our times, the Japanese *nenko* system is widely admired as a highly effective way of motivating the employees of a large-scale corporate enterprise.

The field of labour economics, as it is now called, developed in the context of post-slave and post-feudal markets for labour which slowly emerged in Western Europe after the Black Death. From the time of that catastrophe onwards (and particularly when and where their basic needs and the subsistence of their dependants had been secured), a growing proportion of adult males among populations of working age came to exercise more autonomous control over the hours and intensity of work they chose to put into the production of food, manufactures and services. But over several centuries, as the feudal system gave way to free labour markets and as risks of failing to maintain subsistence wages from season to season only gradually diminished, that choice hardly existed for more than an expanding minority of Europeans. Meanwhile, for most European economies where prevailing technologies of production continued to be labour-intensive, those responsible for the organisation of work attempted to maintain 'authoritarian' systems of control over labour which employers, political elites and their intellectual saratraps argued were necessary to secure the extraction of optimal work loads from workers who would otherwise shirk and evade necessary toil altogether.

Problems for merchants, industrialists, farmers, landowners (and also for royal and local administrators responsible for raising the taxable capacity of kingdoms, perpetually at or on the threshold of war) intensified when wages moved above subsistence levels and leisure preference entered into the calculus of workers, particularly skilled labour in short supply. Thus it is no surprise to find political and ecclesiastical power not only backing the authority of 'masters' but deploying ideology and religious injunctions in order to persuade people to work longer, harder, and without complaint. In England John Wesley, as Reg Ward observed in Chapter 3, was concerned enough about the poor to deplore the 'under-employment of the pre-industrial economy, notwithstanding that the Methodist multiplication of devotions required this surplus leisure'.

Both before and after the Reformation several theologies and forms of organised religion proclaimed on the dignity of work and its role in styles of life conducive to eternal salvation. After Max Weber published his celebrated essay on the Protestant Ethic and the Spirit of Capitalism, theologians and ecclesiastical historians have split the very finest of hairs in scholarly attempts to demonstrate that the published beliefs for varieties of Christianity on offer in Europe differed significantly in the ideological support they lent to the promotion of behaviour conducive to personal success and national economic growth. Alas, historians know too little about changes in interpretation as religious injunctions flowed from authorities and books down to pulpits. They are not too sure, as Chapter 3 again exposes, that the founding fathers of these sects were seriously (even at all) interested in economic growth. But at the level of written theological discourse (which is all that happens to be now available as evidence) historians have detected distinctions between Calvinism and Catholicism and Calvinism and other Protestant beliefs over such economically important matters as usury, rational accountancy, business organisation and the treatment of poverty. Unfortunately the distinctions in print between some of these recommendations for personal economic behaviour (and before they were filtered through churches and regaled to congregations) are more apparent to theologians and clerics (and to modern academics) than they may have appeared at the time to literate but hardly well-educated urban populations, let alone to majorities of labourers who tilled the fields.

Turning specifically to the work ethic: the construction from a plurality of printed texts of perceived differences between Protestant and Catholic religions and among varieties of Protestantism on such matters as the dignity of labour, the productive use of time and its counterpart idleness, and the spiritual value of all kinds of work in the secular domain seems hardly discernible. Even if the 'messages' conveyed to congregations of the faithful followed theological texts *à la lettre* (as historians now read them), they hardly seem clear and distinctive enough to form behavioural foundations for a novel and peculiarly Protestant or Calvinistic work ethic across the industrial regions of Europe. This is not to deny that singular and often peculiar individuals worked beyond the calls of duty or avarice and that they expressed justification for their presumably 'deviant' addiction to work and to their fear and loathing for idleness in religious terms. (Rylands was clearly a case in point.) No doubt the culture of some parishes and congregations accorded higher status to work or (what is more likely) evinced greater intolerance towards idleness than others. Nevertheless, mandates for cultural and community attitudes to toil and its counterpart cannot be convincingly extrapolated from opaque and minor differences between adjacent or even the antagonistic versions of Christian doctrines towards work.

At this end of the twentieth century historians are more likely to search for the sources of extraordinary personal behaviour in relationships between parents and children inside families than among church congregations. That may well be somewhat anachronistic for periods when responsibilities for childhood training and early socialisation may have been more devolved than it is today. Furthermore, and except for a handful of rather famous people, connexions between children and their parents are usually impossible to reconstruct for remote periods of history when the only sources available are religious texts, dealing *en passant* with children and didactic manuals for household management, which also include sections on child care. Among this literature there is evidence of observable variations in the recommendations emanating from several Christian sects on child rearing. If (and it is a big if) most parents took heed of the advice offered by various churches on how best to train their children, they may willy nilly have inculcated attitudes towards work that permanently transformed the productivity of a large enough proportion of a national or regional workforce and thereby made a discernible difference to rates of economic advance for particular places. If modern psychological mechanisms for the explanation of behaviour are transferable back in time to early modern contexts for work, then an *a priori* case based upon religious literature for detectable variations in child-rearing programmes appears to be an altogether more promising line of inquiry than continuing to deconstruct theological texts in search of meaningful words and pages bearing on the development of a Protestant work ethic.

Alas, and even if historians of religious ideas, of intra-familial relations and economic ideology for the early modern period managed to create an *a priori* case for the appearance of a work ethic among selected populations and communities in early modern Europe, its precise significance for the diffusion of capitalism and (what is more important) differential rates of economic growth across space and time will continue to elude us. There can be no doubt that the *prima facie* case for anything approximating to a *high* degree of significance was thrown into the realms of the improbable a long time ago when economic historians exposed the entirely limited degree of correlation between examples of 'successful' urban, regional and national market economies, on the one hand, and the religious persuasion of their inhabitants, on the other. Thereafter, weaker hypotheses that among sub-groups of the workforce held to be important for economic growth (scientists, technologists, merchants, entrepreneurs, skilled workers *et al.*,) members of Protestant sects tended to be represented out of all proportion to their numbers in the relevant population are either untested for most of Europe and more or less refuted for the English industrial revolution.

Far too many factors operate to stimulate or retard the development of local or national economies for simple correlations between high per capita income and the dominance of particular varieties of Christianity across the landscape of Europe to represent anything other than yet another example of ecological fallacy.

Finally, modern economic theory has specified the conditions and data required to establish the case for the significance of a work ethic. They turn out to be stringent and well beyond the sources and information ever likely to become available to historians. Empirically the case requires that the labour and management in any firm or enterprise operate with the same equipment, raw materials and inputs, and that its employees expect to receive comparable levels of pecuniary and other rewards for their work, compared to the labour and management employed by its competitors. If these strong *ceteris paribus* conditions are more or less met and it is then observed that workers in a selected firm or enterprise achieved clear and persistently higher levels of productivity per standardised man hour of labour time employed relative to employees in competitive enterprises, only then is there something to be explained about the motivations of its workers and managers. Economists believe, however, that the gaps in labour productivity that can be measured for modern periods at micro levels (firms, farms, enterprises) and with far more difficulty at macro levels (industries, towns, regions and countries) can normally be accounted for in very large part by difference in capital–labour ratios, the tractability of inputs, technology, the health and skills that people brought to or learned at the workplace, established incentives for pecuniary rewards and promotion, various managerial systems, etc., etc. In modern theories and empirically validated explanations for variations in labour productivity, there is precious little room for gender, culture, race or religion as explanatory variables. Those who wish to argue that things were different for, say, the four centuries or so after the Reformation are, in my view, required to demonstrate that all the other and well-established correlates for variations in levels of labour productivity were either inoperable or of entirely weak significance compared to the diffusion of a Protestant work ethic.

After his acute and interesting analysis of a large group of Methodist businessmen, David Jeremy admitted he could not tell 'how far religion motivated or facilitated their business success'. He also shows greater concern with giving than gaining. In the manner of first-class historians, both David Jeremy and Douglas Farnie make skilful use of circumstantial evidence to show that connexions between religion and economic behaviour were probably not slight. Reg Ward's chapter tells us that they had little to do with anything Wesley may have taught and written. I conclude that at least one Weberian concept, the 'work ethic', might, after long discussion, be allowed to fade into a redundant curiosity in the history of sociological thought. Alas, it may continue to survive as the kind of scholasticism that has for long surrounded Marxist theology and which could hardly have continued to attract the seminal mind of Max Weber.

Part III
Quakers and wealth

7 The Society of Friends and business culture, 1700–1830

Ann Prior and Maurice Kirby

Historians have regularly observed the over-representation of Friends among successful entrepreneurs in the formative years of British industrialisation during the eighteenth and nineteenth centuries. It has also been noted that, given the uncertain and high-risk business environment of the day, the longevity of many of the Quaker business dynasties founded at that time was remarkable. Moreover, Friends' success was achieved with a reputation for honesty and integrity in business. When it is considered that, 'eighteenth-century Englishmen were conditioned to living in a world where indebtedness was endemic and bad debts an accepted concomitant of widespread credit',[1] and that fraudulent activities were commonplace amongst bankrupts, creditors and their solicitors,[2] Friends' reputation for honesty can only be admired. And here may lie the over-riding influence behind the Quaker success story. Casson has argued convincingly for a crucial link between entrepreneurship and business culture:

> With highly subjective information, the quality of entrepreneurship depends on the quality of business culture, [and] the most important aspect of business culture is the extent to which it promotes trust. Trust facilitates co-operation between entrepreneurs, and co-operation is just as important as competition in achieving efficiency.[3]

Recent work on the theory of the firm, building upon an original paper by Coase,[4] has highlighted the concepts of transaction costs and internalisation.[5] As Coase emphasised, the coordination and allocation of resources via competitive markets impose costs on a business. However, these 'transaction costs' may be reduced as a result of internalisation, that is, the supercession of market functions by the individual firm. The focus on internalisation as a cost-reducing strategy has received much attention in recent business history, no more so than in Alfred Chandler's empirical work on the rise of the modern business corporation. However, Chandler has observed that 'as long as legal and personal ties and relationships helped to assure the fulfillment of contractual arrangements, manufacturers usually preferred to buy their supplies rather than invest in and manage the production of these supplies'.[6] Casson has argued similarly that, 'Cooperation between family firms, which use paternalism for internal coordination and reciprocity for external coordination, may achieve better results than a merger which integrates the firms within a larger managerially controlled enterprise.'[7] For Casson, it is the cultural quality, rather than the type of organisation, which is the crucial factor. In this light, it is apparent that the concept of external networks, as an alternative means of reducing transaction costs arising from uncertainty and imperfect knowledge, can be examined in the context of the Coase–Chandlerian view of the theory of the firm. Casson has emphasised the importance of trust in determining the rate of transaction costs. Thus, where trust is low, transaction costs will be relatively high and business performance will be hindered. The membership of the Society of Friends, however, was instilled with a high moral culture, the product in part of an extensive family and kinship network. This, together with an inherited religious code emphasising spiritual priorities, re-dounded to the advantage of Quaker men of business in terms of confidence and expectations.

Although the Society of Friends was by no means unique as a closely knit sect, the degree of internal cohesion and the geographical extent of its family linkages were unusual and distinctive. In a pioneering work, Arthur Raistrick suggested that the Society of Friends was effectually an extended family group in which personal contacts were facilitated by peripatetic ministers and the regular monthly, quarterly and yearly meetings of the Society.[8] At these meetings, many of which involved considerable travel and lengthy periods away from home, it was not unusual for Friends with commercial and business interests to discuss the state of trade and also the possibility of partnership in joint ventures. In the absence of institutional capital markets it was the Quakers' ability to exploit geographically dispersed pools of capital which helped to create a chain of credit and finance with the Society of Friends, not unlike the 'web of credit' which emerged in the Lancashire cotton and Yorkshire woollen industries in the late eighteenth century.[9] But the Quaker financial network was nationwide and even extended overseas, notably to North America. The strength of the chain was reinforced periodically by intermarriage – again on a nationwide scale – especially in industries such as iron, textiles and country banking.[10] External networks with this degree of sophistication were arguably highly conducive to the formation and subsequent growth of the firm in the formative stages of Britain's industrialisation.

It is the concept of family-based networks which provides the rationale of this chapter. Its principal aim is to identify the institutional foundations of Quaker business endeavours in the eighteenth and early nineteenth centuries. Whilst it is accepted that the explanation for the success of early Quaker firms is multifaceted, embracing religious precepts, educational provision and social exclusion, it is contended that the Meeting House system underwrote both commercial stability and confidence by facilitating capital flows in the form of a personalised chain of credit, strongly reinforced by geographically extended family contacts. In this respect the chapter provides firm empirical support for Raistrick's concept of an extended family group. It refines the concept further, however, by focusing attention on the Meeting House as an internalised source of commercial support and advice, facilitated by the close surveillance of business practices. In the first section the chapter highlights the close monitoring of Friends in business at the hands of the Leeds Meeting House, notable as one of the largest gatherings of Quakers in the north of England in the eighteenth century. Evidence taken from the minute books of Meetings outside the area confirms that there was nothing unusual in the way Leeds Preparative Meeting and Brighouse Monthly Meeting, to which Leeds belonged, monitored and advised Friends in business. The second section focuses attention on the assessment of creditworthiness and responses to indebtedness, whilst the third section, in examining the role of Quakers in the foundation of the early railway enterprise, provides impressive empirical verification of the remarkable extent of credit flows on the basis of religious and kinship links. The final section offers some concluding remarks on the nature of Quaker entrepreneurship.

ADVICE IN TRADE

Casson has pointed to the importance of religion in inducing moral conformity, and certainly the influence of the Society of Friends was of paramount importance in the promotion of the honest reputation of the membership. Deeply disturbed by the 'deceitful merchandise and cheating and cozening'[11] which he viewed as the norm in contemporary trade, George Fox demanded of his followers that they act honestly and justly in their business dealings. Honesty in trade, including the avoidance of debt, thus became a condition of membership of the Religious Society of Friends from its inception in the 1660s. But just as the penalty of disownment for 'marrying out' did not stop irregular marriage, disownment for debt could not, in itself, prevent Friends from becoming insolvent. Given the uncertainty and high-risk business environment of the day, it is little wonder that, 'the nature of risk, of attempts to combat risks as well as take them, were a major concern of all eighteenth-century businessmen'.[12] Risk avoidance was certainly an important issue for the Yearly Meeting of the Society of Friends and of the local Meeting House, as the minute books of Leeds Preparative Meeting record. Raistrick has said of Friends in trade that 'no small business stood alone'[13] and this is clearly so: a Friend's concern was also the concern of the Society in general, and the local Meeting in particular. New small businesses were inevitably the most vulnerable, so not surprisingly few escaped scrutiny. Equally significant, however, is the fact that changes in the direction of trade by established businessmen did not go unnoticed. In 1699, when Ben Hornor was of a mind to alter his trade, he first consulted the Preparative Meeting:

> Benjamin Hornor laing before this Meeting his intentions of altering some part of his trade: & keeping Walkfield Markett with cloth; Robert Arthington & Richard Armistead is ordered to discorce him aboute the same, & give advise & consent according as they find the matter.[14]

In response to this request, Robert Arthington and Richard Armistead gave account to the next Preparative Meeting that they 'have received satisfaction aboute his [Hornor] altering part of his trade as formerly mentiond, soe have given consent that he should go on with the same'.[15] Friends seeking advice on 'altering' their way of trading did not always meet with such favourable results. In 1723 when John Thirkell 'acquainted Friends of the Meeting that he thought of altering his trade'[16] five Friends were appointed to look into the matter. According to a minute of the proceeding Meeting, Friends were not convinced that the move would be a wise one:

> Richard Armitstead gave account to this Meeting that he & the other Friends that were ordered met at John Thirkells & discoursed with him about what he proposed in altering his trade and the way he proposed they advised him against, thinking it too hazardous & not suitable for him.[17]

The literature concerned with business failure in the eighteenth and early nineteenth centuries points to a steep increase in failures from about 1750.[18] According to Hoppit, the rise is explained in part by the increased opportunities present in the slowly industrialising economy, coupled with low barriers to entry which low fixed capital requirements allowed. Thus the young and inexperienced were encouraged beyond their abilities to begin concerns. Incoming entrepreneurs in the eighteenth century, as at other times, needed to be aware of their own limitations in making judgements. Overestimation of their business acumen would lower the quality of entrepreneurship. Wrong decisions would be made and confidence undermined leading to withdrawal from the market in an atmosphere of crisis.[19] The Society of Friends, however, was well aware of the impetuosity of youth, and counteracted by internalising judgement of the quality of decision-making by young members intent on business. Friends wishing to set up in business were especially required to seek the consent of the Meeting 'pursuant to an ancient order of this Meeting in the case of young men beginning to trade for themselves'.[20] The proposed undertakings were carefully enquired into, before they met with Friends' approval. John Parker was a case in point. A minute in 1700 recorded that

> John Parker having lade before this Meeting his intentions to set up the clothing trade, saing that his unkles is willing to assist him with wooll & some money; soe this Meeting desires Stephen Elbeck Senior: Robert Arthington & Joshua North to further discorce him therein, giving their advise & consent as in the wisdom of God they see meete, & give an account to the next preparative Meeting.[21]

The appointed Friends reported that they 'have given him [Parker] their advise: & finding [h]is proposalls likely, also consent to set up his said trade'.[22] In 1719, however, Friends were more cautious in the case of Jonathan Watson, 'giving him advice to endeavour to get work for other people when he could, lest by making too much cloth for himself he over run his stock'.[23] Not every proposed venture met with the approval of the Meeting, and Friends were usually, but not always, successful in convincing Members to accept their advice. In 1714, William Pratt acquainted the Meeting; 'that he had a mind to sett up his trade of a broad-clothier'.[24] However, Friends appointed to assess his proposed venture later informed the Meeting that they had spoken with him and advised him 'rather to forbear setting up his trade for some time which he seemed to be willing to'.[25] In 1724, Richard Davison, likewise deferred setting up his trade of a clothier 'for the present', as did Robert Arthington in 1731.[26] Young Friends who attempted to ignore such disciplinary advices found it difficult to avoid censure. After John Atkinson informed the Meeting in 1708 of his design to set up the trade of selling hardware, the Friends appointed were shocked to discover that not only had he begun trading, but that he 'hath overshot himself so (in the trade he entered into without Friends consent) as that they fear he hath not effects to pay his debts withall', Steps were taken against him quickly and firmly, for the minute continued:

> and he appearing at this Meeting was desired to returne people their owne goods which he hath yet remaining, and to pay what moneys he can raise, and to worke at his taylors trade to pay what may still remain.[27]

Although no further minutes concerning new business ventures appear after 1741, reference is made in later minutes to advice of Friends, which show that although the minuting of such matters was discontinued, the rule was still practised. In 1800, for example, the Brighouse Monthly Meeting made the following pronouncement concerning the insolvency of Sarah Steers:

> The women friends inform this meeting that Sarah Steers a young woman of Leeds Meeting who some time ago began shop keeping contrary to the advice of her friends; and who has since been frequently advised to an examination of her affairs, has now become insolvent.[28]

Evidence taken from the minute books of Meetings outside the area is confirmation that there was nothing unusual in the way Leeds and Brighouse Meetings monitored and advised young Friends in business. Bristol Friends, for example, recorded in a minute of 1669 that

> care be taken of such young men that have served out their apprenticeshipp and cannot have their freedom for that they cannot for conscience sake take an oath: that their conditions be looked into and they be incoradged as opertunity shall present from this Meeting . . . 6 Friends are desired to bee assistinge in their advice & otherwise to the young men concern'd as above said.[29]

Philadelphia Monthly Meeting was equally concerned in supporting young Friends entering business, making loans, generally without interest, for setting young men up in trade. In 1713, for example, a young Friend received a loan 'in order for carrying on his trade of candlemaking', and in 1744 another Friend received £10 (to be repaid in twelve months) to buy a stocking weaver's loom.[30]

Moreover, other Meetings were just as strict as Leeds and Brighouse where Friends' business activities met with disapproval. It was shown above how Leeds Friend John Atkinson was compelled to close his hardware shop after his business had been subject to investigation. William Godsalves was similarly dealt with by Lancaster Friends as a minute of 1707 illustrates:

> soon after the last month meeting it did appear that William Godsalves credit was more than his effects would pay for he was prevailed with to shut up

the shop and keep his effects together to pay as farr as it would extras to, which it's feared will fall much short for that he has been very decetfull with Friends.[31]

A Bristol Friend suffered likewise in 1675 when, after enquiry, 'Friends doe advise Peter Hawkins not to sell ale any longer than to dispose of what he hath'.[32] Again, when brothers William and John Hodgetts, members of Stourbridge Preparative Meeting, both left their father in 1773 to go to London 'without his consent and contrary to the advice of Friends', Meeting advised them 'to return home and labour for their parents as they ought'.[33]

Numerous advice and minutes were sent out by Yearly Meeting, stressing the importance of keeping clear and accurate accounts. It is apparent from the minutes that members of the Preparative Meeting were diligent in the oversight of the rule. Although Friends were advised to engage in a regular examination of their affairs, it was not always left to their discretion to do so, as the following entry in 1701 demonstrates:

> Ordered that Robert Arthington & Robert Peart, with what other Friends they are pleased to chuse to themselves doe examine Friends that are traders how they stand, that they goe through the world with a good report, & give account to the next Preparative Meeting what they have done therein.[34]

In seventh month, the appointed Friends reported to the Meeting that 'they hath examnd: into the outward concernes of severall Friends & finds things indifrant well'.[35] Although the task was not completed until tenth month, Friends must have believed the time well spent, for Meeting agreed, 'that a yearly examination be therein'.[36]

Leeds Meeting House was by no means unusual in the close supervision of Friends' business affairs. In 1698 Lancaster Preparative Meeting recorded that:

> Robert Lawson & William Gunson are apoynted to speake to such Friends who its feared is or shortly will be gone into more debt than they will be able to pay and to advise them to clear themselves of debts by such means as the Meeting shall advise otherways that they may be further dealt with.[37]

The following year Lancaster Meeting appointed a committee of weighty Friends to investigate the extent to which local Quakers were 'overcharging themselves in trade etc.'.[38]

Bristol Friends were equally subject to scrutiny as a minute of 1680 illustrates:

> A paper is desired to be proposed against next Meeting, in testemony against publick disorders & particulerly against those who have broaken their promises & engadgments, & run behind hand in their estates, whereby the truth & the profession of it hath manefestly suffered ... That as a prevention of these evills for the future this Meeting may nominate six Friends (at the least) of this Meeting who are desired to take care on the behalfe of the Meeting to admonish & caution all such Friends in such cases, as information shall be given them thereof.[39]

Again, in 1713 an advice from Philadelphia Yearly Meeting required the membership to appoint 'substantial Friends . . . to visit every family amongst us, where they think there is occasion to suspect they are going backward in their worldly estate, and to Enquire and see how things are with them'.[40] Nor was the discipline allowed to relax with time. In 1753 Lancaster Preparative Meeting recorded that five Friends had been appointed 'to have an inspectious eye over Friends in trade and to give advice as they may see occasion'.[41] Croydon Friends recorded in 1782 that the membership should 'frequently examine the state of their affairs, & that such as maybe suspected of any deficiency be duly visited'.[42] Similarly, in 1791 a Monthly Meeting in Birmingham appointed a committee whose duty it was to 'remind Friends of the Yearly Meeting's advice that they should inspect the state of their affairs once a year'.[43] Similar committees were appointed in East and West Devonshire Monthly Meetings in 1797[44] and 1794.[45]

Entries continued to appear regularly, in both the Preparative and Monthly minutes, concerning Friends' inspection into the state of their affairs. Leeds Friends were thus regularly advised in business and this advice was not so much available as compulsory. The minutes do record instances of rebellion, but for the most part Friends appear to have complied, and it is highly likely that culture influenced this compliance. As Casson has commented,

> Many cultural elements are implanted during childhood, with those subjected to similar religious training and secular education within a particular community acquiring broadly similar values and beliefs to which everyone in a group conforms, individual members are often not aware of its influence. This in turn means that they are not naturally critical of these beliefs. This subjective approach to culture is a useful antidote to the view that culture reflects a mystical 'collective will'.[46]

Friends believed that they had a collective responsibility both to help one another to attempt to live up to their professed beliefs, and to protect the Society from disrepute. From a religious perspective, then, the discipline of the Meeting was accepted because it was recognised as ethically sound. After all, as Windsor has argued, there was no point in being a Quaker if the ethics were unacceptable.[47] There is, however, a further important point to be considered in this interaction of business and religion in that Friends must have recognised the advantage which compliance afforded to their business concerns. And here we need to look at credit and creditworthiness.

THE OVERSIGHT OF DEBT

Credit was the life-blood of Britain's industrialisation. Schumpeter has described the 'new combination of means of production, and credit' as 'the fundamental phenomenon of economic development'.[48] In a low liquidity economy with underdeveloped financial institutions, entrepreneurs resorted to credit as a gap-filling medium. The granting of credit, 'the choicest jewel the tradesman is trusted with',[49] was therefore vital to any business undertaking. But the granting of credit involved a judgemental decision made with imperfect knowledge. The decision to extend credit relied on personal experience, or at least a warm recommendation from an intermediary.[50] The close monitoring of business activity within the membership allowed Leeds Friends to improve market knowledge, and advantaged both debtor and creditor alike.

As debtors, Friends were able to have their creditworthiness confirmed by those appointed to examine their accounts. Any reluctance to comply would raise suspicions that all was not well, and therefore put creditworthiness at risk. Likewise, a change of trade might result in loss of creditors' confidence until the new venture proved viable. This might never be achieved if credit was withdrawn. For young and inexperienced Friends starting out, the ability, after Meeting's close enquiry and approval, to promote a business venture as likely to succeed, can only have been invaluable. The intervention of the Preparative Meeting in the business activities of its members reinforced the creditworthiness of those members, lessening the chances of a business starving for want of capital. At the same time, greater confidence in a prospective debtor's ability to repay reduced the perceived risk of business failure through losses in unpaid debt.

Close internal surveillance of business conduct and the availability of a personalised credit network did not mean that Friends in business never failed. To the great distress of the Society, and despite the time and care spent in oversight, Friends were not always successful in avoiding irredeemable debt. Isichei has noted that the 'Records of any city Meeting are full of examples of those who failed'[51] and Leeds minute books are no exception to this. The many entries concerning debt suggest that Friends, in general, had no special flair for business. Nevertheless, an examination of the minutes relating to insolvency reveal that the close internal control exercised by the Meeting in the oversight of debt is of considerable importance to the Quaker success story. Miles has pointed to the West Riding's local attorneys' records as 'a stark reminder of the hazards of lending money on private security'.[52] In a business environment of high risk to creditors, many business failures were the result of losses from unpaid debt. Indeed, before 1850, bankruptcy became increasingly commonplace, afflicting many thousands of businesses and individuals, and through them and their creditors, affecting Britain's economic development in general. The poor state of commercial morality, demonstrated by the widespread existence of fraudulent practices, was both a cause and effect of the law relating to bankruptcy so that credit and confidence, vital to industrial progress, were often undermined.[53] This state of affairs was lamented by contemporaries. Defoe, in his essay on bankruptcy, was critical of the procedure at law[54] but Friends were denied by the rules of the Society from seeking redress from fellow Friends by way of the bankruptcy law. However, it would appear from Defoe that Friends were not much disadvantaged. Indeed, they stood to gain by way of reduced transaction costs. In instances of default, the damage done to creditors was lessened when the debt was, at least in part repaid. Having a debtor thrown into prison might give a creditor the satisfaction of revenge, but was hardly likely to result in satisfaction of the debt. A debtor free to work, and under obligation over time to discharge the debt was, to both creditor and debtor alike, a far healthier prospect. Further, the intervention by law penalised not only the defaulter but also the creditor. Legal fees once discharged against residual assets often left little, if anything, to compensate the unpaid creditor.

Defoe also portrayed vividly the devious and immoral conduct practised by dishonest debtors. Fuelled by his own experiences, he passionately denounced those who took goods fraudulently without means or intent to pay, by secreting assets to avoid their seizure and frequently absconding. Further, the law on bankruptcy, 'tends wholly to the destruction of the [honest] debtor, and yet very little to the advantage of the creditor'.[55] Defoe went on to suggest an alternative procedure in case of failure in business which was remarkably close to that adopted by the Society of Friends. Defoe, although a Dissenter, was not himself a Quaker. However, he clearly recognised the advantage to Friends in business which accrued from the Society's internalisation of the management of debt. Where it was reported to the Leeds Preparative Meeting that a Friend was thought to be unable to discharge his debts, local Friends were appointed to investigate the matter. As in all such cases, if the Friend in question was indeed found to be insolvent, Meeting first concerned itself with righting, as far as possible, the injury which had been done to others. Pratt has noted that bankrupts were disowned, unless honest efforts were made to repay creditors, and Leeds Friends firmly upheld this view.[56] An insolvent Friend was immediately required to relinquish the whole of his assets for the equal benefit of his creditors. When, in 1768, John Horsefall, a Leeds Friend, was found to be unable to discharge his debts, local Friends appointed to investigate the matter informed the Meeting, that they 'understand that he [Horsefall] has given up his effects into the hands of some of his creditors for the use of the whole; they are further desired to see how same is done, and give account to this Meeting'.[57] However, it was almost a year before the matter was concluded satisfactorily, when account was given that Horsefall had 'given up all his effects for the use of his creditors, & that the same have been distributed to most of them & the rest may receive their share when they please to call for it'.[58]

It was often the case that the giving up of the whole of a Friend's assets was not sufficient to discharge the debt. However, this did not release the debtor from his obligation, nor the appointed advisors from their duty. John Horsefall took a year to repay all his creditors, but it often took much longer. Richard Wilkinson became insolvent in 1721, and gave up 'what he hath to his creditors towards paying them'.[59] In 1723, Zacharias Hopkins, one of the original Friends appointed to assist Wilkinson in the matter, informed the Preparative Meeting that 'Richard Wilkinson acquainted him that he had paid some more of his debts, but understanding that severall yet is unpaid, Richard Armitstead & John North are still desired to continue the case about the same.'[60] Towards the end of 1724 account was given that Richard Wilkinson had 'paid so farr of his debts as is believed he is of ability to doe at present, yet he is desired to endeavour to pay the rest as soon as he can'.[61]

The obligation to pay one's debts remained, no matter how long it took. As a minute from Brighouse, the Monthly Meeting to which Leeds belonged, dated 1804 records:

> Brighouse Friends inform us, that Joshua Lees of that place, as appears by minute of this Meeting, dated 12th month 1767, then fell short of paying his just debts, has now fully discharged the same: which account this Meeting receives with much satisfaction.[62]

It is important to bear in mind that whilst Friends belonged to the same religious society, they were not an homogeneous group. As Corley has emphasised, 'first and foremost they were individuals',[63] and some Friends found it more difficult than others to live up to their principles. Meeting, well aware of this human failing, was diligent in the oversight of Friends who were back-sliders. When Joseph Gelder became insolvent in 1756, Meeting was plainly concerned as to his intentions in the matter and three Friends were appointed to visit 'and make proper inquirey into the cause of his failure and how far he has acted agreeable to the advice of Friends in giving up his effects for the payment of his debts'.[64] When the Meeting was later informed that Gelder had 'pretended he had given up all his effects' the same Friends were deputed to visit again and 'advise them to be very punctual in delivering what they have to their creditors'.[65] Either the suspicion had been unfounded, or Gelder had had second thoughts, for a subsequent minute stated that he had been spoken to and 'gave for answer they had not secreted any effects nor has this Meeting any complaint from his creditors'.[66] Where the power of persuasion failed, the threat of disownment might produce the desired result, as in the case of Joshua Hole Junior in 1772:

> Whereas some time since Joshua Hole junior fell short in paying his just debts, & two Friends were then appointed to speak to him & advise him therein who now give account that he has not acted according to their advice, therefore Robert Arthington, John Elam & Samuel Briscoe are desired to speak to him & his wife give them such advise as they think proper & make report to our next Meeting.[67]

Hole responded by sending to Meeting a statement of his accounts which was judged to be unacceptable and so 'the same therefore is returned to him', the bearer being desired to inform him that

> if he does not give the Friends before appointed more full & satisfactory information of his affairs in time to be examined & fully considered before our next Prepar Meeting his case is intended to be laid before the Monthly Meeting.[68]

Hole must have valued his membership above his assets, for the clerk to the Meeting later recorded that

> as he has paid a composition to most of his creditors which they agreed to accept in full of their debt (this Meeting) desires John Armitage & Benjamin Kaye to have his case under their care and see that he pay according to agreement.[69]

Hole was not reported to the Monthly Meeting for his transgression, but was left in no doubt that he must conform if he desired to remain a member of the Society.

A disownment paper drawn up by the Monthly Meeting at Lancaster shows that the same obligation towards creditors was required of Lancaster Friends, as Deliah Jackson learnt to his cost in 1753. Jackson despite the repeated advice of Friends had not only 'absented himself from his creditors' but 'took with him some valuable effects'. For such 'unwarrantable actions' Jackson was disowned.[70] In 1758 Friends of Settle Monthly Meeting had also offered 'repeated and pressing advices' to Thomas Blakey to give up what he had for the benefit of his creditors. However, Blakey had 'so long as is in his power, avoided resigning his all for the equal use of his creditors' and was disowned for his transgression.[71]

That Friends did not tolerate those who refused to accept the discipline is confirmed by the case of Hannah Jepson in 1815. The discipline demanded in case of failure that no preference should be given to any creditor. Friends appointed to visit Jepson, however, reported that she 'signed an instrament which empowered the assignees of one of her creditors to seize the property which she had in her possession'.[72] For this act, Hannah Jepson was disowned. In 1772 Friend Thomas Dean was disowned by Settle Monthly Meeting for the same offence after Meeting learnt that

> he has transgrest the rules of Friends in paying some of his creditors more than the stipulated five shillings in the pound, whilst others have got nothing, & whereby it seems most probable he has rendered himself unable to pay several of them anything or at least the stipulated 5s in the pound.[73]

John Evans was another Friend who was disowned in like circumstances in 1827 after Warwickshire North Monthly Meeting's judgement 'that he has acted in a very unjustifiable manner in giving a preference to one of his creditors to the disadvantage of the rest'.[74] A paper written by the Friends appointed in the case of Isaac Cross, a member of Lancaster Preparative Meeting, illustrates the fact that Friend Cross was yet another offender who had been given repeated advice to make an equal assignment of his property but instead had 'made partial payments' and thus forfeited his membership of the Society.[75]

It was not unusual for a businessman faced with insolvency to abscond leaving his debts unpaid. Although Friends were not immune from this 'unworthy' practice, escape from creditors could prove difficult to accomplish. Whilst Meeting could not prevent Friends in debt from absconding, the minutes show that the national network was a valuable aid in locating the culprits, and sometimes successful in retrieving the situation. In 1815, an insolvent Friend, Samuel Raleigh, left Leeds for Liverpool but did not escape from oversight:

> The Overseers of Leeds Meeting give account, that Samuel Raleigh has fallen short of paying his just debts, and that he has removed to Liverpool: John Broadhead & Samuel Grimshaw are directed to inform Friends of Hardshaw Monthly Meeting thereof, request them to visit him on our behalf, and inform us the result.[76]

Hardshaw Monthly Meeting acted promptly in the matter and a reply was received in time for the next Meeting:

> Your minute dated the 18th of 8th month 1815 respecting the failure of Samuel Raleigh in the payment of his just debts, and his subsequent removal to Liverpool was produced at Hardshaw Monthly Meeting on the 24th, we were appointed by said Monthly Meeting to visit him there upon your behalf & inform you the result – We have accordingly had an interview with him wherein he appeared candid & open; he attributed his failure in a great measure to his own & his wife's long indisposition, by which they were prevented from giving their attention to his business, which it required, & partly to some heavy losses in various articles of his trade; but did not express any concern on account of the loss which his creditors were likely to sustain by his insolvency.[77]

As a result of this communication, Raleigh was disowned.

The same efficient use of the network in extending the Oversight of the Meeting, and the same careful enquiry on behalf of others, are clearly recorded in Monthly Meeting minute books in general. Devonshire House Monthly Meeting, for example, recorded in 1826 that Friends had visited William Ward on behalf of Brighouse Monthly Meeting and it was their belief that 'he does not appear sensible of much delinquency attributing his failure to the circumstances of his creditors refusing to allow him time'. A later minute recorded that Brighouse had forwarded William Ward's disownment paper with a request that Devonshire House Friends deliver it to him.[78] Similarly, in 1791 Grace Church Street Monthly Meeting received a request to visit Nathan Gill on behalf of Lancaster Friends. Those Friends appointed to the case reported that Gill 'declines giving the Meeting further satisfaction respecting his misconduct having he says, done all in his power, to satisfy his injured creditors' and that he would 'make them full compensation if it ever be in his power'. However, the minute went on to state that he was 'not as humble as they would have liked regarding injured creditors'.[79] After receiving this report Gill was sent a certificate of disownment by Lancaster via Grace Church Street Meeting.

The same procedure was followed by Birmingham Friends as a minute of 1793 records:

> Thomas Horne having brought a reproach on our religious society by not fulfilling his engagements, this Meeting requests the Monthly Meeting of Arundel & Chichester (within the compass of which we are informed they now are) to deal with him on our behalf and acquaint us with the result thereof.[80]

The case went no further than this, however, after Chichester informed Birmingham of Friend Horne's decease.

It would be inaccurate to say that every Friend who failed in business dealt with complete honesty towards his creditors. The Leeds Preparative Meeting minutes show that some were hesitant, or even very reluctant to comply with the discipline, and that others did not comply at all. For the most part, however, Meeting's oversight of debt, intended to assist Friends to keep to truth, and to protect the Society from scandal, also acted to serve the creditors' best interests.

It is apparent from the above minutes that the Meeting House did not regard the collective responsibility towards their members and the Society as being limited by locality. Moreover, the minutes reveal the crucial role played by the national Meeting House network in the extension of oversight beyond local boundaries. The minutes with regard to migration are further evidence of the importance of the network in the oversight of Friends. A local Meeting House did not accept newcomers professing to be Friends at face value. Where Friends wished to migrate to an area which lay outside the vicinity of their local Meeting, they were first required to obtain a certificate from the Monthly Meeting. The intention of the certificate was to inform the adoptive Meeting of the newcomer's clearness from any irregularity, and this included clearness from debt. Such was the case in 1710, when Henry Thompson of Armley, acquainted the Preparative Meeting with

> his intention of removing himself to London, & also that if he findeth not busieness there to his satisfaction he intendeth to transport himself into America. So that the representatives from this Meeting may be capable to give the Monthly Meeting account of his clearness from all debts, they with the assistance of William Benson & Gervase Elam are desired to see that all his debts be paid, & that he be clear from other intanglements, as marriage etc., and this Meeting giveth way to Henry to lay his intention before the Monthly Meeting, the said persons appointed finding him clear, not otherwise.[81]

The minutes of Monthly Meetings outside Brighouse are further evidence of the importance that the Society attached to the giving and receiving of certificates of removal in cases of migration. Moreover, clearness from debt was a main concern both in the drafting of these certificates and in their minuting. In 1784, for example, Peel Monthly Meeting received a certificate for a young Friend newly arrived from Carlisle. The Monthly Meeting there had certified that 'he was born of parents in good esteem amongst us, and as he grew up diligently attended our Meetings, being of a sober and orderly conduct' but had also certified that the young man had 'left clear of debt' before 'recommending him to your care and oversight'.[82] In the same way Devonshire House Monthly Meeting recorded in 1787 that a certificate had been brought in from Brighouse Monthly Meeting on behalf of Empson Middleton 'imparting that they do not find, but that he left them clear of debt'.[83]

To give a certificate of clearness, which included clearness from debt, to departing Friends was to give the holder an invaluable reference as to his or her creditworthiness. Crucial to any business venture, proof of creditworthiness in an age of personalised local credit must have been a particularly valuable asset to a Friend attempting to start up in business who was unknown to local traders. At the same time, the extension of oversight could act to remove the creditworthiness of Friends who attempted to avoid the discipline. In 1738, when Joshua North took it upon himself to remove to a new area without a certificate, Meeting clearly felt it had a duty to inform that area's Meeting. North had informed the Meeting of his intention 'to sett up his trade of a linnen weaver & linnen draper' and four Friends were appointed to advise him. When, at the next Meeting, Joshua Siddal gave account of their discovery 'that the young man had begun trade in Bradford, not having a certificate from where he served his apprenticeship the matter referred for him to acquaint Bradford Friends with state thereof'.[84]

Bristol Friends felt the same obligation to acquaint Friends in Ireland in the case of Charles Woodward in 1678. Woodward was clearly out of favour with the Meeting since he had been advised to 'setle here close to his labour, & labour dilligent therein, that thereby he might become more capeable to discharge those debts he had contracted'.[85] From a minute of the next Meeting, however, it is apparent that this advice had been ignored by Friend Woodward:

> This Meeting being informed by William Thield & James Stirrige that Charles Woodward is gon hence intending for Ireland. This Meeting therefore desires Thomas Gouldney (& 4 others) to write a short paper & signe per order of this Meeting, directed to Friends in Ireland & elsewhere to caution them to beware of him.[86]

Similarly, when William Hancock removed to America in 1798 without requesting a certificate, East Devon Monthly Meeting forwarded a copy of the following minute to Philadelphia Monthly Meeting by way of a warning:

> [Hancock] is, we understand by accounts received, settled somewhere in the neighbourhood of Philadelphia. We think it necessary to inform you respecting him, that sometime before his removal, he failed in business, owing to his having unsuccessfully engaged in severall undertakings not only without any capital of his own, but with a considerable debt of his deceased Father's which he engaged to pay in order to support the credit of his family, whereby many individuals were injured in their property, and great reproach was brought on our Holy Profession.

The minute also clearly illustrates the extent to which the Discipline was routinely accepted as a fact of business life within the Society for it continues:

> his case of course became an object of this Meeting's concern and attention, but he being, during the exercise of our labours towards him, unexpectedly affected with a temporary derangment of mind, it was judged expedient to suspend them; and as he left his neighbourhood in this affecting situation and shortly after it pleased Providence to restore him, removed to America, they were never resumed. We therefore refer his case to you for such further extensions of care as may be in the wisdom of Truth appear advisable.[87]

Friend Hancock would, no doubt, have been fully aware that a request for a certificate would not have been forthcoming from the Meeting House, given his insolvent state, as Charles Merrifield, another East Devon Friend, learned to his cost in 1829. Merrifield, intent on removing, requested a certificate for himself and his family from the Meeting House. According to the usual procedure in these circumstances Friends were appointed by the Meeting to make the necessary enquiries before drawing up a certificate. In this case, however, the Friends appointed informed a later Meeting that they had 'found there was some obstruction on account of his not having fulfilled an engagement'. The Friends also reported to the Meeting that despite several interviews with Merrifield they had been unable to prevail upon him to clear the debt. Although further efforts were made by Friends 'with a view to removing the obstruction which appears to exist to issuing a certificate of removal on his behalf',[88] Merrifield persisted in his refusal and was eventually disowned for his conduct. The Meeting, however, did not find the circumstances applicable in the case of Merrifield's wife and children and a certificate of removal was duly prepared by Friends on their behalf.

The Meeting House network thus facilitated the flow of information between localities, at a time when communications in general were poor. The resulting increase in market knowledge can be viewed as an aid to creditworthiness in upright migrant Friends, and also as a means of debt retrieval. At the very least, the system acted as a damage limitation exercise, removing the creditworthiness of suspect Friends by forewarning or disownment.

Quaker family firms were thus advantaged by valuable and exclusive externalities arising from the effectiveness of their supportive network. Collective responsibility for honesty in business led to the internalisation of guidance in good business practice, and improved commercial judgement. Transaction costs were reduced as confidence was increased. Credit flowed more easily, as the following case study will show, expanding business opportunities. Friends could invest with confidence in other Friends, knowing that their concerns were overseen by those whose only vested interests were the good name of the Society, and the desire that Friends 'walked in truth'.

THE STOCKTON AND DARLINGTON RAILWAY COMPANY

There can be few more outstanding examples of the role of external networks in facilitating the foundation and early operation of a successful business than the Stockton and Darlington Railway, the original joint stock pioneer of steam locomotive traction.[89] Dismissed by transport historians as fulfilling little more than a precursory role in the inauguration of the 'Railway Age' after 1830, the Stockton and Darlington Company came to occupy a vital strategic position in the development of the rail network of northern England. Fortuitously located in relation to mineral deposits, it also served as a 'fuel artery' for the expanding metallurgical trades of south Durham and north-east Yorkshire. By the early 1870s Teesside was the most important iron-producing centre in the world, an achievement which had been dependent not only on natural resource endowments and efficient transport services, but also on extensive credit networks focusing on the Stockton and Darlington Company.[90]

The early pre-operational history of the Stockton and Darlington Railway was marked by a long gestation period. Originally conceived in the 1760s as a canal project for the localised distribution of coal, it was dependent for its eventual inauguration in 1821 on a combination of technical change, entrepreneurial foresight, and effective credit networks. It is well known that the initial technological breakthrough was provided by the steam locomotive, especially as developed by George Stephenson. It is equally celebrated that the railway was dependent for its entrepreneurial leadership and financing on members of the Society of Friends. Quaker involvement was epitomised by the interrelated Pease and Backhouse families of Darlington, the former with involvement in the woollen trade, and the latter presiding over a banking partnership with its own note issue. As a public joint stock company with a capital in excess of £100,000 the Stockton and Darlington Railway demanded a broad base of financial support and it was in anticipation of a shortfall of funding prior to their application for parliamentary sanction that the leading Quaker promoters resorted to their own financial network. It was this that enabled the subscription list to be closed at the end of December 1818. Of the 1,209 shares of 100 each, the majority were subscribed locally. Thus the Backhouses were prepared to invest £20,000 and the Peases £6,200. A further large subscription came from the Quaker, Benjamin Flounders of Yarm. In total, two-thirds of the subscriptions were from local sources, and in this respect the project was comparable with canals and other succeeding railway companies.[91] The remaining third was obtained from extra-regional sources, principally from within the Society of Friends. Thus the Gurney banking partnership of Norwich, related by marriage to the Backhouses and subsequently to the Peases, was committed to the extent of £20,000, whilst Thomas Richardson of London, Quaker bill-broker and cousin of Edward Pease, was prepared to invest £10,000. Further large subscriptions were forthcoming from the Quaker community of Whitby, some of whose members enjoyed filial ties with their co-religionists in Darlington. As Edward Pease's son, Joseph, stated to Quaker cousins in Leeds on the day the subscription list was closed, the scheme for 'a Darlington Railway' was 'so popular amongst Friends that about £80,000 stands in the name of the members of our Society'.[92]

That the original Quaker promoters could not rely on local sources of finance alone was recognised formally in the Stockton and Darlington Company's prospectus which provided for the appointment of a Quaker-dominated committee of bankers and financiers in London charged with the task of obtaining extra subscriptions. This extensive use of the Quaker financial network meant that in the context of subsequent railway promotions the Stockton and Darlington project was a special case. The customary practice was followed of obtaining sub-scriptions from interests in trade, commerce and banking, yet this was a scheme for a public joint stock company which in important respects replicated a close family partnership. Quaker financiers and relations in London, Norwich and Leeds were prepared to invest in the unfamiliar venture of a public railway because the risks were mitigated by the commitment of their Quaker 'cousins'. The investment of the Gurneys and Thomas Richardson was an indication of the confidence that they placed in the sound judgement of their Darlington relatives. It is reasonable to presume that Quakers outside the north-east of England had little independent means of evaluating the commercial prospects of the Stockton and Darlington project. As a transport innovation it was unprecedented and geographically remote. But they did know that their northern 'cousins' were birthright members of the Society of Friends with unimpeachable records of honesty and scrupulousness in business dealings. The entrepreneurial leader, Edward Pease, was well known as a deeply conservative, evangelical Quaker, a regular attender at the London Yearly Meeting and observer of a frugal personal lifestyle. Moreover, it is salutary to note that the principal reason for Jonathan Backhouse's resignation as treasurer to the Stockton and Darlington Railway in 1833 was his wish to embark upon full-time ministry for the Society.

Confirmation of the extensive Quaker commitment to the Stockton and Darlington Railway is provided by the evolving pattern of share ownership in the company following its incorporation in 1821. By the end of 1822 there were 69 proprietors who, collectively, owned 463 of the individual shares valued at £100. The leading shareholders, owning five or more shares are indicated in Table 7.1

The Quaker and banking influence is unmistakable and this feature of the

Table 7.1 Principal shareholders in the Stockton and Darlington Railway Company, December 1822

Proprietor	No. of shares
*Jonathan Backhouse (banker, Darlington)	50
*John Backhouse (banker, Darlington)	20
John Baxter (Darlington)	10
*Henry Birkbeck (banker, Lymm, Norfolk)	20
Richard Blanchard (Esquire, Northallerton)	10
Robert Chaloner (Esquire, York)	10
*Joseph Gurney (banker, Norwich)	50
*Joseph John Gurney (banker, Norwich)	20
*John Kitching (merchant, Stamford Hill, Middlesex)	16
*William Leather (banker, Wakefield)	15
Thomas Meynell (Esquire, Yarm)	20
Richard Miles (timber merchant, Yarm)	5
Annie Peacock (spinster, Danby Hill, York)	10
*Edward Pease (merchant, Darlington)	30
*Joseph Pease Jr (merchant, Darlington)	5
Leonard Raisbeck (Esquire, Stockton)	15
*Thomas Richardson (bill-broker, Stamford Hill)	50
*William Skinner (banker, Stockton)	5
*William Skinner Jr (banker, Stockton)	5

Note: * denotes Quakers.

Source: PRO, RAIL 667/3, Stockton and Darlington Railway Management Committee Minutes, 13 Dec. 1822.

shareholding list was reinforced in subsequent years. By July 1823, when the number of shares had risen to 537, Edward Pease had increased his holding to 35 shares, Thomas Richardson to 55, and John Kitching to 22.[93] Table 7.2 also illustrates several substantial new holdings, all of them from within the Society of Friends:

Table 7.2 New share holders in the Stockton and Darlington Railway Company, July 1823

Proprietor	No. of shares
*Edward Backhouse (banker, Sunderland)	
*Robert Barclay (banker, Lombard Street)	20 (collective holding)
*Joseph John Gurney (banker, Norwich)	
*Robert Barclay (banker, Lombard Street)	10
*Simon Martin and family (banker's clerk, Norwich)	5
*George Newman (leather seller, Godalming)	10
*Henry Newman (leather seller, Bermondsey)	26
*John Newman (leather seller, Worcester)	6
Josiah Newman (leather seller, Ross, Hertfordshire)	5
*Thomas Newman (leather seller, Bermondsey)	10

Note: * denotes Quakers.

Source: PRO, RAIL 667/3, Stockton and Darlington Railway Management Committee Minutes, 25 Jul. 1823.

After this date there were few shareholdings of note before the opening of the railway in September 1825, the exceptions being those of David Bevan, Quaker banker of Lombard Street (10 shares), George Stacey, chemist of London (8 shares) and, most significant of all in view of an impending marital alliance with the Gurneys, the acquisition of a further 45 shares by members of the Pease family.[94]

The pattern of shareholding was not, however, the only indication of Quaker financial commitment. Recent research has highlighted the Stockton and Darlington Company's borrowing record during the early critical phases of its operations after 1825, when liquidity problems were acute in the face of the non-completion of the branch lines to collieries and deep uncertainties concerning the reliability of locomotive traction.[95] By 1830 these difficulties had been resolved, but only because the company had been sustained financially by the Quaker credit network. For example, the Gurney banking partnership agreed to the postponement of the repayment of debts incurred in 1824. According to an agreement negotiated in January 1827, the outstanding sum was to be redeemed in four equal instalments in the period July 1827 to January 1829. It was also agreed that a further £20,000 borrowed from Overend, Gurney and Co. should be repaid in two instalments in January and July 1828.

The subsequent history of the Stockton and Darlington Railway provides further ample evidence of the effectiveness of Quaker financial networks, notably in relation to the founding and industrial development of Middlesbrough and the expansion of the Stockton and Darlington Company itself. Its status as a family firm was confirmed by the Peases' continuing role as the dominant entrepreneurial force throughout its independent existence.[96] No member of the family ever served as chairman of the company or of any associated undertaking. This can only have been the result of deliberate policy: why pursue the shadow of titular office when the substance of power was guaranteed by Quaker wealth and finance?

CONCLUSION

It is conventional to regard the latter half of the eighteenth century as the period when Quaker financial networks were most active. The preceding section has demonstrated that in the north-east of England such networks extended well into the nineteenth century in a general context of improving institutional arrangements for capital formation. What emerged on Teesside after 1820 was not only a new and geographically compact metallurgical district with excellent transport facilities along the 'fuel artery' of the Stockton and Darlington Railway, but also a group of firms linked together by Quaker finance and the inevitable ties of kinship which had long been a permanent feature of the Society of Friends. For the Stockton and Darlington Company in particular, the effect of personalised networks was to extend the boundaries of the firm in ways which contributed not only to its own growth and stability but also to regional economic growth and structural diversification. As a commercial enterprise, therefore, it was unusually advantaged and its experience in this respect provides impressive confirmation of the extent to which successful entrepreneurship rested on the reduction of transaction costs via access to external networks. So too in the case of the Leeds Preparative Meeting and the Brighouse Monthly Meeting, their records provide valuable insights into the world of the Quaker businessman. Moreover, evidence from the minutes of Meetings outside the area confirms that there was nothing unusual in the way that Leeds and Brighouse Meetings monitored and advised Friends in business. As the chapter has demonstrated, Friends intent on business pursuits were obliged to seek the advice and approval of their fellow Quakers. But far from this acting as a stultifying influence on aspirant entrepreneurship, it could open the door to a sophisticated credit network as an essential means of commercial survival in the eighteenth and early nineteenth centuries. The strength of the network was reinforced by collective adherence to the Quaker code of conduct as set forth in the London Yearly Meeting advices, together with extensive intermarriage, giving access to geographically dispersed pools of capital. As the relevant records show, however, the network was also buttressed strongly by a system of internal communications which served to limit the adverse consequences for commercial confidence and stability of irredeemable debt.

NOTES

1 M. Miles, 'The Money Market in the Early Industrial Revolution: The Evidence from West Riding Attorneys c1750–1800', *Business History* 23: 140, (1981).

2 S. Marriner, 'English Bankruptcy Records and Statistics before 1850', *Economic History Review* 2nd series, 33: 358, (1980).

3 M. Casson, 'Entrepreneurship and Business Culture', in J. Brown, and M. B. Rose (eds), *Entrepreneurship, Networks and Modern Business* (Manchester, 1993), p. 30.

4 R. H. Coase, 'The Nature of the Firm', *Economica* 4: 386–405, (1937).

5 See, for example, O. E. Williamson, *The Economic Institutions of Capitalism: Firms, Markets, Relational Contracting* (New York, 1985), and P. J. Buckley and M. C. Casson, *The Economic Theory of the Multinational Enterprise* (London, 1985).

6 A. D. Chandler, *Scale and Scope: The Dynamics of Industrial Capitalism* (Cambridge, MA, 1990), p. 38.
7 Casson, 'Entrepreneurship and Business Culture', p. 43.
8 Arthur Raistrick, *Quakers in Science and Industry* (Newton Abbot, 1968), pp. 34, 45, 335.
9 See Pat Hudson, *The Genesis of Industrial Capital: A Study of the West Riding Wool Textile Industry c. 1750–1850* (Cambridge, 1986); Sidney Pollard, 'Fixed Capital in the Industrial Revolution in Britain', *Journal of Economic History* 24: 299–314 (1964).
10 On the interrelatedness of Quaker families see, for example, Verity Anderson, *Friends and Relations: Three Centuries of Quaker Families* (London,1980) and R. L. Brett (ed.), *Barclay Fox's Journal* (London, 1979). Quaker banking networks are analysed in L. S. Pressnell, *Country Banking in the Industrial Revolution* (London, 1956).
11 J. L. Nickalls (ed.), *Journal of George Fox* (London, 1986), pp. 37–8.
12 J. Hoppit, *Risk and Failure in English Business 1700–1800* (Cambridge, 1987), p. 16.
13 Raistrick, *Quakers in Science and Industry*, p. 28.
14 Leeds University Library Special Collections (hereafter LULSC), Leeds Preparative Meeting Minutes (hereafter LPMM), E1, p. 71.
15 LULSC, LPMM, E1, p. 72.
16 LULSC, LPMM, E2, p. 83.
17 Ibid.
18 See, for example, Hoppit, *Risk and Failure*, pp. 49–51; S. Marriner, 'English Bankruptcy Records', *passim*.
19 J. A. Schumpeter, *Business Cycles: A Theoretical, Historical and Statistical Analysis of the Capitalist Process*, cited in Casson, 'Entrepreneurship and Business Culture', p. 47.
20 LULSC, LPMM, E2, p. 160.
21 LULSC, LPMM, E1, p. 80.
22 Ibid., p. 82.
23 LULSC, LPMM, E2, p. 54.
24 Ibid., p. 26.
25 Ibid.
26 Ibid., p. 92; p. 136.
27 LULSC, LPMM, E1, p. 216.
28 LULSC, Brighouse Monthly Meeting Minutes (hereafter BMMM), R1, p. 246.
29 R. Mortimer (ed.), *Minute Book of the Men's Meeting of the Society of Friends in Bristol, 1667–1686* (Bristol, 1971) p. 21.
30 F. B. Tolles, *Meeting House and Counting House: The Quaker Merchants of Colonial Philadelphia 1682–1763* (New York: 1963), p. 59.
31 Lancashire Record Office (hereafter LRO), Preparative Meeting Minutes Lancaster (hereafter PMML), FRL, 2Axxvii, p. 115.
32 R. Mortimer, *Minute Book of the Men's Meeting*, p. 98.
33 Friends Meeting House Birmingham (hereafter FMHB), Stourbridge Preparative Meeting Minutes (hereafter SPMM), 170/171.
34 LULSC, LPMM, E1, p. 98.
35 Ibid., p. 102.
36 Ibid., p. 111.
37 LRO, PMML, FRL2Axxvii, p. 98.
38 M. Mullett, *Radical Religious Movements in Early Modern Europe* (London, 1980), p. 42.
39 R. Mortimer, *Minute Book of the Men's Meeting*, p. 153.
40 F. B. Tolles, *Meeting House and Counting House*, p. 73.
41 LRO PMMML, FRL,2Axxvii, p. 46b.
42 Friends House Library London (hereafter FHLL), Croydon Preparative Meeting Minutes (hereafter CPMM), 11c, p. 8.

43 FMHB, Warwickshire North Monthly Meeting Minutes (hereafter WNMMM), 11/23.
44 East Devon Record Office (hereafter EDRO), East Devon Monthly Meeting Minutes (hereafter EDMMM), 874D/M40, p. 200.
45 West Devon Record Office (hereafter WDRO), West Devon Monthly Meeting Minutes (hereafter WDMMM), 1444/7/1, p. 58.
46 Casson, 'Entrepreneurship and Business Culture', p. 40.
47 D. B. Windsor, *Quaker Enterprise: Friends in Business* (London, 1980), p. 168.
48 J. A. Schumpeter, *The Theory of Economic Development: An Enquiry into Profits, Capital, Credit, Interest and the Business Cycle* (Cambridge, MA, 1934), p. 74.
49 D. Defoe, *Complete English Tradesman*, vols 1–2, (New York, 1889), p. 274.
50 Hoppit, *Risk and Failure*, p. 163.
51 E. Isichei, *Victorian Quakers* (London, 1970), p. 486.
52 Miles, 'The Money Market', p. 139.
53 Marriner, 'English Bankruptcy', p. 366.
54 D. Defoe, 'Of Bankrupts', in H. Morley (ed.), *The Earlier Life and Works of Daniel Defoe* (London, 1889), pp. 110–23.
55 Ibid., p. 110.
56 David H. Pratt, *English Quakers and the First Industrial Revolution: A Study of the Quaker Community in Four Industrial Counties – Lancashire, York, Warwick and Gloucester, 1750–1830* (London, 1985).p. 29.
57 LULSC, LPMM, E3, p. 98.
58 Ibid., p. 107.
59 LULSC, LPMM, E2, pp. 67–8.
60 Ibid., p. 84.
61 Ibid., p. 93.
62 LULSC, BMMM, R2, pp. 9–10.
63 T. A. B. Corley, 'How Quakers Coped with Business Success: Quaker Industrialists 1860–1914', in D. Jeremy (ed), *Business and Religion in Britain* (Aldershot, 1988), p. 169.
64 LULSC, LPMM, E3, p. 27.
65 Ibid., p. 28.
66 Ibid.
67 Ibid., p. 131.
68 Ibid., p. 133.
69 Ibid., p. 134.
70 LRO, FRL, 2Bii.
71 LULSC, Settle Monthly Meeting Minutes (hereafter SMMM), H4, pp. 257–8.
72 LULSC, BMMM, R3, p. 205.
73 LULSC, SMMM, H6, p. 135.
74 FMHB, WNMMM, 15/27.
75 LRO, FRL 2BV8.
76 LULSC, BMMM, R3, p. 217.
77 Ibid., p. 221.
78 FHLL, Devonshire House Monthly Meeting Minutes (hereafter DHMMM), 11/b/2. p. 383.
79 FHLL, Gracechurch Street Monthly Meeting Minutes (hereafter GSMMM), 11/b/1.
80 FMHB, WNMMM, 11/23.
81 LULSC, LPMM, E1, p. 242.
82 FHLL, Peel Monthly Meeting Minutes (hereafter PMMM), 11/b/5, p. 2.
83 FHLL, DHMMM, 11/b/2, p. 6.
84 LULSC, LPMM, E2, p. 175.
85 R. Mortimer, *Minute Book of the Men's Meeting*, p. 127.
86 Ibid.
87 EDRO, EDMMM, 874D/M40, pp. 224–5.

88 EDRO, EDMMM, 874D/M42, p. 25.
89 This section is based in part on M. W. Kirby, *The Origins of Railway Enterprise: the Stockton and Darlington Railway, 1821–1863* (Cambridge, 1994).
90 I. Bullock, 'The Origins of Economic Growth on Teesside, 1851–81', *Northern History* 9: 79–95 (1974).
91 See, for example, J. R. Ward, *The Finance of Canal Building in Eighteenth-Century England* (London, 1974); S. A. Broadbridge, 'The Sources of Railway Share Capital', in M. C. Reed (ed.) *Railways in the Victorian Economy: Studies in Finance and Growth* (Newton Abbot,1969), pp. 184–211.
92 Durham County Record Office, Pease Family Papers, U418e PEA, 46/19, Joseph Pease Jnr. to W. Aldam and T. B. Pease, 26 Dec. 1818.
93 Public Record Office (hereafter PRO), RAIL 667/3, Stockton and Darlington Railway Company Management Committee Minutes, 25 Jul. 1823.
94 Ibid.
95 Kirby, 'Quakerism', pp. 115–18. PRO, RAIL 667/3, Stockton and Darlington Railway Company Management Committee Minutes, 26 Jan. 1827.
96 Kirby, 'Quakerism', pp. 115–21. See also M. W. Kirby, *Men of Business and Politics: The Rise and Fall of the Quaker Pease Dynasty of North-East England, 1700–1943* (London, 1984).

8   Changing Quaker attitudes to wealth, 1690–1950

T. A. B. Corley

WESLEY'S CONDEMNATION OF RICHES

Towards the end of his long life John Wesley (1703–91), the founder of Methodism, was increasingly concerned about those of his flock who were accumulating wealth. Earlier, he had pointed out fairly gently that it was not good enough for the rich to use part of their money for charitable purposes; rather, he urged, 'gain all you can, save all you can, give all you can'. The rich were no more than stewards of their material possessions, and must make sacrifices. Otherwise, they would fall into the sins of covetousness and of sensual pleasures associated with wealth.

Wesley's advice on this topic became more insistent in his final decade. By then, a number of Methodist businessmen had followed his injunctions about thrift and hard work and found themselves with comfortable fortunes; they regarded it as their right to derive pleasure from the rewards of their labours. His sermon of 1780, 'On the Danger of Riches', issued a categorical warning that Christ's ban on the laying up of treasures on earth was as absolute as that on adultery or murder. They could keep back only the necessities and conveniences of life, reasonable provision for dependants after their death, working capital and just enough over to avoid falling into debt. By 1788, he was castigating wealth as a mortal danger to the soul and a hindrance to entry into the kingdom of heaven. Methodists had a stark choice between enjoying affluence in this life and through frugality postponing happiness to the next world.[1]

Wesley practised what he preached, and gave away as much as £30,000 in all from the profits of his very successful publishing business. However, this example, and the uncompromising messages in his sermons, appear to have had little effect on his wealthy adherents. In one of his last sermons (1790), he spoke almost despairingly about their failure to heed his warnings on this subject. He doubted if over the past half-century he had convinced as many as fifty 'misers' about the sin of covetousness.

Economic historians, such as R. H. Tawney, have tended to dismiss as futile Wesley's efforts to publicise the evils of excessive wealth-holding, as no more than 'conspicuous exceptions' to the prevalent timid religious atmosphere of 'morality tempered by prudence', one 'softened on occasion by a rather sentimental compassion for inferiors'.[2] For the purpose of the present enquiry, the stand taken by Wesley provides a benchmark against which to judge the attitudes of Quakers to this topic. However, a further dimension can be provided by seeing how secular, or non-religious, views on wealth evolved over the centuries. This is done in the following section, before the Quaker response is fully discussed.

EMERGING VIEWS OF ECONOMISTS ON WEALTH

The editor of Wesley's sermons has identified one barrier to rich Methodists after the mid-1770s heeding his denunciation of wealth: namely, the influence of Adam Smith's *Wealth of Nations*, published in 1776. Indeed, Wesley may have had Smith in mind (without mentioning him by name) when he stated, not entirely accurately, that no previous opinion-makers had to his knowledge denounced riches.[3] In fact, Smith had written both as a philosopher and as an economist, and he did not argue purely from the standpoint of self-interest. In helping to turn economics into a rigorous discipline in its own right, he adopted a more subtle approach.

Until nearly the end of the eighteenth century, the world of learning had been broadly divided into natural or physical sciences, on the one hand, and 'unscientific' subjects such as moral and political philosophy, on the other. The emerging social sciences, most notably economics, were seeking patterns into which the individual activities of people fell, and from which laws, or tendencies, could be deduced. While, of course, not being capable of being tested in a laboratory, those laws had scientific characteristics, and were also value-free in the sense of not depending on any religious principles such as predestination or the divine will.[4]

To demonstrate how scientific laws operated in human societies, Adam Smith used the concept of the invisible hand. Even though all individuals in an economy might be pursuing their selfish ends, this invisible hand ensured that all their actions worked themselves out for the benefit of everyone. Present-day economists show that Smith was merely describing the operations of the fully competitive and flexible market, with its in-built automatic equilibrating mechanism.[5]

Properly read, once his qualifications about harmony, benevolence and the natural law have been taken into account, Smith's work is seen not to have condoned selfishness as such or wealth for its own sake. In an earlier philosophical treatise, *The Theory of Moral Sentiments* (1759), he maintained that 'the great and most universal cause of the corruption of our moral sentiments' was 'the disposition to admire the rich and powerful and despise the poor'.[6] However, in *The Wealth of Nations* he was little interested in the rich, but saw the entrepreneur's goal as the accumulation of capital; he castigated merchants not because they were wealthy but because collectively they reckoned to conspire against the economic interests of other groups. He approved of the state taking action to safeguard property rights, and as a principle of taxation ranked equity above the ability to pay.

However, seventy years later John Stuart Mill, in his *Principles of Political*

Economy (1848), felt it desirable to see the gap between the rich and the poor narrowed. The existing system of private property could be fundamentally altered through the exercise of the human will, for example, by taxing unearned fortunes more heavily than those built up by 'industry and economy'. Yet until such radical changes eventually took place, the iron laws of Ricardian economics would continue to operate, with all the accompanying drift towards inegalitarianism.[7]

Then in 1890, Alfred Marshall took the argument a stage further in his *Principles of Economics*. Originally a mathematician, he had become an economist in order to understand the phenomenon of poverty, and saw current inequalities of wealth as needlessly great. 'The drift of economic science during many generations has been with increasing force towards the belief that there is no real necessity, and therefore no moral justification for extreme poverty side by side with great wealth.' Here, then, was 'a serious flaw in our economic organization'. Also in 1890, he told the British Association that taxes should be levied on the rich; even though entrepreneurs were wealth-earners, depriving them of some wealth need not seriously check the overall accumulation of capital.[8]

Marshall's outspoken views chimed in with the policies of later British governments in introducing or increasing taxes on the rich. In 1848, as in 1890, the standard rate of income tax was no higher than 3p in the £, but by 1938 had risen to 25p, while a series of allowances at the lower range and additions such as the supertax higher up the scale had gone some way towards making it a progressive tax. As to wealth, the graduated estate duty of 1894 represented a more or less effective impost on capital, successive increases in its rate by 1938 raising the yield nearly ninefold. The bitter and protracted battles between the Liberal Government and the House of Lords from 1909 onwards show clearly how the state's employment of fiscal measures for redistribution purposes was beginning to bite among the wealthy.

Thus, by the early twentieth century, the previously implicit assumption that the distribution of income and wealth in Britain was more or less 'appropriate' had given way to the need for relatively heavy taxes on the wealthy. One economist who did speak up for them was John Maynard Keynes in 1919, on the grounds of their having been the creators of capitalism over the past century. Europe, he wrote, had been 'so organized socially and economically as to secure the maximum accumulation of capital', most of which passed into the hands of those least likely to consume it. He continued,

> The new rich of the nineteenth century were not brought up to large expenditures, and preferred the power which investment gave them to the pleasures of immediate consumption. In fact, it was precisely the inequality of the distribution of wealth which made possible these vast accumulations of fixed wealth and of capital improvements which distinguished that age from all others.

Keynes saw in this state of affairs the main rationale of the capitalist system.

> If the rich had spent their new wealth on their own enjoyment, the world would long ago have found such a regime intolerable. But like bees they saved and

accumulated, not less to the advantage of the whole community because they themselves had narrower ends in prospect.[9]

In his *General Theory* of 1936, Keynes stated, 'I believe that there is social and psychological justification for significant inequalities of income and wealth', although admittedly not such wide disparities as then existed.[10] Keynes thus posed the dilemma over wealth in capitalist societies, that unless entrepreneurs are permitted to retain (most of) the fruits of their enterprise, they will not come forward in the first place, or at least not use their talents to the full. On the other hand, in 1958 J. K. Galbraith, as a critic, specifically identified the three basic attractions of wealth: first, 'the satisfaction in the power with which it endows the individual'; second, 'the physical possession of the things which money can buy', and third, 'the distinction or esteem that accrue to the rich man as a result of his wealth'.[11] Clearly, the second or financial aspect is the one that would be easiest to control. Since exhortation from outside seems of little value, the apparatus of the state is the only effective way of curbing personal riches, by taxation and/or by direct action, such as curbing monopolistic practices.

Nowadays, economists working in the field of the public economy – the former public finance – regard the state, or the public sector, as having certain economic functions. A key function is to optimise the distribution of income and wealth, although in some societies a drive for greater economic efficiency has tended to sideline this goal. Adam Smith's invisible hand, or the present-day unfettered market, allows the rich to get richer, usually at the expense of the poor. To the extent that such inequality is deemed to be socially and economically harmful, the state should be required to correct this 'market failure'.[12]

To sum up the argument so far, John Wesley may seem nowadays to have been too single-minded in his invectives against wealth. Most firms that grew rapidly during the Industrial Revolution needed above all ample working capital; perhaps many Methodist enterprises failed to survive through their assets being curtailed. Certainly, the number of successful Methodist businessmen in that era was far smaller, in relation to the denomination's size, than that of the Quakers or Unitarians. With the above background it is now possible to examine how far Quakers were able to reconcile their principles with the gaining and holding of wealth by many adherents.

THE QUAKERS AND WEALTH, TO 1895

Quakers, or members of the Society of Friends, were not particularly numerous in Britain, totalling between 14,000 and 16,000 in 1850, or roughly one in 2,000 of the UK population, then 27 million. By 1950 they were some 20,000 out of a population of 50 million. Yet during the eighteenth and nineteenth centuries there was a disproportionately large number of Quaker entrepreneurs. Various reasons have been given for this phenomenon.

The Quaker educational system, for boys, was both practical and business-orientated; members were debarred from the professions for their refusal to swear oaths, and in families the virtues of hard work and pertinacity were instilled from a tender age. Just as importantly, the ramifications of the 'Quaker Counsinhood' were valuable in facilitating, say, the raising of capital and the dissemination of useful business knowledge. Reckless trading and bankruptcy were penalised by disownment, and Quakerly insistence on goods being of high quality and sold at fair prices attracted consumers in an era of steadily increasing disposable incomes.[13]

Unlike most other Christian denominations, Quakers had no laws or rules imposed from outside. Instead, they regarded the priesthood as something held in common with all believers, who through their faith enjoyed the spiritual experience of direct contact with God. There was no regular recited form of worship, the emphasis being on stillness to allow the inner light – which came from the Holy Spirit – to be felt.

To foster the ethos of Quakerism, the Society's ultimate decision-making body, the Yearly Meeting, drew up Queries to be answered in writing each year by local Monthly Meetings, the answers being summarised by the regional Quarterly Meetings. On the basis of these answers, the Yearly Meeting often sent out to these meetings 'counsel', which in 1738 was codified under heads such as 'Covetousness' and 'Trade' in a volume of *Christian and Brotherly Advices*, revised roughly once a generation. A complementary set of General Advices, issued from 1791 onwards, came to be read at Sunday meetings for worship. Strict integrity in commercial transactions was enjoined, and the perils of striving after money for its own sake emphasised. The 1883 General Advices gave reminders that 'we must account for the mode of acquiring, as well as for the manner of using, and finally disposing of our possessions'. Other advices warned against becoming 'entangled with the cares of this world' as well as against the 'snare of accumulating wealth'. They thus counselled 'manifesting Christian moderation and contentment in all things'.[14]

The Yearly Meeting's counsel echoed the writings of the Society's founder, George Fox (1624–91), who stated that the holding of wealth tended seriously to dim the inner light. In 1690 he deplored the practice of bringing up some young people in fashionable and worldly ways, because parental indulgence made them 'brittle, peevish, fitful spirits that will not abide heavenly doctrine, admonitions, exhortations and reproofs of the Holy Ghost', or the inner voice of a properly trained conscience. As he admonished some Friends in the ministry travelling to America, 'Have a care to keep down that greedy, earthly mind, that raveneth and coveteth after the riches and things of the world, lest ye fall into the low region . . . and so lose the Kingdom of God'.[15]

Like the Society he founded, Fox did not go as far as Wesley in a blanket condemnation of wealth. The affluent could set an example to others if they lived simply and were generous in their philanthropy; otherwise the guidance of the Holy Spirit would be crowded out by preoccupation with 'riches and the things of the world'. Hence a distinction grew up between plain and gay (or worldly) Quakers, according to their manner of life and especially the recreations they pursued; dancing and theatre-going were severely frowned on. Friends were then a sect that largely lived apart from the world, having their own distinctive forms of dress and of speech, exclusive in being debarred from marrying outside (under penalty of disownment) until fairly late in the nineteenth century.[16] To the plain members who implicitly followed the advices, therefore, the ostentations associated with riches were particularly abhorrent.

Some private letters or diaries of successful businessmen may be quoted on this issue. The Liverpool merchant, James Cropper (1773–1840), in 1827 reminded his two young partners that power and responsibility could not be separated, saying:

> Too many are looking on wealth and [financial] independence as the road to pleasure and enjoyments; now if we consider these the gifts of an all-bounteous Creator who is no respecter of persons and who bestows his gifts in greater or less abundance on particular individuals, we shall be satisfied that they are all in trust and for the good of the whole Human family . . . Let those to whom Riches are intrusted humbl[y] endeavour to do their duty and then trust in the Mercy and Goodness of God.[17]

A more familiar and pithy observation is by the railway magnate Edward Pease (1767–1858), who in 1844 wrote in his diary, 'The accumulation of wealth in every family known to me in our Society carries away from the purity of our principles, adds toil and care to life and greatly endangers the possession of heaven at last.'[18] The corn merchant, Joseph Sturge (1796–1859), often aired this topic in his correspondence. To a nephew he wrote, 'Surplus wealth brings always increased temptations, and of course increased responsibility, to those who wish rightly to use it.' And again,

> One of the things which has struck me most forcibly with regard to wealth, is the curse it often proves to children . . . If I want any young person to help me in any benevolent or religious object, . . . the children of the rich, too often, will not only do nothing themselves, but like 'the dog in the manger', try to obstruct those who do.[19]

These reflections indicate how deeply the question of wealth was exercising the conscience of thoughtful Quakers. Others concerned themselves with the associated problem of poverty, most notably Joseph Rowntree (1836–1925) in the early 1860s. Having estimated the number of the poor in Britain as 1 million out of 29 millions, Rowntree attempted to establish a link between poverty and crime. He deemed charitable works to be inadequate substitutes for more wide-ranging policies; in a neat epigram, he insisted that charity 'creates much of the misery which it relieves, but does not relieve all the misery it creates'. He denounced the state, and the Church of England as its poodle, for tenaciously maintaining vested interests that blocked radical progress on the condition of the poor. Yet when preparing to speak on this issue to Quaker audiences, he was told that some of his remarks were too strong for 'weak brethren'. That opinion was given by the chocolate manufacturer Joseph Storrs Fry (1826–1913), a leading figure in the Yearly Meeting, who preferred not to see things stirred up.[20]

Indeed, between about 1860 and 1910, when many of its most influential members were businessmen, the Yearly Meeting was unable, and perhaps unwilling, to face the social problems that were all too evident in the economy as a whole. These problems intensified in the lengthy period of the 'great depression' from the early 1870s almost until the end of the century: a time when the wide disparity between rich and poor was for the first time being charted with any precision. The parliamentary *Return of Owners of Land* in 1874 was collated and extended by John Bateman in *The Great Landowners of Great Britain and Ireland* (1876). As to the poor, the non-Quaker Charles Booth revealed by statistical means both the extent and the types of poverty in his survey of London, undertaken in 1889: techniques followed by Joseph Rowntree's son Benjamin Seebohm in his *Poverty: A Study of Town Life* (1901), which covered the city of York.[21]

These uncomfortable findings took some time to receive attention in the Yearly Meeting. In 1883, its members offered no tangible succour to the poor when they pronounced that it was the Heavenly Father's will that all his children should be rich in faith. The meeting was then dominated by a group of evangelical Quakers with individualistic, theological and inward-looking views. Its conclusions were not subject to voting, and the 'sense of the meeting', intended to reach a position of unity rather than unanimity, could only act as a drag on change of any kind.

Even so, a new spirit was about in the Society, which in time led to serious debates on social questions. An important prelude had been the setting up of the Home Mission Committee in 1882, with the task of carrying the faith to the many in Britain who had no direct contact with organised religion. This practical experience of what later became known as 'outreaching' brought home to that Committee that multiplicity of the country's social problems. Thanks to its efforts, the 1895 Yearly Meeting authorised the holding of a conference at Manchester to discuss in broad terms Quakerism's role in the modern world.

The Manchester Conference of 1895 put social issues firmly on the Quaker agenda. Led by younger Friends such as John Wilhelm Rowntree (1868–1905, another son of Joseph) and Edward Grubb (1854–1939), its deliberations challenged the prevailing quietism by standing ready to come to terms with the latest scientific thought.[22] Before his early death, J. W. Rowntree strove to encourage more thorough and wide-ranging studies of social conditions. In his eloquent words,

> There is a notable stirring of social conscience. The existing order is challenged. Poverty in its hideous shape is regarded not as a fixed institution but as a social disease, an evil too great to be borne. That the many should suffer a stunted life while a few enjoy the freedom of wealth and leisure is a contradiction of brotherhood that cannot be glozed over by the application of a few stock platitudes.[23]

To Rowntree and his colleagues, high unemployment and the gulf between rich and poor were some of the gravest defects in society, ones that Quakers should be prepared to strive unceasingly to put right. The 1895 conference proved to be thus a landmark in Quaker concern about problems of wealth and poverty.

THE QUAKERS AND WEALTH, 1895–1950

In non-Quaker Britain many organisations, from the Christian Socialist movement in mid-century to the Fabian Society from 1884 onwards, had proposed measures to tackle the social issues of the day. Not unexpectedly, therefore, once these issues had been very publicly aired at the Manchester conference, a Socialist Quaker Society (SQS) was mooted, and launched in 1898.[24] Its founders, not generally prominent in the Counsels of the Yearly Meeting, held their own separate conference at the time of the 1898 Yearly Meeting, to discuss the most effective methods of spreading socialist ideas among the Society's members. Its general approach can be seen from one founder's argument that industrialists had a responsibility, if they were faithfully to follow the inner light, to produce goods that were socially useful and to return to the community as much as they received.

Such radical sentiments, and the mere existence of such a body as the SQS, were far from welcome to the Yearly Meeting, still dominated by successful employers who felt that they were pursuing the inner light to their own satisfaction. For some years the SQS was banned from using the facilities of the London head office, then at Devonshire House in the City of London. However, its success as a pressure group emerged when a rival, the more moderate Friends Social Union (FSU), was set up in 1903 for the study of social questions. Founded by such notables as George Cadbury, Seebohm Rowntree and Edward Grubb, it enjoyed both respectability in mainstream Quakerism and the contempt of the SQS for its persistence in favouring philanthropy to ease social ills rather than more radical steps.

The SQS's journal, *The Ploughshare*, from 1906 onwards provided a kind of running commentary on the Liberal Government's social programme, such as the introduction of pensions and health and unemployment insurance, against the hostility of the rich. Articles stressed that a tenth of the British population held nine-tenths of the country's wealth: a shocking state of affairs that only socialist policies could remedy. One article in 1912 even proposed a comprehensive state medical service, on the pattern of the educational facilities provided by the public sector since 1870.

Underlying all these discussions on society and its evils was the problem of wealth. As more and more British businesses turned themselves into joint stock companies and became giants through growth or mergers, the issues were seen to be less about personal riches and more about corporate wealth and the economic power these giants could exert.[25] On the FSU's prompting, in 1907 the Yearly Meeting set up a Committee on Social Questions, which reported in 1910. The Yearly Meeting adopted from its report a new query to be put to members at quarterly, monthly and local meetings. Did they take a living interest in the social conditions of those around them, and did they seek to understand the causes of social wrongs and to help to remove them?

The First World War added a new dimension to social concerns. A conference held at Llandudno in September 1914 concluded that war was not an isolated phenomenon but sprang from a struggle between nations for markets and spheres of influence. Hence social malfunctions caused strife on an international scale, just as at home they were responsible for poverty, unemployment and industrial disputes between employers and the workforce.

Once the issues of war and the social condition had become linked in this manner, they were bound to remain high on the Quaker agenda. The 1915 Yearly Meeting, again acting on a recommendation from the FSU, set up the War and Social Order Committee. That body set aside questions about the origins of war, and concentrated on devising a set of seven (later eight) principles for establishing a proper structure of society once peace returned. These principles, known as 'Foundation of a True Social Order', were adopted by the Yearly Meeting of 1918. They declared that this new social order should be directed not to material ends but to co-operation and goodwill between groups at every level of society. 'Service, not private gain should be the nature of all work', they continued. Moreover, 'the ownership of material things, such as land and capital, should be so regulated as best to minister to the need and development of man'.

Ironically enough, these wartime pronouncements, while helping to establish the SQS as an 'insider' body rather than a gadfly, terminally undermined its reason for existence. In 1919 its journal, *The Ploughshare*, closed down, and the SQS itself was finally disbanded five years later. By then, it could claim that its investigative work had passed to others.

The War and Social Order Committee continued in being until 1928, each of its successive conferences making pronouncements that would have seemed unacceptably radical even a few decades earlier. This increasing freedom of expression doubtless reflected the changing composition of Quakerism in Britain. By the inter-war years, the substantial exodus of wealthy businessmen, together with the final removal of all barriers to Quakers joining the professions, materially transformed the make-up of the Society's membership and direction. Thus middle-grade civil servants, local government officials, school teachers, social workers, solicitors and surveyors were beginning to predominate at all levels; there was increasing pressure for business meetings to be held on Saturdays, rather than during the week when only the retired or self-employed could attend. These professional people were not risk-takers striving to build up capital, but mostly salary-earners in secure jobs. They were therefore likely to take a more hard-line attitude towards wealth than their entrepreneurial predecessors had.

To be sure, the work of the War and Social Order Committee was not much to the liking of the still quite numerous Quaker business people. They felt that its pronouncements were too theoretical and did not always take account of real-life conditions in industry and commerce. In 1918, a conference of Quaker employers, chaired by one of the Rowntree family, was held to discuss the broad topic of Quakerism and Industry.[26] Much of its time was spent on the topical question of industrial relations, and its report welcomed the opportunities for collective bargaining set out in the Whitley Report of 1917/18 on relations between employers and employees; that had recommended joint representative committees in firms to settle problems in this area.

After complaints had been aired in the Yearly Meeting that the War and Social Order Committee lacked popularity and did not represent the views of the Society as a whole, in 1928 it was disbanded and replaced by a nominated Industrial and Social Order Council with what was considered to be a more adequate constitution. Despite the new council's terms of reference being to consider how to apply basic social principles to the outstanding issues, it came under criticism for hesitating to explore the root causes of social ills.

Two more meetings of Quaker employers were held between the wars, in 1928 and 1938. These had remarkably little new to say; hence their deliberations, while no doubt helpful to the participants themselves, inevitably made little impact on thought in the Society as a whole. The Second World War from 1939 to 1945 once again heavily disrupted ordinary life but at the same time provided an opportunity for new thinking. Undoubtedly the most important wartime pronouncement by the Industrial and Social Order Council was the Social Testimony which it adopted in 1944, and which was approved by the 1945 Yearly Meeting.

Almost prophetically, this Social Testimony contributed an environmental touch, as follows:

> The resources of the world have been given to all men individually and for their corporate life. To all men they are given, to all men in common ownership they belong. And although these resources may be administered by particular individuals, groups or nations, any system which limits their availability for all men and women, regardless of colour or creed, is hindering Christian fellowship and the divine order.[27]

By then, wealth was being interpreted not narrowly in terms of private fortunes, or even as corporate assets, but as global resources. It would soon become clear that many of these resources, once used up, could never be replaced.

The fourth conference of Quaker employers, held in 1948, was on the subject of Central Planning and Control. Its proceedings were influenced by the Social Testimony of 1944, and also by the programme of the Labour Government since 1945, such as nationalisation, the introduction of the welfare state and national economic planning. The report acknowledged that until lately, business people had not on the whole been accountable to the community for their economic actions. However, they must in future expect to have their commercial freedom curtailed for the benefit of other sections of society, for instance over the siting of factories. Although no fewer than 120 business people attended, and the under-35s made a distinctive contribution to the debates, the Quaker employers' conference was never held again.

Developments in Quaker social thought since the late 1940s appear to have been modest; one historian has spoken of a 'post-war retreat' in this area.[28] The Yearly Meeting wound up the large and unwieldy Industrial and Social Order Council in 1957 and appointed a much smaller Social Order Committee (later the Social and Economic Affairs Committee) to take its place. Being a nominated panel of experts, it was criticised as concerning itself with narrow aspects of society rather than with society as a whole.

The fortieth anniversary of the eight-part 'Foundations of a True Social Order' in 1958 coincided with a national conference on Industry and the Social Order. This conference made some interesting pronouncements: for example, that most British people were rich in material possessions, and to that extent would find it difficult to enter the kingdom of heaven. However, it confessed itself as being powerless to produce 'blue prints, or even ground plans' of the structure of an ideally just society, and admitted a 'sense of difficulty and difference [diffidence?]'. Therefore it could do no more than put its collective self in God's hands. 'Indeed, our consciousness of the extremity of our plight serves to underline our affirmation that with God all things are possible.'[29] Clearly, the conference had not thrown up the man of the moment, such as a John Wesley or J. W. Rowntree, both of whom had been well aware that the divine assistance came to those who assisted themselves.

CONCLUSION

For any survey of how religion and society in Britain have interacted with one another over the past centuries, the Society of Friends makes an instructive case study. From its foundation in about 1650 until the mid-nineteenth century, Quakers were rather inward-looking, set apart from the rest of the community by the Society's form of non-hierarchical organisation and worship, a distinctive way of speaking, dress and behaviour, a sharing of the civil authority's punishments and disabilities through 'sufferings' as a means of holding to their beliefs and values, and an almost universal tendency, until after the mid-nineteenth century, to marry within the Society. They nevertheless readily transacted with non-Quakers to make a living, and many became wealthy from these commercial dealings.

Perhaps in consequence, the testimony of British Quakers about the evils of wealth were never as wholehearted as it was over the issues of war and of strong drink. Displays of affluence by members could be subjects of comment or warnings as long as plain-living Quakers were so visibly distinguishable from the rest of society. Yet worldly behaviour all too often proved to be an intermediate stage before resignation took place. For the young people in the worldly Ashworth cotton dynasty, the inner light was clearly dim almost to extinction, so that a daughter about to resign and marry in the established church could write, 'I am desirous of expressing the feeling of sincere esteem which I shall always entertain for a community in which I was born and in which I leave so many dear friends.'[30] Quakerism thus suffered considerable loss of membership by the wealthy, who appear to have looked forward to greater social acceptance in affluent Church of England circles.

The tea-dealer Henry Tuke Mennell (1835–1923) later made the celebrated remark, 'A carriage and pair does not long continue to drive to a Meeting House',[31] but this may well simply have applied to Quakerism a saying that had become common among Nonconformist denominations generally. To be sure, not all resignations from the Society were in order to join the established church; some members fell out over such practices as reading the Bible in Meeting. As shown above, marked changes in attitude, towards less tolerance of wealth, occurred when influential Quaker bodies became less and less dominated by business magnates and more and more by professional and salaried people who enjoyed adequate incomes but few riches.

On the complementary issue of poverty, few really poor people were members of the Society, which seems to have come relatively late to linking the problem of wealth with that of widespread poverty in an increasingly affluent nation. About the sole early exception to this disregard was Joseph Rowntree. The starting up of mission work in Britain itself, institutionalised in the Home Mission Committee of the early 1880s, at last brought home to members the complexity of social problems and the need for serious thought about them.

For Quakers who from then on came to recognise the need to correct the plainly intolerable social ills at home, the overriding problem was that only society as a whole, in the form of the state, had the necessary power and authority to enforce such corrective action. Yet for two centuries at least, the state had represented only a section of the community, the property-owning class which pertinaciously strove to make the lives of Quakers and other recusants a misery, if not to obliterate them altogether. Only with the extension of the franchise and the removal of religious disabilities did the state begin to show itself to be an ally and not an enemy of Quakers – except over such issues as war and military service. Perhaps a realisation sooner of the state's potential role in curbing excessive wealth could have made Quaker efforts to this end more effective, as the Society moved from a narrow sect into a respected denomination. As it happened, however, no clear line of progress on the issue discussed in the present chapter can yet be discerned.

ACKNOWLEDGEMENTS

An earlier draft of this chapter was offered to the 65th Anglo-American Conference of Historians on 'Religion and Society' at the University of London in July 1996. Owing to an unQuakerly bomb-scare at Senate House, it could not be discussed, but I greatly benefited from private exchanges of view with Professor D. J. Jeremy and Dr D. A. Farnie, and later with Mr W. P. W. Barnes. I am very grateful to Mr E. H. Milligan, retired librarian of Friends House, London, for much help over this and earlier writings on the Quakers, and to the library staff there for assistance in tracing items which he had recommended.

NOTES

1   A. C. Outler (ed.), *The Works of John Wesley* (Nashville, Tennessee) Sermon 50 'The Use of Money', vol. 2, pp. 263–80 (1985); Sermon 87 'The Danger of Riches', pp. 227–46 and Sermon 108 'On Riches', pp. 518–28, vol. 3 (1985); Sermon 131 'The Danger of Increasing Riches', vol. 4, pp. 177–86 (1987).

2 R. H. Tawney, *Religion and the Rise of Capitalism*, (New York, 1947), p. 161.
3 Outler (ed.), *Works of John Wesley*, vol. 3, pp. 227, 229.
4 S. Zamagni, 'Economic Laws', in J. Eatwell, M. Milgate and P. Newman (eds) *The New Palgrave Dictionary of Economics* (London, 1987) vol. 2, pp. 52–4.
5 A. Smith, *The Wealth of Nations* (1776, ed. E. Cannan, London, 1961), vol. 1, p. 477; M. Blaug, *Economic Theory in Retrospect*, 2nd edn (London, 1968), pp. 58–9.
6 A. Smith, *The Theory of Moral Sentiments* (1759, ed. D. D. Raphael and A. L. Macfie, Oxford, 1976), pp. 50–4.
7 J. S. Mill, *Principles of Political Economy* (1848, ed. W. Ashley, London, 1909), especially p. xxiii.
8 A. Marshall, *Principles of Economics* (1890, 9th edn, London, 1961) vol. 1, pp. 713–14; A. C. Pigou (ed.), *Memorials of Alfred Marshall* (London, 1925), pp. 282–3.
9 J. M. Keynes, *The Economic Consequences of the Peace* (London, 1919), pp. 18–19.
10 J. M. Keynes, *The General Theory of Employment, Interest and Money* (London, 1936), pp. 373–4.
11 J. K. Galbraith, *The Affluent Society* (Harmondsworth, 1962), p. 80.
12 R. A. Musgrave and P. B. Musgrave, *Public Finance in Theory and Practice* (New York, 1973), pp. 10–14.
13 T. A. B. Corley, *Quaker Enterprise in Biscuits: Huntley & Palmers of Reading 1822–1972* (London, 1972), pp. 3–10, and 'How Quakers Coped with Business Success: Quaker Industrialists 1860–1914', in D. J. Jeremy (ed.), *Business and Religion in Britain* (Aldershot, 1988), pp. 164–87.
14 *Book of Christian Discipline of the Religious Society of Friends* (London, 1883), pp. 226, 243; J. Child, 'Quaker Employers and Industrial Relations', *Sociological Review* NS 12(3): 293–315 (1964).
15 *A Journal or Historical Account of . . . George Fox* (Leeds, 1836), vol. 2, p. 447.
16 The marriage question for Quakers in the earlier period, not always well understood outside the Society, is briefly explained here. The Yearly Meeting strongly deplored marriages with non-Quakers, annual reminders being issued on this matter: husband and wife needed full unity of outlook in an era when they might be heavily penalised for non-payment of tithes or for refusing service in the militia. Lord Hardwicke's Act of 1753 and the Marriage Act of 1836 made Quaker weddings legal only if both parties were members of the Society; hence marriage to a non-member could only take place before a 'hireling priest' or (from 1837 onwards) the registrar: both equally obnoxious to devout Quakers. Not until the Marriage (Society of Friends) Acts of 1860 and 1872 could non-members be married according to Quaker usage.
17 Letter from James Cropper, 12 January 1827, quoted by S. Chapman, 'Ethnicity and Money Making in Nineteenth Century Britain', *Renaissance and Modern Studies* 38(1): 35 (1995).
18 Sir A. E. Pease, *The Diaries of Edward Pease* (London, 1907), p. 202.
19 H. Richard, *Memoirs of Joseph Sturge* (London, 1864), pp. 48–9.
20 A. Vernon, *A Quaker Business Man* (London, 1958), pp. 60–2.
21 These works are discussed in W. Hagenbuch, *Social Economics* (Welwyn and Cambridge, 1958), pp. 148–78.
22 R. M. Jones, *The Later Periods of Quakerism* (London, 1921), vol. 2, pp. 971–9.
23 J. W. Rowntree, *Essays and Addresses* (London, 1905), p. 242.
24 P. D'A. Jones, *The Christian Socialist Revival 1877–1914* (Princeton, 1968), pp. 367 ff.; T. Adams, 'The Socialist Quaker Society 1898–1924', unpublished MA thesis, Lancaster University, 1985 (in Friends House Library).
25 W. H. Marwick, *Quaker Social Thought* (London, 1969); D. J. Jeremy, *Capitalists and Christians: Business Leaders and the Churches in Britain 1900–1960* (Oxford, 1990), pp. 355–9.
26 Ibid., pp. 162–73.

27 London Yearly Meeting of Religious Society of Friends, *Christian Faith and Practice in the Experience of the Society of Friends* (London, 1960) para. 545.
28 Marwick, *Quaker Social Thought*, p. 32.
29 Society of Friends, *Christian Faith and Practice*, paras. 547–9.
30 R. Boyson, *The Ashworth Cotton Enterprise* (Oxford, 1970), p. 252.
31 P. H. Emden, *Quakers in Commerce* (London, 1939), p. 231.

Part IV
Ethnicity, religion and wealth

9 Ethnicity and money making in nineteenth-century Britain[1]

Stanley Chapman

No one doubts the importance of the search for motivation in the eighteenth- and nineteenth-century drive to the acquisitive society and, in particular, the emergence of aggressive entrepreneurship out of the more relaxed lifestyles of earlier centuries.[2] Research on the 'consumer revolution' of eighteenth-century England is widening our understanding of the demand side, but tells us nothing of the men who supplied the goods in ever increasing quantity and variety. More than two generations of sociologists have argued the possible connection between the Protestant ethic and the 'spirit of capitalism', but the Weber thesis has now finally been laid to rest,[3] and little has been found to put in its place. Meanwhile economists, belatedly developing an interest in entrepreneurship, have focused on the critical importance of cultural values drawn from society and particularly 'the ethic of achievement'. Presumably such values were built on historical experience, though economists, having turned their backs on history for some years, are scarcely qualified to pursue this line.[4] However, sociologists and economists would agree that Britain makes an appropriate location for historical study of money-making, for Weber was an Anglophile while recent research in economics sometimes starts with comparison of entrepreneurial performance in Britain and some competing economies. It seems an opportune moment for social historians to return to the roots of their subject to see if they can help colleagues with an old problem.

A current development in the focus of research in British economic and social history can help us. Economic historians were so long absorbed in the development of the industrial regions of the north of England and of Scotland that the metropolitan area has been substantially neglected. Social historians can scarcely claim a better record. Research on London not only rectifies an imbalance, it also opens a window on a region with a much greater international orientation than the manufacturing regions. During the eighteenth century London became the international metropolis as well as developing its role as the fulcrum of the English regions. In its former capacity it became a fully international city, not simply in the commodity and financial sense, but more significantly in its population and outlook. Closer study of the driving forces of this international community must illuminate any study of the changes in the values of capitalism. It is certainly a study Weber would have approved of, for his antecedents included some of the most prominent and successful Anglo-Saxon families trading and manufacturing in London and Manchester.

It is now a fairly familiar notion that a large part of the enterprise responsible for marketing the produce of eighteenth- and nineteenth-century Britain came from merchants of foreign extraction. Not only Huguenots and Jews, but Germans, Greeks and a variety of other continentals flocked to take advantage of trading opportunities, while others again came from the new frontiers of the world – from America, Australia, South Africa and India – to the hub of international trade. At first the focus was London, but from the end of the eighteenth century, Manchester, Leeds, Bradford, Liverpool, Nottingham and other centres of commerce featured a high percentage of foreign-born merchants. Such statistics as we have suggest that the migration was a very substantial one. The earliest comprehensive London directory, that of Mortimer, listed 1,316 merchants and factors in 1763, more than three-quarters of whom had non-English surnames. A little over a century later, in 1870, Manchester's mercantile community contained at least 420 foreign-born merchants, the majority of them Greek (200) and German (153). German-born merchants conducted most of the export trade of Bradford and Nottingham in the middle decades of last century. Though some came to escape religious persecution or anti-Semitism, most came simply to take advantage of trading opportunities.

The migrants brought expertise in particular commodities and export markets and often useful credit facilities with overseas customers. From an early date there is evidence of superior education. But the most enduring characteristic of the settlers was their various cultural and religious commitments which were cultivated in settlement enclaves and family networks, and which survived within integrated family groups to the second and third generations. The life of these socio-religious trading elites in the great centres of British commerce was evidently a potent factor in British hegemony in international trade in the nineteenth century, and in the economic and cultural development of several of our great cities.[5] This chapter will focus on the peculiar pressures experienced by certain minority groups in British commerce, which, perhaps rather surprisingly, so often led to conspicuous success.

Little has been written about these socio-economic groups in relation to their achievements in trade. This is probably not so much for want of interest as paucity of source material. Commercial correspondence survives in a few places, but merchant autobiographies are very rare and the kind of personal papers that reveal the motivations of an entrepreneur even scarcer. The most that can be attempted is to look at a handful of representative merchants for whom good material is available to try to identify characteristic attitudes and business policies. The word representative evidently requires clarification. The most that can be attempted is to identify entrepreneurs that came from typical backgrounds and rose to the top of the mercantile hierarchy in their respective sectors of trade. In each sector there was a pyramid of wealth, status and economic power. Those at the apex invited the emulation of lesser merchants, not simply because they were successful, but because they transmitted standards and practices of the trade along the chains of credit. Lesser merchants sent their sons to greater merchants for training, and the most successful families inter-married, reinforcing each others' commercial ethics and drawing on each others' most profitable policies. 'Representative' therefore uses the word in the sense that a captain is representative of his team or a prime minister of his cabinet, by no means identical to all, or necessarily typical of the group, but representing standards to which most feel constrained to be loyal.

The subjects chosen for close study are N. M. Rothschild, representing the German–Jewish connection, Joshua Bates, representing both the Puritan and American connection, and Pantia and Stephen Ralli, who stood at the head of the large colony of Greek merchants in Britain last century. It may be objected that Rothschild was a banker, but in fact he came to England as a textile merchant, and retained an interest in trade throughout his life.[6] Similarly, it could be objected that Bates, as a partner in Baring Bros., was also in banking, but it will be shown that in his lifetime the firm's main interest was still in trade. Ralli Bros. also appear in Skinner's London Banks, but again their principal interest was in trade. In conclusion to this chapter, some comparisons will be made with merchants who were members of comparable minorities but British-born, in particular some Quaker and Scottish merchants, groups both known to be particularly well represented in the mercantile community and having their own religious ideologies.

One final general point must be made. It is simply that life-long commitment to money-making, whether by British or foreign-born entrepreneurs, must be seen as exceptional, and this is no less true of Victorian entrepreneurs. Walter Bagehot explained the position well in his classic work *Lombard Street: Description of the Money Market* (1873) when he wrote that most merchants 'have a good deal of leisure, for the life of a man of business who employs only his own capital, and employs it nearly always in the same way, is by no means fully employed'.[7] Consequently we see established merchants taking long vacations and early retirement, and giving a great deal of their time to politics, religion, music, theatre, science, literature and other intellectual pursuits. Some purchased country estates while their sons went into the learned professions and the arts. This process is as readily observed in the lives of many German and American as British men in trade. It is not possible to illustrate the point at length here, but reference to the mercantile ancestry of Max Weber, the author of *The Protestant Ethic and the Spirit of Capitalism*, shows a body of telling evidence. Weber's forebears were Schunk, Souchay & Co., who around 1835 were the richest Anglo-German trading house in Britain, but a close study of the lives of the partners and of the next generation, some of whom were just as successful in trade, exhibits frequent diversion into intellectual and social activities.[8] Another way of looking at the matter is to observe how science, music, politics and religion of the major centres of mercantile settlement (London, Manchester and Bradford) were enlivened by the newcomers.[9]

GERMAN JEWS: N. M. ROTHSCHILD (1777–1836)

All five Rothschild brothers acquired their father's pleasure in business but the London partner Nathan (N. M.) was inseparable from his work. 'I do not read books, I do not play cards, I do not go to the theatre, my only pleasure is my business,' he wrote in 1816. Saloman and Amschel seem to have had modest ambitions but Nathan and James were insatiable. 'Are you somebody like David Reiss who feels he is fortunate if he obtains cheap remittances amounting to £10,000?' Saloman inquired rhetorically. 'No, you want the whole of Frankfurt, the whole of Paris, the whole of Amsterdam . . . [N. M.] seems rather upset if somebody else does any business transactions with London. He feels that he more or less owns London.' James seems to have been a kindred spirit. Thus he writes to his brothers in March 1818:

> As everybody here [in Paris] knows that I am buying, we have to show that we are the masters of the exchange market . . . I am telling you in confidence that my big deal [the Hamburg claim for 37.5m reparations payment from France] is three-quarters concluded . . . It is submitted for signature to the Chief . . . You can imagine that I would love to be a sterling millionaire in Paris so as to laugh at the whole world.

The next day he adds, 'Thank God, we get all that is due to us without trouble; I never doubted that if we continue in this way we will become the richest people in Europe.'

It is by no means unusual to find successful entrepreneurs with a lust for business, but in the case of Continental Jewish families the psychological need for achievement and the attainment of higher status by innovational creativity seem to have been greater. Carl writes: 'While I was with Saloman in Paris we talked about business activity. It is needed more in Frankfurt than in other places because in Frankfurt a Jew can acquire prestige only through business.' Nathan, who appears to have had little interest in fine clothes, titles, etiquette, art, mansions or entertaining, insisted that 'as long as we have a good business and are rich everybody will flatter us'. The brothers' correspondence shows that anti-Semitism made them deeply anxious, and they wanted nothing better than to raise themselves above its odium. The central role of the Court Jews in the history of Europe has been traced back to the Renaissance, when the rise of strong centralised monarchies allowed a few Jews to insert themselves into the changing social hierarchy. In most of the 240 territories that comprised the so-called Holy Roman Empire the Jews were accepted and granted the right to found their own communities, not in any spirit of tolerance of their religion so much as a means of fostering the prosperity of the state. The princes needed experienced financial agents and advisers capable of carrying through their mercantilist programmes and the more successful Jewish money lenders, who were not inhibited by Christian ethics and guild and corporation controls, filled this role admirably. Selma Stern's valuable work on *The Court Jew* has identified and defined the type with commendable clarity:

> Though the Court Jew was a product of his time, a product of the particular combination of Court absolutism, mercantilism and baroque culture, he was

nevertheless not merely an automaton created by the ruler and blindly carrying out his will . . . He possessed a remarkable degree of industriousness and restlessness, a great interest in speculation and action, a strong desire for success, a lust for money and profit, an ambition to climb higher and higher and to assimilate as completely as possible to his environment in speech, dress and manners . . . Nevertheless, he remained a Ghetto Jew, whose experience and fate bound him to his community and kept him confined within its religious and social organisation.

This portrait, though referring primarily to the sixteenth and seventeenth rather than later centuries, fits the Rothschilds and their German–Jewish connections remarkably closely, and their correspondence illustrates and elaborates these themes without changing them in any significant way. Reference is made to the Maier Amshel principle, that everything is to be risked to be able to make contact with a great prince, and it is better to deal with a government in difficulty than one that has good fortune on its side. Relations with the courts of Prussia, Austria, Denmark and Britain were cultivated with the conviction that 'A court is always a court and it always leads to something. . . . Business transactions with royalty always end in a profitable way.' It is worth while accepting thin profit margins in order to establish a connection, and if 'one wants to stay in business one should not try to make too much profit . . . in peace time one has to be more than glad for a profit of half a per cent'. In the limited space available we can provide only two illustrations of the working of this principle. 'Today [28 March 1816] I concluded a minute transaction with Denmark,' James writes; 'I made a profit of £10 which is really nothing to rave about but thereby I came into contact with the Court.' A few months later he is writing, 'You are perfectly right in saying that we do not need any new business transactions. If, on the other hand a Minister recommends a transaction one has to take it seriously.[10] We cannot afford to lose the Prussian Court.' In England the influence of the Court was obviously much less dominant, but N. M. applied the same principles to important officials, notably Herries, Wellington, and Lord Stewart, the British ambassador in Paris, with the quite extraordinary result that his first million pounds was won under government guarantee in 1815.[11]

In Britain the dividends for government patronage also came in the form of increased status and credit standing. Already at the close of 1814 N. M. could write, 'My bill in London is better than Bethmann [the leading banker] in Frankfurt because everybody feels honoured to speak to me.' Acceptance as a first-class house meant entry to an elite in which it was possible to pick and choose one's clients, not only in Britain, but throughout the rapidly growing international economy, which was now increasingly focused on London. It is at this point that we must emphasise the second distinctive element in N. M.'s success, an element that belonged to his personal genius rather than family tradition. To conduct the colossal acceptance business that he built up in the decade or so after the Napoleonic War evidently required an almost super-human mental register of the fluctuating creditworthiness of hundreds of merchant houses through Europe. No doubt his total dedication to business contributed much to this achievement but, when proper allowance has been made for this, much must be attributed to facility in instant and accurate judgement. If there is any substance in the journalistic tradition of Rothschild infallibility, it must surely apply to his arbitrage business, for it was well known to contemporaries that he had lost money on some state loans, and made little on others. Arriving in Britain at the opportune moment of unprecedented expansion of overseas trade, and the wartime collapse of a sequence of less resilient enterprises, young Rothschild was able to forge his eminence as a government financier to the opportunities for financing international trade. He was by no means the first (or last) merchant to be involved in government financing, but most had come to it late in life as the climax of a successful career in trade. N. M. came into the orbit of government finance at a relative early stage of his career – in 1814 aged 37 – and spent most of the remainder of his life (1816–36) capitalising on his break-through. Outstanding entrepreneurial success has sometimes been achieved through the linking of two distinct traditions, and N. M. Rothschild's career offers the most dramatic illustration of this phenomenon in the fusion of the long Central European tradition of the Court Jew with the equally distinguished English tradition of the merchant financier.

The revealing Rothschild correspondence does not leave their motivation in any doubt. The long and dangerous experience of the Court Jews committed them to taking extraordinary risks to win social acceptance by the favour of princes and by their wealth. The Rabbinic tradition was an assurance of the highest integrity. At the close of the French Wars N. M. Rothschild became the richest commoner in London, but he never found time to enjoy his wealth. Instead, he established a dynasty that used its fortune and influence to raise the status of English Jewry at large. The house of Rothschild, that is to say, was a vehicle for improving the legal status and social reputation of a downtrodden religious minority, even to the third generation.[12]

AMERICAN PURITANS: JOSHUA BATES (1788–1864)

The important role played by American merchants in the main period of British industrialisation has, as yet, scarcely been recognised. In the eighteenth century North America became the foremost destination of British exports,[13] and after the Revolution American merchants became much more than local agents of British merchants. In 1833 Joshua Bates, giving evidence to the Parliamentary Select Committee on Manufacturers, Commerce and Shipping, maintained that the capital employed in the export of British manufacturers to America was 'almost entirely' American and that three-quarters of the cotton imported into Britain was shipped in American vessels.[14] The word 'capital' here evidently means 'fixed capital' for in his evidence to the Bank of England Bates acknowledged the crucial role played by English credits, but the large part played by American merchants cannot be doubted.[15] In several British centres it is clear that American firms were the pace-setters. In Liverpool, the premier port for the American trade, Brown Shipley emerged as the premier merchant house soon after the French Wars.[16] In

Manchester, A. & S. Henry took a comparable lead and held it until after mid-century, when they were overtaken by the New York importer A. T. Stewart.[17] In London, the most dynamic merchant from the late 1820s to the early 1860s was arguably Joshua Bates, a neglected figure, but because of Baring Brothers' position as the leading Anglo-American accepting house, of singular importance.[18] Material has been published on all these firms, but only in the case of Bates can we draw close to the real entrepreneur of the enterprise.

Bates's puritan background is amply revealed in a few of the letters written by some of his Boston circle following his arrival in London in 1828. After a page-and-a-half of pious reflections and exhortations, a close connection of his early years wrote to him:

> I consider labour one of the greatest blessings conferred on mortals for it makes us active and industrious, useful to ourselves and all around. It gives health to the body and a good relish for sleep. Many have said to me why do you work so hard? I have replied that I never considered that I worked too hard as long as I had a good relish for my food by day and quiet and refreshing sleep by night. I observed your activity and industry while you was [*sic*] serving your apprenticeship with Mr Gray and have no doubt but your application and attention to business are greater than ever.[19]

There is no clearer exposition of the Protestant work ethic from an entrepreneur in the period, nor better commendation of a young exemplar of it.

However Bates's dedication to work soon appeared to go far beyond that required by Protestant morality. Within four or five years he terminated Barings' long-standing credit business with Russian wool exporters, launched new trading ventures to North America and the Far East, and opened a branch in Liverpool. Another American friend of his Boston youth did not mince his words:

> I do not think you at all avaricious, but deem you one of the most ambitious men alive. You are not content with having, by your own efforts, raised yourself from the situation of an obscure clerk to the *head* of the first house in Europe (I may say in the world) but you are now striving to extend the business of that house beyond precedent, and to accomplish this are sacrificing health, comfort and probably life ... Your business in this country [the USA] has gone on quite prosperously under the care of our friend Ward, who has quite exceeded the most sanguine expectations we ever formed.[20]

Far from being contrite about this avuncular message Bates appears to have cherished the thought of being the head of the first merchant house in Europe, which probably had not occurred to him (at any rate in so many words) at the time. A year later, when he gave evidence to the government inquiry just mentioned, the *Edinburgh Review* reported Bates as 'managing partner of the house of Baring Bros. & Co., perhaps the most extensive, and certainly one of the best informed merchants in the country',[21] but Bates recorded in his private diary that this periodical had styled him as the first merchant of the country.[22] As a matter of fact, Barings had less than half the capital of Rothschilds at this period.[23]

One could easily say that Bates was simply a workaholic and leave it at that, except that such people need some purpose or motivation. In this instance, the Protestant work ethic provides the moral justification, or mores, but is by no means the whole story. No doubt Bates came of a New England religious background, but his diaries do not show a particularly religious man; there are practically no references to scripture, or to the divine will (even on the tragic loss of his only son), or even to church attendance or charities.[24] Bates evidently became inured to long hours at his desk because he came to trade without benefit of capital and connections and had to strive for some years to establish himself, but the dedication to business long outlived this period. The diaries suggest two further factors, the struggle for personal prestige, using Baring Bros. as a vehicle, and the search for social acceptance in the upper reaches of English society through the Baring family network. In the first he was very successful, winning distinction for himself and his firm, but in the second he was largely disappointed.

For most of the thirty-three years of the diaries (1830–1863), Bates made only sporadic references to his firm's capital and profits, and then only in the context of the distinction of the house and his own contribution to it. The more arresting passages are reserved for the status of his firm while the most deprecatory ones refer to the low standing of American bonds. A few examples must suffice here. When Barings came through the 1837 crisis unscathed he recorded:

> It is a source of pride and satisfaction to me that by foresight on the part of myself and partners our House has never discounted a bill and never had aid from the Bank [of England] in any way, so that our skill and judgement have excited the admiration and astonishment of everybody.

Then in 1840:

> It cannot be denied that, but for the exertions of my house, the Bank of England would have stopped payment, as also Jourdon [the US Bank], and bills on Peabody for a large amo[unt] would have gone back to America and the confusion would have been very great.

(Meanwhile, Baron Rothschild had refused to contribute anything to the Bank's relief.) After the success of the Russian £5.5m loan in 1850, Bates wrote:

> I don't know that B B & Co can stand any higher, they are undoubtedly the first commercial firm in the world which is a great achievement when it is considered that there is no stain on their fame of any kind; we are always liberal to all, honest as a matter of course. We work hard, perhaps too hard.

The flavour of these remarks is in stark contrast with those on the United States. 'There never was a country so disgraced in point of credits as the United States of America by the repudiation [of the debts] of some of the States and the inability of others to meet their engagements.'[25]

Despite all these achievements and so much commercial virtue, Bates was never fully accepted by the Barings. At the end of 1835, after seven years in partnership, he was recording:

I am quite aware that too much falls on me. To talk to everybody [calling at the office], sell the goods, draw the plans for operations ... require a vast deal of thought and hard thinking too, then I have all the disadvantage of not being supported by my partners.[26]

Three years later he complained: 'I have now lived about 20 years in England and cannot recollect that anyone ever *offered* me any act of civility. I do not see that I have made any friends, although I have in many other places.'[27] The advent of steamships at this time cut the trans-Atlantic voyage to thirteen or fourteen days and brought many more Americans to London, introducing some relief to Bates's social isolation, but scarcely changing the attitude of his partners. In 1844 he was in despair again:

The return of Lord Ashburton [from the United States] has renewed the mortification and pain I have always felt in consequence of my social position. On joining the house of B B & Co when Lord A. was a partner, I found that he and Mr Mildmay did not consider that by forming a co-partnership with me they had incurred the so-called necessity for and intercourse with me and my family in our social relations.

A more-than-generous financial assignment by Bates to his partners had done nothing to relieve the situation.[28]

It seems strange on the face of it that Bates did not return to America with his fortune at this time for he was already aged 56 and had a capital of £800,000. His retirement had been predicted by an American friend, William Sturgis, so early as 1832:

I think the time will come when you will feel inclined to return to this country [the United States] and seek in the friendly relations of social intercourse for a species of enjoyment which is not found in the artificial and formal arrangements of European society ... my friend Cushing ... has returned *very rich* but finds himself almost a stranger in his native land and with a constitution impaired by too much devotion to business in a climate not favourable to 'length of days'.[29]

Bates never did return to settle, and it can only be inferred, with the help of some other letters, that his striving for status overcame all other considerations. Sturgis compared his passion for fame with that of the young soldier braving the cannons for the sake of military glory.[30] Perhaps his American upbringing persuaded him that celebrity must ultimately be won from the value of his accumulated capital and the weight of his commercial integrity, an assumption that no Englishman would have cherished for long, at any rate at this period.

GREEK ORTHODOX MERCHANTS: PANTIA RALLI (D.1860) AND STEPHEN A. RALLI (1829–1902)

By 1840 the Greek merchants trading from London and Manchester were almost certainly the most numerous foreign group in these centres, but they were not popular with the English or with other alien merchants. This was not entirely a disparagement of the Greeks as an ethnic group, for the description 'Greek' was used loosely to include practically all traders from the Middle East, including significant numbers of Armenians, Turks, Arabs and Jews, all subjects of the Ottoman Empire through this period.[31] Nevertheless 'pure' Greeks were much the most important element, both numerically and in wealth, and the indictment was clear, as the reports of the Bank of England's Agent (manager) in Manchester show. In 1852 he was writing to the Bank directors that:

> In most cases I have no very great confidence in the *stability*, as regards means, of our *Greek* customers, but consider them in general as a *security* on which we have no very fast hold; a small portmanteau and a few pounds would enable some of them to be a *long way* out of our reach in a very short time. While we had only a *few* firms in the market they *did well* and conducted their business very satisfactorily, *but* owing to the greatly increased influx of small and almost unknown adventurers, the *credit* of the *Greeks* has been injured to an extent from which it will be a long time before it thoroughly recovers.[32]

Failures among the Greek houses were, it was said, kept very quiet by the parties involved in order that they might extricate themselves from their difficulties more favourably. Creditors and banks seemed to have had no significant knowledge of the capital, connections or prospects of even the better known firms, but because of the glutting of British export markets it was easy for the more plausible of them to obtain supplies of Manchester goods for the markets of the Middle East.[33]

All this might have been regarded as a relatively temporary aberration, but there was a string of Greek failures in 1860 and severe setbacks following the Overend Gurney crisis in 1866.[34] In the meantime, *The Bubbles of Finance*, a popular parody on the Levant trade published in 1865, cleverly depicted the typical Greek trader as a sly, unscrupulous entrepreneur who was nevertheless loyally supported by his 'clan'. He was never to be trusted unless he could offer the most solid security. Something of the jealousy of the indigenous merchant population comes through in the same source:

> If the Manchester Greeks thrive, prosper, and increase during the next 25 years as they have done in the last quarter of a century [i.e. since 1840], more than half the buying, selling and agencies of the most important trade in England will be in their hands. As it is, all throughout the ports of the Levant – at Smyrna, Salonica, Alexandria, Beirut and Constantinople – the Greek importers of English goods make large fortunes where the local English merchants can barely make a living.[35]

This was not gravely misleading, at least in the sense that the British consular officials in these towns had reported to Palmerston that a large part of the trade was already in Greek hands in 1848.[36] The Greeks suffered severe competition in the mid-1860s, but that was much more to do with the growth of German commerce and German–Jewish finance than any resurgence of indigenous British enterprise.[37]

The Bank of England Agent provided a fair perspective when he recognised that the early Greek arrivals included a number of firms of substance. By mid-century, when there were some 200 Greek houses in Britain, over thirty of them had discount accounts at the Bank of England, two of them (Ralli Bros. & Spartali and Lascardi) for the maximum credit allowed to any firm (£30,000).[38] Ralli's were the pioneers of Greek mercantile enterprise in Britain, opening an office in London in 1818 for the import of grain. Spartali & Lascardi were a leading firm of ship owners. The capital of Ralli Bros was in excess of £500,000 in 1850,[39] which compared favourably with the top British mercantile houses at the period.[40] However, it must be conceded that other Bank of England account holders in the Greek community were still a long way behind the two leaders. Thus, to take a couple of examples, Cassavetti Cavafy & Co. traded Manchester goods from bases in London, Liverpool, Manchester, Alexandria and Cairo with a capital of only £20,000 to £30,000.[41] The partner in Ionides Bros., a firm that built up an important shipping line, still had little capital in the 1850s and the senior partner spoke only poor English.[42]

This situation has been described at some length because it provides the essential background to understand the otherwise incomprehensible policies of successive heads of Ralli Bros. The firm originally consisted of five brothers from Chios (Kios) who dispersed from their trading base in Constantinople to Odessa, Marseilles, London, Manchester and Liverpool.[43] It was Pantia Ralli, the youngest of the five brothers, and probably the most able, who first organised the system of trading in cargoes of grain while they were still in transit from the Black Sea ports, 'a system which for more than two generations [*c.*1820–*c.* 1880] was the recognised rule and custom of the corn trade in England'.[44]

It was also Pantia Ralli who established the autocratic control and disciplined system which enabled Ralli Bros. to stamp its authority on the Levant trade and trading community. The system that he established included the rule that no partner or employee was allowed to 'lead a life unduly luxurious or extravagant' or to take part 'in any other combination or enterprise whatsoever'. A second rule was established in 'the iron discipline which regulates the relations of superiors and inferiors, and which, indeed, pervades the entire organisation'. These rules, together with 'absolute probity in all transactions', 'have been religiously maintained irrefragable for close upon an entire century', a Greek hagiographer wrote in 1902. The London families from Chios nicknamed Pantia Ralli 'Zeus', admitting the moral influence he exercised over them.[45]

So anxious was Pantia to safeguard the reputation and credit of his firm that it never issued 'paper' (bills of exchange) but did a cash business to the extent of its available means.[46] The system was reported to Baring Bros. in 1863:

When they [Ralli Bros.] buy goods in New York and New Orleans, they pay cash and draw against them [Barings] on London; when they sell goods in America (this being an important branch of their business) they remit the net proceeds to the London firm.[47]

This conservative policy protected the firm from the vulnerability of so many small houses in the recurrent trade crises, but capital only built up slowly for some years. In 1832 Ralli Bros.' capital was, as we have seen, probably between £80,000 and £100,000. The partnership divided after Pantia Ralli died in 1860, Scaramanga & Co. taking over the Marseilles, St Petersburg, Taganrog and Rostoff interests. Stephen Ralli, while retaining the traditional interest in Alexandria and Smyrna, refocused his part of the old house on the United States and India (establishing a branch in Calcutta in 1851, and in Bombay in 1861).[48] Thereafter profits and capital increased rapidly: to £1.2m in 1878, £2m in 1880, and £3m in 1901, according to the Bank of England. Barings, who probably had more direct access to the firm, recorded £4.2m in 1902, perhaps half of which was Stephen Ralli's share in the partnership.[49]

In 1851 Pantia Ralli had brought his nephew Stephen from Marseilles to London to train as his successor. From this time, we read:

> the prestige and interest of the firm absorbed the very soul of the young Stephen Ralli, and filled it with a sort of religious cult. His devotion to work became a veritable passion ... He was austere ... undisturbed by the accumulation of wealth ... counting ostentation as a thing derogatory to the dignity of man.[50]

He 'entirely abstained' from 'active politics', his only relaxation being the comfort of his home and his wife, herself a Ralli. Evidently he was utterly loyal to the strict system formed by his uncle, and more financially successful with it. But why should a rich and successful merchant have devoted his whole time and entire career to expanding the business? Though he came of a persecuted minority in the Ottoman Empire, he did not have the same need as, say, the Rothschilds to win religious toleration or democratic rights for his people. The answer to the question is broadly indicated in his obituary in *The Times* in 1902:

> An organisation so enormous could be successfully maintained and developed only by a constant and unremitting devotion to duty, and the unsparing labour necessary on the part of a principal already possessed of immense wealth was more to the advantage of those who subsisted by the continuance of the business. Stephen Ralli did not labour for money; that he considered as an object quite secondary to the prestige of the firm. His exceptional commercial talents may therefore be said to have been second to his great moral and intellectual endowments ... But it was in the Greek community that he held permanently the dignity of Doyen and the post of Mentor. His authority was supreme and his ruling undisputed.[51]

In other words, like his uncle, Stephen Ralli used his firm as a vehicle to dominate the Greek community and in particular to raise the moral standing of this clannish group in Britain. Respectability was more than a watchword of the Victorian age, for the word spelt social acceptance, and for that the most able entrepreneur was willing to devote his entire life.

ALIEN AND BRITISH IDEOLOGIES

The three important entrepreneurs examined in this chapter were extraordinarily wealthy men who exercised great influence in the nineteenth-century mercantile world, especially in their own socio-religious groups. However, it seems that none of them sought money for its own sake or sought to live in luxury. Their wealth was simply a way of winning esteem in the essentially hierarchical mercantile world, and of demonstrating that their motives in public life could not be impugned. The element common to these men is the struggle for social acceptance for themselves and their grouping, primarily by the winning of pre-eminent status for their respective firms. Each was looked up to and set standards for the other (less successful) trading families of the group. It seems unfair to make direct comparisons between these single-minded foreigners and the indigenous mercantile community, but some comparisons with British religious minorities active in trade could help to explain why the newcomers were so successful. Here again the literature is scarce, but it is possible to learn something of the leading entrepreneurs from two British minorities, the Quakers and the Scots.

So far as nineteenth-century trade is concerned, the Quakers probably found their greatest influence in Liverpool, where we know quite a lot about three interrelated families, the Rathbones, the Croppers and the Bensons.[52] The group was largely schooled and inspired by the leadership of William Rathbone III (1726–89), much as Jews were to acknowledge the moral authority of the Rothschilds and Greeks the Rallis. The Quaker standard was spelt out by James Cropper to two of his young partners in 1827:

> Remember my dear Sons that power and responsibility are inseparable. Too many are looking on wealth and independence as the road to pleasure and enjoyments; now if we consider these the gifts of an all-bounteous Creator who is no respecter of persons and who bestows his gifts in greater or less abundance on particular individuals, we shall be satisfied that they are all in trust and for the good of the whole Human family . . . Let those to whom Riches are intrusted humble endeavour to do their duty and then trust in the Mercy and Goodness of God.[53]

However, Quaker service and charity, though widely admired, were seldom beneficial for the accumulation of capital in the firm. The Rathbones found that dedication to public work had reduced their trading capital to £80,000 in 1842, and that of Cropper, Benson & Co. was probably at about the same level.[54] Eminence was achieved by good works, characteristically requiring more and more time away from the family business, which sooner or later declined. The Quaker experience is known to have been duplicated in the experience of some other entrepreneurs who were religious dissenters.[55]

The Scots were particularly prominent in the trade to India, though few of them were more successful than Ralli Bros. at the end of the century. The records which best disclose the mind and purpose of entrepreneurs in the business are those of Jardine Skinner & Co., a firm that was closely connected with Jardine

Matheson & Co., famous for its leading role in the trade to China.[56] Here as elsewhere the key to success was hard work. When David Jardine went out to Calcutta in 1840 his London correspondent wrote, 'You will at all events find plenty of work and the very existence of our business depends upon everyone sticking closely to it and thinking of nothing else.'[57] After four years' toil Jardine was in no doubt about the qualifications required for a mercantile career in India:

> No-one shall ever be my partner until he is capable of taking a certain lead in some department of the office ... Money and connections are entitled to a certain weight in every house of business, but if they alone are looked to and no notice taken of talent, efficiency, industry, zeal and ability, what a pretty firm J S & Co or any other firm would be.[58]

However, he did not live long enough to impress his will permanently on the firm, for both he and Skinner died in the cholera epidemic of 1844.

By 1863 there were other considerations in filling partnership vacancies. C. B. Skinner, the head in Calcutta at the time, recommended and succeeded in appointing someone who was

> an honourable and conscientious man of business, painstaking and plodding, but not clever or apt in initiating measures. This certainly when he comes to be head of house is a disqualification, but not in our case sufficient to weigh against the positive advantages of being a *gentleman*, respectable and respected, of honourable principles, well known to most of us, and already thoroughly acquainted with Calcutta and its trade and acclimatised to India.[59]

This of course is only one incident, but there are several later indications of the preference for acceptable club men over entrepreneurs.[60] Given the conditions of life for the British in India and the Far East, this is not altogether surprising, but it helps to explain the much faster growth rates of firms conducted on a different set of assumptions, either because they were outsiders (like Ralli Bros.) or rather eccentric recluses who shunned the social life, like Sir David Yule.[61]

It may seem vain attempting to reach any conclusion from such a small number of case studies, but because each is in some way representative of a major trading and financial group some generalisation is possible. A large and important part of British commercial and industrial success last century was clearly the consequence of an influx of foreign merchants. They brought expertise in overseas markets, mercantile experience and sometimes capital, but their most important contributions were their alternative cultures. Traditionally in Britain, successful merchants had translated their fortunes into leisure and landed estate, religious idealists had distributed their profits to charities and their talents to civic service, and expatriate merchants had typically dissipated their time at clubs and sport. By contrast, talented immigrants kept their own company and single-mindedly dedicated themselves to their business activities. The difference, according to the evidence assembled here, can be attributed to the determination of minority groups to achieve somewhat contradictory aims: the sustenance of their particular culture and acceptance into the upper ranks of British society. The benefits to Britain were twofold. The *mélange* of socio-religious groups and cultures in our trading centres made a major contribution to the success of the economy in the nineteenth century.[62] And the high standards of personal integrity introduced by single-minded religious minorities sustained and reinforced the emergence of the City of London as the world financial centre. Recent experience suggests that the value of such inputs has by no means disappeared with the passage of time.

NOTES

1 This chapter was originally published in *Renaissance and Modern Studies* 38 (1995), pp. 20–37.
2 N. McKendrick, J. Brewer and J. H. Plumb, *Birth of a Consumer Society* (London, 1982); Lorna Weatherill, *Consumer Behaviour and Material Culture in Britain 1650–1760* (London, 1988); Carole Shammas, *The Pre-Industrial Consumer in England and America* (Oxford, 1990).
3 H. Behmann and G. Roth (eds), *Weber's Protestant Ethic: Origins, Evidence, Contexts* (Cambridge 1993), especially Chapter 4 by Guenther Roth.
4 Mark Casson, *Enterprise and Competitiveness: A Systems View of International Business* (Oxford, 1990), Chapter 4. See also M. Casson, *The Economics of Business Culture* (Oxford, 1991).
5 S. D. Chapman, *Merchant Enterprise in Britain from the Industrial Revolution to World War I* (Cambridge, 1992), especially Chapters 5, 10.
6 S. D. Chapman, 'The Foundation of the English Rothschilds: N. M. Rothschild as a Textile Merchant', *Textile History* 7 (1977).
7 W. Bagehot, *Lombard Street* (14th edn, London, 1873), p. 204.
8 H. Lehmann and G. Roth (eds), *Weber's Protestant Ethic*, pp. 102–20; G. Roth, 'Between Cosmopolitanism and Ethnocentrism: Max Weber in the 1890s', *Telos* 96: 7–13 (1994); S. D. Chapman, *Merchant Enterprise*, pp. 91, 144–5. For a small merchant with comparable attitudes to business, see P. W. Gaddum, *Henry Theodore Gaddum: His Forebears and his Family* (privately published, Manchester, 1973).
9 Bill Williams, *The Making of Manchester Jewry, 1740–1875* (Manchester, 1976); R. H. Kargan, *Science in Victorian Manchester* (Manchester, 1977); E. C. Black, *The Social Politics of Anglo-Jewry, 1880–1920* (Oxford, 1988); W. E. Mosse (ed.), *Second Chance: Two Centuries of German-Speaking Jews in the U.K.* (Tübingen, 1991); S. Stern, *The Court Jew* (Philadelphia, 1950).
10 Rothschild Archives, London. This section summarises a more substantial treatment in S. D. Chapman, 'The Establishment of the Rothschilds as Bankers', *Jewish Historical Society Transactions* 29, (1988).
11 Ibid. and N. M. V. Rothschild, *The Shadow of a Great Man* (London, 1982), p. 22.
12 *Dictionary of Business Biography*, article on Lord Rothschild, vol. IV (London, 1985).
13 R. Davis, *The Industrial Revolution and British Overseas Trade* (Leicester, 1979), p. 14.
14 *Select Committee on Manufactures*, Parliamentary Papers, 1833, VI, pp. 53, 59.
15 S. D. Chapman, *The Rise of Merchant Banking* (London, 1984), p. 109.
16 Bank of England (hereafter B of E), Liverpool letters, 17 July 1827. A. Ellis, *Heir of Adventure* (London, 1960), Chapter 4.
17 Anon., *Fortunes Made in Business*, vol. III (1887), Chapter 4. H. E. Resseguie, 'Alexander Turney Stewart and the Development of the Department Store, 1823–76', *Business History Review* 39 (1965), pp. 301–22.
18 For the context, see John Orbell, *Baring Bros. & Co. Ltd.: A History to 1939* (London, 1985); and S. D. Chapman, *Merchant Banking*.
19 Guildhall Library, Baring Bros. Archives, HC5.1.14, 28 September 1828. Spelling and

punctuation in this and subsequent letters have been modernised. Hereafter cited as BBA (G).

20 BBA(G) HC5.1.5, 11 June 1832.

21 *Edinburgh Review*, 58 (1834), p. 42.

22 Joshua Bates diaries, in private ownership, 14 October 1833. Hereafter cited as JB diaries.

23 S. D. Chapman, *Merchant Banking*, p. 40.

24 JB diaries, 4 March 1837, 7 January 1840. Cf. J. H. Clapham, *The Bank of England: A History* (London, 1944) vol. II, p. 69. M. E. Hidy, *George Peabody, Merchant and Financier* (New York, 1978) pp. 164–5.

25 JB diaries, 4 June 1842, 30 January 1850. Cf. Hidy, *George Peabody*, p. 167, for a similar contemporary comment.

26 JB diaries, 27 December 1835.

27 JB diaries, 15 July 1838, 23 September 1838.

28 JB diaries, 24 June 1844.

29 BBA(G) HC5.1.5, 31 December 1832. Bates had 35 per cent of Barings' total capital of £1.35m in 1858 – diaries, 1 January 1858.

30 BBA(G) HC5.1.5, 11 June 1832.

31 J. Scholes, *Foreign Merchants in Manchester*, MS, Manchester Public Library.

32 B of E Manchester Letter Books, VII (1852) pp. 4–6. The italics indicate underlining in the original. This source subsequently referred to as B of E M.

33 B of E M, numerous references, notably IX (1853) p. 2, X (1856), p. 73.

34 S. T. Xenos, *Depredations, or Overend Gurney & Co. and the Greek Oriental Steam Navigation Co.* (London, 1869) especially p. 113.

35 [M. R. L. Meason], *The Bubbles of Finance* (London, 1865), p. 5.

36 Public Record Office FO 83/111, reports from Alexandria, Beirut, Cairo, Odessa, Salonica, Varna, and so on.

37 V. A. Zolotov, *Khlebnyy Eksport Rosii Cherez Porty Chernogo i Azouskogo Morey u 60–9OE Gody XIX U* (Rostov, 1966), pp. 224–39 (*Russia's Grain Exports through the Black Sea and Azov Ports 1860–1890*).

38 B of E Ms. 3394, Greek Firms' Accounts 1848–52.

39 B of E M X p. 32. P. Herlihy, 'Greek Merchants in Odessa in the 19th Century', *Harvard Ukranian Studies* 3–4: 403 (1979–80), refers to three leading Greek houses with fortunes of between £80,000 and £100,000, one of which was evidently Rallis.

40 S. D. Chapman, *Merchant Enterprise*, pp. 90–1, 158, 183, 270, 291.

41 S. D. Chapman, Merchant Enterprise, Chapter 5.

42 A. C. Ionides, *Ion: A Grandfather's Tale* (Dublin, 1927). B of E M X (1857), p. 60, Liverpool X (1849) p. 77.

43 [Jack Vlasto], *Ralli Bros. Ltd.* (London, 1951), p. 9.

44 J. Gennadius, *Stephen A. Ralli* (London, 1902), p. 40.

45 Ibid., p. 24.

46 Ibid., pp. 23–4.

47 BBA(G) HC 16.2, 1 June 1863.

48 Nottingham University Archives, Brandt Circulars, 30 December 1865, 1 July 1866. BBA(G) HC 16.2, 1 June 1863. *Select Committee on Indian Currency*, Parliamentary Papers, 1893–4, LXV, evidence of S. A. Ralli, pp. 133–4.

49 B of E Discount Office records (unlisted). Baring Bros. 'Character Book' 1878–1902, at the Bank.

50 Gennadius, *Ralli*, pp. 26, 34.

51 Obituary in *The Times*, 30 April 1902.

52 The best source is still W. Rathbone, *A Sketch of Family History during Four Generations* (London, 1894).

53 Letter Book of James Cropper (1773–1841), owned by Mr J. Cropper, Tolson Hall, Kendal. Letter dated 12 January 1827.

54 Rathbone, *Family History*, p. 67.

55 For a valuable case study, see R. A. Church, *Kenricks in Hardware: A Family Business 1791–1866* (London, 1969).

56 M. Greenberg, *British Trade and the Opening of China* (Cambridge, 1951).

57 Cambridge University Library, Jardine Skinner MSS, typed extracts, blue book 1, p. 1, 4 April 1840. Hereafter cited as JS.

58 JS, blue book 2, p. 24, 10 June 1844.

59 JS, green book 4, 3 March 1860.

60 JS, blue book 1, 17 May 1894.

61 *The Times*, 4 July 1928.

62 In merchant banking, it has been shown that Anglo-German houses grew faster than the older aristocratic houses: see S. D. Chapman, 'Aristocracy and Meritocracy in Merchant Banking', *British Journal of Sociology* 37: 180–93 (1986).

10 The Weber thesis, ethnic minorities, and British entrepreneurship

W. D Rubinstein[1]

The 'Weber thesis' – the celebrated theory first proposed by the famous German sociologist Max Weber (1864–1920) in 1904–5 which posits a salient causal connection between Protestantism and capitalism is perhaps the best-known theory ever propounded by any sociologist; the notion of a 'Protestant work ethic' has passed into the popular consciousness.[2] The 'Weber thesis' continues to fascinate both sociologists and historians, with the role of (especially) Protestant Dissenters in Britain 'sparking' the British Industrial Revolution seen by many social historians as highly significant. Despite the fame of the 'Weber thesis' and the popularity of its ideas, it also remains true that (in my view) quite a few searching questions about it remain to be addressed and answered. It is the aim of this chapter to examine the thesis from a variety of original perspectives.

The 'Weber thesis' may perhaps be read as an attempt by a German liberal, on the one hand, to respond to extreme German conservatives who viewed capitalism as 'Jewish' – in particular Werner Sombart (1863–1941) in works published from 1902 on (Sombart was later a supporter of the Nazi regime) – and, on the other, a response to Marxism, which sees modern capitalists as comprising a new elite adversarial to Europe's pre-modern elites which largely remained in power in the Edwardian period. In contrast to either extreme, Weber saw *both* German capitalism and Prussia's political and military elites as emerging from the Reformation and, moreover, implicitly or explicitly saw Protestant Germany as both 'modern' and sharing all-important commonalities with those other leading 'modern' and Protestant nations, America and Britain. By origin, Weber was himself a liberal German Protestant who also had Huguenot ancestors and close relatives who had become wealthy as merchants in Britain. The Souchay family of Manchester and London, merchants, several of whom left fortunes of between £200,000 and £300,000, originally French Huguenots, provided one of Weber's great-grandfathers, and Weber, like many German liberals of his day, was a pronounced anglophile.[3] Although a consistent critic of Wilhelmine German politics, and involved in Germany's liberal Democratic Party during the brief period of his life in the Weimar Republic prior to his premature death in 1920 at the age of 56, Weber was also certainly a German nationalist in the ethnic/nationalist sense of so many Germans of his day; more specifically he believed that what he termed (in 1917) *Herrenvolk* would be 'called upon to be helmsmen of the world's course', and would probably have preferred an alliance between Germany, Britain, and America to govern the world. It is also worth making the explicit point that Weber was not Jewish or of Jewish descent, unlike so many innovative central European social commentators of his day, but an 'Aryan' German Protestant, writing as a senior German academic; nor was he a Marxist and, indeed, the whole endeavour of the 'Weberian' approach to sociology is to offer an alternative to Marxist analysis.

Much of the evidence presented by Weber in support of his 'thesis' is anecdotal and lacks any kind of statistical grounding. Much of it, too, is very dubious. For instance, one type of 'evidence' used by Weber is that of the injunctions in Benjamin Franklin's *Poor Richard's Almanacs*, with their pithy sayings advocating thrift and hard work taken as evidence of Protestant America's support for capitalism, notwithstanding the fact that Franklin was a freethinking Enlightenment Deist and was certainly not writing from a 'Protestant' viewpoint. Weber in fact presents no quantitative evidence of any kind in support of his thesis. Nevertheless, many recent British historians are convinced that there is 'something' to the 'Weber thesis', with, for example, Everett E. Hagen noting that more than half of the entrepreneurs and inventors mentioned in T. S. Ashton's *Industrial Revolution* were Protestant Dissenters. Michael Flinn, along with many other historians, has taken the association between Protestantism in its British context and successful entrepreneurship to be almost self-evident, stating in his essay 'Social Theory and the Industrial Revolution' that 'I propose ... (in common with most historians of the Industrial Revolution) to take a substantial disparity between the proportion of non-conformists in society and the proportion who were successful entrepreneurs as an assumption basic to any further argument', thus rather neatly avoiding the question centrally at issue.[4] Despite a number of such efforts, there have been few detailed studies of this question which are either exhaustive or satisfying.

It seems to me that there are several separate questions which must be addressed and answered in any attempt to come to grips with the accuracy of the 'Weber thesis' for modern Britain, especially for the Industrial Revolution.

First, since apart from small numbers of Catholics, Jews and Eastern Orthodox adherents, everyone in Great Britain was nominally Protestant, Weber – and certainly many of the historians who have followed him – have implicitly or explicitly postulated a division between Anglicans and Protestant Dissenters (including, it seems, adherents of the Church of Scotland) in their attitudes towards capitalism. Is such a dichotomy plausible in the British context, likening *de facto* the attitude of the Church of England towards wealth, entrepreneurship, and business life to that of the Catholic Church on the continent? Indeed, are the stances of the various Dissenting sects towards capitalism sufficiently similar to make the grouping of them together plausible, the Dissenting sects ranging from the religious groups founded in the seventeenth century like the Independents and Quakers to those founded in the nineteenth like the Mormons, and differing very widely among themselves in religious doctrine and practice?

Second, and most critically, there is a possible central question about the Weber thesis which must be addressed when seeking to understand it, the question of whether it was the explicit teachings and doctrines of religious bodies which engendered any ability by its adherents to perform successfully as capitalists, or, on the contrary, a variety of distinctive group characteristics and salient features *unrelated to* religion or religious doctrine which might engender entrepreneurial success. These unrelated characteristics might include, for instance, the kinship networks and national/international links so characteristic of small, endogenous religious groups; the 'ghettoisation' of such groups either in commerce or finance at a time when such pursuits were forbidden to the mainstream, or in certain types of trades where, for whatever reason, a particular group clustered; and the disinclination or legal or social impossibility of such groups producing a 'haemorrhage of talent' into the 'idle rich', landed gentry, or *rentier* class in subsequent generations as (so it is often argued) would be commonplace among entrepreneurial families from the mainstream.

There seems to be no doubt that Weber himself, and many subsequent scholars who have explored this topic, have taken it for granted that it was the religious teachings and doctrines of Protestantism, especially Calvinist Protestantism, which engendered the nexus with capitalism, specifically what Weber termed the 'this-worldly asceticism' which viewed hard work, thrift, sobriety and a deliberate eschewing of conspicuous consumption or luxurious display as the elements which were religiously commanded by Protestantism; Protestantism also viewed worldly success as a sign of God's grace. Crucially, too, Protestantism broke with Catholicism in permitting the charging of interest. Other historians researching this topic have viewed the Protestant educational process, and the values and syllabuses of Protestant Dissenting academies, as fundamental to explaining why Protestants allegedly did well as capitalists.

Consciously or not – and this very crucial distinction remains to be drawn out fully in the literature – many historians who use the notions of the 'Weber thesis' as valuable to explaining entrepreneurial behaviour mean something entirely different, namely the *non-religious* characteristics and attributes of minority ethnic groups which advantage the likely wealth-generating abilities of these groups. Certainly clear-cut distinctions between the religious and non-religious components of the 'Weber thesis' are seldom made or delineated with rigour – as, indeed, it may be difficult to do, given the complexities and ambiguities of this whole surprisingly complex subject.

Among non-religious characteristics of religious or ethnic groups, in particular, the existence of kinship networks, national and sometimes international, typical of such groups as Quakers, Unitarians, Huguenots, and overseas Scots, is perhaps the most important. Kinship networks arguably assisted materially in entrepreneurial success by sharing and diminishing risks, supplying capital and low-interest loans, providing honest partners, providing accurate information about markets, opportunities, and local conditions, and producing a pool of like-minded marriage partners for dynastic formation. As well, it is likely that the internal means of moral sanction aimed at penalising disgraceful conduct by errant members of these 'cousinhoods' were also effective as well, especially before limited liability and modern capitalisation techniques.

The problem with this view for the purposes of assessing the 'Weber thesis,' however, is that not only Protestants formed these networks. The various Jewish 'cousinhoods' which have existed in modern times, especially the celebrated intermarried financial families of Anglo-Jewry like the Goldsmids, Montefiores and Mocattas, functioned in precisely the same way, if anything, on a far vaster international scale. So, too, however, did the nineteenth-century Anglo-Greek families like the similarly intermarried, phenomenally wealthy mercantile dynasties headed by the Rallis, Schillizzis and Vlastos, Germans like the Schroeders and Goschens, and, indeed, American business families in London like the Peabodies and Morgans. So, too, do overseas Chinese, Indians, Lebanese, and many other groups of this kind, both in Britain and elsewhere. Indeed, the mercantile dynasties of virtually any ethnic minority behave in strikingly similar ways, especially when located overseas or remaining outside the normal status system of their own country for whatever reason.

If this is indeed the case, it seems perfectly clear that religious doctrine and practice *cannot* be the central explanatory factor for the association between certain religious groups and success in capitalism. At best, the explicit teachings of particular religious doctrines might offer necessary but not sufficient reasons for the success enjoyed by these groups, for it is also clear that not all religious minority groups have any notable association with success in capitalism. For instance, Roman Catholics (including the Irish) in Britain have no reputation for forming entrepreneurial 'cousinhoods' of this kind, although objective research and evidence might very conceivably identify more prominent Catholic business-men in modern Britain than one might expect (a point addressed shortly). In contemporary Britain, among recent 'coloured' immigrant groups, certainly Hindus and Sikhs, and conceivably some African groups like Nigerians, enjoy a reputation for entrepreneurship, while West Indians and probably Pakistanis plainly are not known for forming entrepreneurial networks, for reasons about which one might speculate.

If one argues that it is not the *non*-religious but the specifically religious doctrines or teachings among some groups which account for their entrepreneurial success, there are still a host of questions and considerations which must be addressed in validating this claim. Two in particular stand out. First, on careful reflection there is little necessary or obvious nexus between religious doctrines and entrepreneurial success. It is not obvious that thrift, hard work, asceticism, etc., lead to entrepreneurial success. They may be necessary preconditions, although even that is very arguable, but they are obviously not sufficient ones. Such qualities as low cunning, an eye for bargains and untapped potential markets, and an ability to cheat one's suppliers or customers with a straight face and without doing irreparable harm to one's reputation, surely come to mind as more relevant qualities for the successful entrepreneur than thrift. Above all, a successful entrepreneur must identify, enter and exploit a niche market, especially one with high barriers to further entry. It is not clear how any of these things are relevant to Protestant religious doctrine or any other. Second, even granting that religious doctrine is relevant to entrepreneurial success, it is also unclear how ministers or teachers of religion engender these qualities in their adherents, even if they can be taught at all. Ministers have presumably denounced adultery, fornication and drunkenness for several thousand years, yet it is not self-evident that these forms of behaviour have disappeared or indeed diminished, either in the past or today. Among few ministers of religion, of any religion, were or are sermons likely to be confused with lectures at business schools, even, say, among the Protestant ministers of 'Gilded Age' America. Plainly, the nexus here, if there is one, is far more subtle, presumably entailing not direct advice on business practices but on ancillary qualities like 'rational' behaviour and, indeed, thrift and hard work. This is presumably what Weber had in mind, although it, too, seems to take us away from religion as such.

One central relevant point in my opinion which cannot be emphasised too strongly is that place – place in the overall economy – is more important than effort. For instance, any moderately competent stockbroker will automatically become wealthier than the most energetic shopkeeper in the world – provided, of course, that the shopkeeper remains a shopkeeper, and does not develop a chain of shops. Thrift, hard work, ascetic living, and so on are for the most part quite irrelevant to this generalisation. It may well be that particular religious and ethnic groups tended to be found, as entrepreneurs, in particular trades or areas of the economy which were inherently lucrative. Certainly, for example, there were a very significant number of successful Jews and other foreign groups in the City of London, especially Greeks, Germans and Americans. Throughout modern history the City has certainly been at the very centre of wealth-generation in Britain, the place where more fortunes, and larger fortunes, were probably earned than any other locale. For this reason, Jews and other foreign groups were clearly overrepresented among Britain's top British wealth-holders in modern times (although Jews probably comprised a markedly lower percentage of Britain's wealth elite than was the case in Germany). Protestant Dissenters *may have* congregated disproportionately in heavy industry, especially the ownership of textile factories, which were, if successful, lucrative enough, though not often productive of the very largest fortunes.

Jewish entrepreneurial success is, of course, legendary throughout modern history and, with post-Holocaust and multi-cultural eyes, a subject which many historians (both Jewish and, especially, non-Jewish) are naturally reluctant to address explicitly, although I note with satisfaction that, for instance, Dolores Augustine's recent work on German wealth-holders in the Wilhelmine period examines this question frankly and objectively.[5] The early twentieth-century Socialist Zionist theorist, Ber Borochov, noted two characteristics of the economic structure of Jewry in eastern Europe at the time, that more Jews were to be found in the economy the further one 'moved from nature' as he put it, with virtually none in agriculture or mining, but a great many in urban commerce and, second, that the economic profile of Jewry had the form of 'an inverted pyramid,' with many at the top and few at the bottom[6] – I might note, a most inadequate and peculiar description of the economic state of Russian Jewry, renowned not for its wealth but its poverty. Borochov, incidentally, regarded these group characteristics as both lamentable and as the cause of much anti-Semitism, and he, together with many other early Zionists, specifically turned to Zionism, with its aim of re-establishing a Jewish state, in order to give Jews a 'normal' socio-economic structure.

Apart from their kinship networks, Jews became renowned for their entrepreneurial abilities for a host of other reasons, a list so long that no brief resumé could enumerate them. Throughout medieval, early modern and modern history these include: the complete absence of a peasantry or pre-modern aristocracy or military caste; great familiarity with working in the medium of portable or personal wealth rather than in real property, with Jews until modern times often forbidden to own land; almost universal literacy among male and, indeed, female Jews; and a view of the Jewish community as forming one people, with a lack of internal hereditary distinctions or permanent differences in status, engendering intra-communal Jewish charity and self-help as a norm. These are the non-religious reasons. In terms of the Jewish religion other reasons may be offered as well. Unlike some forms of Christianity, Judaism has never viewed poverty as good in itself, or wealth as evil in itself, although it is also strikingly true that Judaism has never really viewed the acquisition of wealth as a sign of God's grace, perhaps because once the king or local ruler learned of Jewish wealth, Jews seldom enjoyed it for long. The fact that the Jewish religion is so obsessively oriented around the calendar and based largely on chronologically defined sacred events, may also have produced a more 'modern' outlook (in Weber's sense). As is so often the case, separating the religious and non-religious elements here is very difficult, but in the case of the Jews virtually all of the group characteristics were strongly supportive of entrepreneurial success.

Having said this, there are two important points, perhaps central, in understanding the value of the 'Weber thesis' which also must be made but which, so far as I am aware, have not been made before. First, the advantages almost certainly enjoyed by small kinship networks and 'cousinhoods' in an earlier phase of capitalism – down to, say, the second quarter of the nineteenth century – may well have been negated by economic developments thereafter, from, say, the 1820s and the dawn of the railway/steamship age. Many of the advantages of risk-diminution, 'insider' information about local conditions and credit-worthiness, the provision of honest business partners, etc., probably entered much more fully into the public realm than before, becoming more widely available to all entrepreneurs regardless of their backgrounds.

Indeed, it is entirely possible that most of these kinship networks became disadvantageous and counterproductive at that point, for instance by restricting access to public and outside sources of investment and credit and handicapping exceptional entrepreneurs with an overrestrictive, overly-lengthy, family or group process of decision-making. Moreover, the natural desire among most members of by now well-established social groups for financial and economic security and for safe, risk-free investments may well have deterred entrepreneurial risk-taking, working with a host of other social pressures and constraints as such families entered the 'Establishment'. It is thus paradoxically true that the normal interpretation of the 'Weber thesis,' wherein an *individual* entrepreneur, animated by a lifetime of religious-based hard work and thrift, may well be a more relevant 'ideal type' among nineteenth-century capitalists than among those of the previous period. There would appear to be some evidence for such an interpretation. First of all, 'New Dissent', with its Methodist businessmen – so allegedly characteristic of nineteenth-century factory capitalism – is far less productive of, or reliant upon, kinship networks or 'cousinhoods' of the type found among Quakers or Unitarians than were the sects of 'Old Dissent', producing instead (it would seem) the classical ruggedly individualistic 'self-made man' of popular depiction, who was, indeed, driven by religion to practise lifelong abstemiousness, thrift, ceaseless work and the other Protestant virtues. Second, the type of urban factory capitalism which grew strongly in Britain from the second quarter of the nineteenth century, and which reached its apogee around 1880 or so, appears to have produced more individual entrepreneurs, among whom no salient group or kinship networks may be readily discerned, than was the case among capitalists of the previous era, who were more notable for such networks. (I base this upon my study of everyone who left £100,000 or more – rather than £500,000 or more – in Britain during the nineteenth century, which is now nearing completion.) It is possible, therefore, and perhaps likely, that a searching study of Britain's leading capitalists and businessmen in 1880 would find more confirmatory evidence for the 'Weber thesis' than a similar study of business entrepreneurs in 1780, that is, where religious commitment can be singled out as important to their business success and who were also 'rugged individualists' in the sense of enjoying no group or communal connections or the advantages therefrom. As with so much in this unusually complex subject, however, proving or disproving such a contention appears to be very difficult, without an agreed-upon definition of what a successful entrepreneur might be or comprehensive biographical evidence about their religious identities.

The second point of importance relates as well to the small kinship networks of 'cousinhoods', including both the Protestant groups like Quakers and Unitarians, and non-Protestant groups like Jews, and, especially elsewhere in Europe, Greeks and Armenians. In the context of British society one characteristic which all of these groups have in common in my view is that they characteristically combine a high degree of marginality with high self-esteem, a combination which, almost certainly, greatly facilitates high achievement in any field.

The crucial point here is not that they were excluded (or excluded themselves) from the normal status system and normal status achievement within the British 'Establishment'. Other groups were also excluded, and if marginality is a *sine qua non* for achievement, especially entrepreneurial achievement, then Catholics would surely be more advantaged than any other group, yet they are unknown as entrepreneurs. Nor is high self-esteem a *sine qua non* for entrepreneurial achievement, or every scion of the aristocracy would be a great entrepreneur. High self-esteem is obviously a difficult concept to define, and still more to verify, but it may centrally revolve around a notion of 'Chosenness' and specialness in a positive sense which is shared by groups like the Jews (whose group *raison d'être* is 'Chosenness') and small groups of Protestant Dissenters, like the Quakers and Unitarians, which combine a sense of moral superiority with a shared sense of historical persecution; such groups are, significantly, often philo-semitic and view themselves as a kind of reincarnation of the ancient Hebrews. In my opinion, high marginality combined with high self-esteem may be key characteristics of most groups which are over-productive, sometimes phenomenally over-productive, in any intellectual or cultural field. In contrast, Catholics in Britain combine high marginality with low self-esteem, while Anglicans, the majority and in some respects the most interesting group and the group most difficult to explain, may combine low marginality and high centrality with mixed and varied self-esteem. It would seem, however, that the groups which were most overrepresented as successful entrepreneurs were groups like the Quakers, Unitarians, and Jews who had these characteristics in common. Quite possibly, these groups were also grossly overproductive of intellectual and cultural achievements in general, although this is more debatable and complex.

One central mystery about the application of the 'Weber thesis' to the British experience which needs much more attention is the position of Anglicans. My study of non-landed wealth-holders leaving £500,000 or more between 1809 and 1939 suggested that Anglicans were probably neither overrepresented nor underrepresented, but formed a component of Britain's wealth structure approximately representative of their overall percentage in the British population, although one can of course debate what that percentage actually was, depending upon which estimates of religious sectarian numbers one employs. This is, if not peculiar, at least something which requires further investigation. Unlike Dissenters, Anglicans (apart from the great landowners) had no reputation for any success at capitalist entrepreneurship. More importantly, not being a minority group, Anglicans could presumably not benefit from the kinship networks so common among religious and ethnic minorities. It is possible that other facets of status recognition and affiliation in fact acted as substitute kinship networks of a kind – the 'old school tie' among the public schools and universities, urban guilds and livery companies, especially in London and older commercial cities like Bristol, perhaps kinship networks based upon partnerships formed by former inhabitants of the same town in London or abroad, and so on. As well, the fact that Anglicans could arguably have actually been economically disadvantaged by lacking effective kinship networks in the manner of other minorities might well have been balanced by the propensity (for whatever reason) of Anglicans to be found as entrepreneurs disproportionately in the more lucrative mercantile and financial sectors of the economy (as, say, stockbrokers, merchants, large-scale retailers, and shipowners) rather than in heavy industry and manufacturing, and in all trades associated with the land. Anglicans may well have benefited, too, from favoured treatment, *de facto* or *de jure*, throughout the Empire, as well as in the professions, especially the law. Nor should it be forgotten that until the mid-nineteenth century the Church of England was itself a fairly significant generator of large fortunes of the 'Old

Corruption' type among its bishops and other high church dignitaries, and among the practitioners of the old Ecclesiastical Courts, which vanished in 1858. Of course, Anglicans alone were allowed to matriculate or graduate from the two old English universities until the 1870s. One assumes that this worked to produce the 'haemorrhage of talent' away from business life, but this assumption has never been realistically tested, and it might well have been economically advantageous to have attended an old university. Finally, the very important and broadly based Evangelical movement among Anglicans may have produced similar character traits among its adherents as did Dissent: a constant preoccupation with being judged by a stern God, with unremitting toil and self-denial as a result. There were certainly significant numbers of Anglican businessmen who were religiously devout, endowing or building churches and contributing generously to missionary societies and the like. Yet the very ambiguous nature of the Church of England as it had evolved by the nineteenth century, being both 'Protestant' and 'Catholic', and containing both a 'Low' and 'High' wing (as well as a 'Broad Church' of the majority of clerics) precludes any definitive conclusions about the likely effects of Anglican doctrine upon personal behaviour.

To complicate matters still further, several other major religious denominations within Britain must also be considered. In Scotland, Presbyterianism (after 1843, divided into three or more rival factions) to a Weberian was presumably a clear-cut example of Calvinistic Protestantism engendering business entrepreneurship. Certainly Scottish entrepreneurship, particularly in Glasgow and Dundee, among overseas mercantile Scots, and among the Scots–Irish Presbyterians of Belfast, was legendary, yet can it be shown that Scottish entrepreneurship was significantly more successful than entrepreneurship elsewhere in Britain? If Scottish Presbyterianism produced the positive results which are alleged, why did it manifest itself most strikingly only after about 1860 rather than long before? There is also the matter of Roman Catholicism: the nexus, if any existed, between English Catholics and business life remains totally unexplored so far as I am aware. There were a number of wealthy English Catholic business dynasties, for example the Taskers and the Eyres, and one wonders how underrepresented, if at all, English Catholics (as opposed to Irish Catholics or Irish Catholics in England) actually were among Britain's nineteenth-century entrepreneurs.

This brings us to the last crucial question concerning the 'Weber thesis' in its British aspects: how, empirically, does one test its accuracy? There are several key variables in any such test – how to define the group of 'entrepreneurs' to be examined; how to identify their religion in a statistically meaningful number of cases, given the habitual lack of detailed knowledge about the youth or private lives of many businessmen; whether to count an entrepreneur's original or adult religion when these differed, or indeed, their ancestral religion in cases where one's great-grandparents, say, had been Quakers or Unitarians; how to assess the impact of religious-based schooling, and so on. Even more fundamentally, the mere fact of belonging to a particular religion in itself says virtually nothing about the degree of religious belief of any particular individual, and still less about how, if at all, religious affiliation affected entrepreneurial ability. Even prominent and lifelong association with a religious group, generous donations, and so on, may be only loosely connected with business behaviour. Furthermore, the Victorian period – if we are studying entrepreneurs and businessmen from that time – was an era when religion dominated virtually all public debate and most written discussion: it was impossible *not* to be influenced by the religiosity of the time, just as today it is, in Britain at least, virtually impossible to be anything but secular in one's world-view, at least for the great majority of people.

There are other attendant confusions and pitfalls which have also intruded into any attempt to 'operationalise' the 'Weber thesis'. Many studies include not only entrepreneurs and businessmen but also inventors, innovators and engineers, who do not, strictly speaking, belong in any attempt to test empirically the 'Weber thesis'. For example, Everett E. Hagen analysed the religious backgrounds of ninety-two entrepreneurs and inventors mentioned in T. S. Ashton's *The Industrial Revolution*, discovering that 41 per cent of the Englishmen and Welshmen in this study were Dissenters, 58 per cent Anglicans.[7] But Hagen's study – and probably others – lumps together entrepreneurs and inventors, groups conceptually un-related. Many notable inventors were notoriously bad at marketing their inventions, while most entrepreneurs invented nothing. Similarly, several generations of the same family are sometimes included in such studies, or representatives of families of a later generation from the original entrepreneur, further adding to the potential confusion.

So far as I am aware – and I may well be ignorant of other relevant research – only a handful of wide-ranging attempts to test empirically the 'Weber thesis' in its British context have ever been made. Hagen's study has been noted. David Jeremy studied the religious affiliations of 1,181 persons with entries in the *Dictionary of Business Biography*.[8] Of those whose childhood or adult religion was known – a small minority of the total number of entries – 14.2 per cent were Nonconformists in childhood and 17.3 per cent Nonconformists in adult life. Unfortunately, it is almost certainly the case that the number of Anglicans was greatly underestimated by the fact that little information survives about them – only 6.3 per cent were found to be Anglicans in childhood and 15.1 per cent in adult life. However, the religious affiliations of no less than 74.2 per cent of all entries in the *DBB* in childhood were unknown, together with the adult affiliations of 63.7 per cent, making far-reaching conclusions difficult to draw, entirely apart from any question as to how comprehensive or significant the persons chosen for entry in the *DBB* were in any case. My own study of Britain's top non-landed wealthholders deceased between 1809 and 1939, in my book *Men of Property*, found that 51 per cent of millionaires and 56 per cent of half-millionaires whose original religions were known were Anglicans. My guess is that both types of studies, if truly comprehensive and searching, would find fairly similar results: that, very broadly, overall religious affiliation in British society and religious affiliation among business leaders were fairly similar, with two exceptions: Jews and other European immigrant groups like Greeks were greatly overrepresented, while Catholics were underrepresented, although possibly not by as much as one might think. The overrepresentation of Jews and other Europeans was probably due to two factors: their concentration in the lucrative City of London and the non-religious factors which enhanced their likely success, especially the international knowledge and trustworthy partners which flowed from their kinship networks. In the case of Jews, in a capitalist and largely 'modern' society like Britain their overall percentage in the wealth structure was almost certainly lower than on the continent. Additionally, Nonconformists probably were disproportionately to be found in manufacturing industry, especially at a level of wealth just below the very top, for reasons which may suggest some affinity between Nonconformity and factory capitalism.

Everyone who has investigated the 'Weber thesis' in a sophisticated way during the recent past has, I think, agreed on how elusive a concept it presents, and how subtle, rather than clear-cut, are the connections between religion and entrepreneurship. In many respects, it is a great credit to Max Weber that he should have enunciated a sociological theory which is still closely studied nearly a century later and about which no firm conclusion has ever been reached. Most scholars would, I think, agree that there is 'something' to the 'Weber thesis', but what that something is, and what the limitations of that connection actually are, remain more opaque now than in 1905. This is probably not a paradox: Weber was writing at a time when the chiefly Protestant states of Britain, Prussia/Germany and the United States were at the absolute zenith of their economic ascendancy. Since that time, we have seen many other nations and peoples advance economically, and several of the original leaders fall behind. Fitting Weber's insight into a subsequent century of economic history makes its assessment, if anything, far more difficult than it was in his lifetime. This leads on to a final query: has the decline of active religiosity in Britain since the early part of the century been a factor in Britain's alleged economic decline? Since Dissent has declined more than Anglicanism, can this be linked in any way with the decline of British manufacturing industry? Or has this factor been quite irrelevant to the multitude of other factors which have so often been advanced to explain Britain's economic decline?; that is, if there has indeed been a decline.

NOTES

1 For other works relevant to this topic see also my include *Men of Property: The Very Wealthy in Britain Since the Industrial Revolution* (London, 1981); *Elites and the Wealthy in Modern British History* (1987); and *Capitalism, Culture and Decline in Britain, 1750–1990* (London, 1993).

2 Max Weber's *Die protestantische Ethik und der Geist des Kapitalismus* appeared in *Archiv für Sozialwissenschaft und Sozialpolitik*, Vols xx and xxi (1904–05). The first English translation appeared in London in 1930 as *The Protestant Ethic and the Spirit of Capitalism*. It was translated by Talcott Parsons and contained an introduction by R. H. Tawney. Historians might debate the degree to which the notion of a 'Protestant work ethic' had penetrated to the English-speaking world before 1930. Weber had a gift for a felicitous phrase which entered ordinary speech: he also coined the term 'charisma' to describe the magnetic and irrational qualities of a great leader.

A host of works from both history and sociology appeared in English in the 1960s and 1970s which discussed the 'Weber thesis'. These included Robert W. Green (ed.), *Protestantism, Capitalism, and Social Science: The Weber Thesis Controversy* (Lexington, Mass., 1973), S. N. Eisenstadt, *The Protestant Ethic and Modernization: A Comparative View* (New York, 1968), Everett E. Hagen, *On the Theory of Social Change* (Homewood, Ill., 1962), and Kurt Samuelsson, *Religion and Economic Action* (New York, 1961). The last work, translated from the Swedish original by E. Geoffrey French, is an unequivocal attack on the Weber thesis.

The 'Weber thesis' has also been discussed by many social and economic historians of modern Britain, e.g., M. W. Flinn, 'Social Theory and the Industrial Revolution', in Tom Burns and S. B. Saul (eds), *Social Theory and Economic Change* (London, 1967). See also the discussion of this subject in my *Men of Property: The Very Wealthy in Britain Since the Industrial Revolution* (London, 1981), pp. 145–63, which is derived from a study of the religious backgrounds of wealth-holders leaving £500,000 or more from 1809 to 1939.

Discussions of the 'Weber thesis' then went into abeyance for a decade or two, but have recently reappeared. See the essays in Hartmut Lehmann and Guenther Roth, *Weber's Protestant Ethic: Origins, Evidence, Contexts* (Cambridge, 1993) and, generally on this subject, David Jeremy (ed.), *Business and Religion in Britain* (Aldershot, 1988). See also Norman Stone, 'The Religious Background to Max Weber', in W. J. Shiels (ed.), *Persecution and Toleration: Papers Read at the Twenty-Second Summer Meeting and the Twenty-Third Winter Meeting of the Ecclesiastical History Society* (Oxford, 1984).

Earlier versions of this chapter were read at the section on 'Wealth and Religion' at the annual Conference of Anglo-American Historians, University of London, July 1996, and at the Economic History Seminar at Oxford University, January 1997. I am most grateful for the comments and suggestions I received on these occasions.
3 See the interesting essay by Guenther Roth, 'Weber the Would-Be Englishman: Anglophilia and Family History,' in Lehman and Roth, op. cit.
4 Hagen, op. cit., pp. 294–309; Flinn, op. cit., p. 25.
5 Dolores Augustine, *Patricians and Parvenus: Wealth and High Society in Wilhelmine Germany* (London, 1994).
6 Ber Borochov, 'The National Question and the Class Struggle', (1905) in Arthur Hertzburg (ed.) *The Zionist Idea: A Historical Analysis and Reader* (New York, 1959), 352–60.
7 Hagen, op. cit., especially pp. 303–4.
8 David Jeremy, 'Religious Links of Individuals Listed in the Dictionary of Business Biography,' in Jeremy (ed.), *Business and Religion in Britain*, pp. 188–205.

11 Ethnicity, religion and wealth
A commentary on the uses of Max Weber

Chris Waters

In my own work as a practitioner of what has been termed the 'new cultural history', I often find myself far removed from the concerns of business or economic history. Trade patterns, market formation and entrepreneurial activity seem quite distinct from my own research interests, which focus more on questions of identity and selfhood, on the ways in which experience is both negotiated and understood through language. Interested in the manner by which the subjectivity of historical actors is constituted through discourse, and increasingly preoccupied with the sources of the self, to borrow from the title of Charles Taylor's magisterial study of that name,[1] I find myself often returning to the work of those earlier theorists who first began to offer ways of thinking about the impact of ideas on behaviour and subjectivity. Despite their apparent difference from this project, both of the chapters in Part IV of this volume – and to a large extent many of the chapters in *Religion, Business and Wealth in Modern Britain* as a whole – are at least implicitly concerned with similar issues, with attempting to chart the complex relationship between systems of thought, understandings of the self and what Max Weber termed this-worldly behaviour. Moreover, as many of the authors in this volume are aware, any consideration of the impact of religious ideas on the practices of everyday life is compelled to consider the links between them first elaborated by Weber in his enduring study, *The Protestant Ethic and the Spirit of Capitalism.*[2]

The two chapters under consideration here raise a number of questions about the cultural context of economic life, questions first considered on a broadly conceptual level by Weber. Specifically, Weber was preoccupied with the extent to which the values that emanated from certain religious world views, especially from the various Calvinist sects, influenced the economic behaviour of those individuals who subscribed to them. Both Stanley Chapman and Bill Rubinstein are interested in similar questions; while they remain sceptical about the so-called 'Weber thesis' in general, they nevertheless follow Weber in so far as they share his belief that economic success needs to be understood as the result of a complex array of psychological and social factors that cannot be explained wholly in economic terms.

The 'Weber thesis' has elicited more commentary than most theses put forward by the great modern social theorists. In this sense Rubinstein's chapter builds upon and contributes broadly to an ongoing debate that won't seem to stop. As we all know, Weber didn't always get it right. He had, for example, an axe to grind with German Marxists and conservatives, as Rubinstein aptly notes, which coloured his findings. Moreover, like Leopold von Ranke, the mid-nineteenth-century German historian he deeply admired, Weber was a fervent anglophile who believed that Britain's economic success, and even its enviable political institutions, in part stemmed from its unique seventeenth-century Protestant heritage – a point greatly exaggerated in his work. One can indeed be critical of Weber, but I don't think it is enough simply to batter him over the head with a weighty empirical sledgehammer, as some historians have often been wont to do, dredging up examples of Catholic, Anglican, and even Jewish, captains of trade and industry in order to counter his assertions about the seminal importance of Protestantism for the rise of capitalism.

One of the reasons why an entire academic industry has arisen around the 'Weber thesis' is because it is a thesis that is almost impossible to test empirically; as Rubinstein notes, many of the attempts to do so have not been very convincing. But perhaps the crucial problem with the 'Weber thesis' is not its empirical shortcomings, for it was, after all, merely a 'thesis', but rather its author's dubious reliance on the notion of an 'elective affinity' existing between the Protestant ethic and the spirit of capitalism. Weber never argued that Protestantism directly led to capitalism, or even that Protestants were absolutely necessary for its growth and sustenance. His elusive notion of 'elective affinities' was about as far as he would go, a term he borrowed from Goethe's brilliant novel of the same name. Perhaps it is a concept that makes for good fiction, but it remains analytically imprecise – in ways that Weber seldom was in his subsequent work – when used to assert the existence of links between religious belief and economic behaviour.

Historians have sometimes been quick to dismiss Weber because they cannot always find an explicit causal connection existing between Protestant belief and capitalist behaviour and thus conclude that to search endlessly for such connections is futile. This is indeed the case if we read Weber narrowly, merely looking for a direct correspondence between Protestantism and capitalism. But if we interpret his endeavour rather broadly and admit that there are indeed some conceptual weaknesses in his thesis (such as the notion of elective affinities), there remains much of value for us as practising historians. Rather than dismiss the 'Weber thesis', we might instead expand its terms of reference, adding a social dimension to its logic that would allow us to chart the complex ways in which various forms of group discipline and collective solidarity, derived in part from a religious ethos, often bound members of marginal religious bodies together and in so doing contributed to their economic success.

What revisions, then, do we need to consider in order that we might continue to benefit from Weber's conceptual insights? Moreover, how do the chapters in *Religion, Business and Wealth in Modern Britain*, particularly in this final section of the volume, help us make those revisions? Rubinstein offers important guidance when he asks whether it was the explicit teachings of various religious bodies that engendered a salient nexus with capitalism or a number of group traits, unrelated to religion, that were responsible for that nexus – traits such as close kinship ties within small religious and ethnic groups, those groups' location in crucial venues for entrepreneurial success, their ghettoisation in particular types of trade, and their persecution by society. By posing such questions, Rubinstein rightly suggests that we need to focus less on the narrow relationship between religious belief and economic activity and more on the broader social and political contexts in which that relationship was forged. He also suggests that we might focus on the ways in which the marginalisation of an ethnic or religious group, coupled with the high self-esteem cultivated by members of that group, often combined to provide a fertile ground for economic success. In so doing, he challenges Weber, arguing that religious teaching offered at best a necessary, though seldom sufficient, reason for the economic success of specific groups in society.

Where one might perhaps disagree with Rubinstein concerns his framing the question in rather draconian either/or terms: *either* it was the explicit teachings of various religious bodies *or* the unique characteristics of small, marginalised, cohesive and homogeneous religious groups that were responsible for specific manifestations of economic behaviour. As he argues, we need to focus more than Weber did on the social dynamics of those religious communities engaged extensively in economic activity. This requires that we also pay close attention to those external forces that shaped group dynamics – religious persecution, the exclusion of various religious bodies from the political community, and so on. But this does not mean that we should wholly ignore the actual content of religious belief. Once we have mapped the social cohesiveness of a religious community and traced its importance for business activity, and once we have explored the impact of those external forces that played a role in generating that community's very cohesiveness, we are still left with the question of ascertaining how the religious beliefs shared by members of that community bound it together and offered important guidelines for conduct in a sometimes hostile environment. In the final analysis (and here Weber was surely correct), until recently economic behaviour could not be wholly separated from the content of religious belief, even though the connection between them is elusive and difficult to chart.

As Rubinstein points out, Weber developed his thesis about the Protestant roots of capitalism in part as a response to extreme German conservatives who saw capitalism as 'Jewish'. Chapman, however, makes it clear that British capitalist activity cannot be understood without considering the formidable role played by Jews in its development. He argues that Jews in Britain, often of German origin, were prominent not only in the world of banking and finance but also in the textile trade in northern industrial towns. Moreover, like Rubinstein, he claims that it was more the status of Jews in society – their psychological need for achievement and respect – than the specific content of their beliefs that fuelled much of their economic activity. By offering an illuminating comparison of the factors that motivated Jewish, Protestant and Greek Orthodox men of business, Chapman also suggests that the marginalisation of specific religious or ethnic groups, along with their struggle for social acceptance, were at the heart of their drive for economic success; this, he asserts, was ultimately of greater importance than the specific religious beliefs of those groups. While the evidence for this point is overwhelming, does it invalidate the general arguments put forward by Weber? It certainly hinders the ability to posit an easy link between Protestantism and capitalism. But perhaps it also suggests the need to explore further the complex formation of group identities, the structures of marginalisation experienced by members of specific groups and the role played by a particular religious ethic in giving form and substance to the business activities of members of those groups.

Chapman's comparative focus demonstrates conclusively that no easy connection can be made between religious belief and economic activity. Moreover, like Rubinstein, he also argues that we need to study such groups in the broader social and cultural context in which they operated. This is indeed a worthy goal, although it should not be undertaken at the expense of ignoring belief entirely. Perhaps what we now need is a much more nuanced understanding of the complex relationship among four, quite discrete phenomena: first, the content of specific religious beliefs; second, the logic of those kinship and community ties that bound together individuals who shared those beliefs in a tight-knit, cohesive world; third, the impact of various forces external to that world which influenced its inner dynamics; and, finally, the role played by the interaction of these four phenomena in shaping specific attitudes and business practices. In short, what we need is more sustained and multi-layered studies of the kind that Leonore Davidoff and Catherine Hall provide in their analysis of English middle-class formation, *Family Fortunes*.[3] It is through this work that we can understand how religious ideology, family and kinship networks, community organisations and specific business practices are linked together in a complex and mutually reinforcing manner. Davidoff and Hall dissolve the distinctions between the public and private spheres by showing how, within the late eighteenth- and early nineteenth-century evangelical family, religious doctrine, mediated within the gendered context of the family and the community, gave rise to a distinctive code of conduct for this-worldly activity. In so doing, they offer an elaboration of many of the links that are considered by the authors in this volume.

In conclusion, then, for all the difficulties we sometimes have with his work, Max Weber remains an extraordinarily imaginative and eclectic thinker. Rather than dismiss that work out of hand, we might continue to build upon it, asking even more sophisticated questions that would allow us to bring together and build upon the discrete insights of social, cultural, economic and political historians. If we do so, then perhaps we can begin to overcome some of the worst excesses of sectarianism within our own profession and develop still further some of the illuminating insights offered by the two chapters under consideration here.

NOTES

1 Charles Taylor, *Sources of the Self: The Making of the Modern Identity* (Cambridge, 1989).

2 Max Weber, *The Protestant Ethic and the Spirit of Capitalism* (transl. Talcott Parsons, London, 1930).
3 Catherine Hall and Leonore Davidoff, *Family Fortunes: Men and Women of the English Middle Class, 1780–1850* (London, 1987).

Index

DATE DUE
